Section 8	Miscellaneous information	
Chapter 8.1	Filing of flight plans	
Chapter 8.2	Control of the manoeuvring area and	
Chapter 8.3	Taxiing	p141
Chapter 8.4	Runway-in-use	p143
Chapter 8.5	Flight priorities	p145
Chapter 8.6	Wake turbulence separation	p147
Chapter 8.7	250kts below FL100	p154
Chapter 8.8	Speed control during arrival	p157
Chapter 8.9	Telephone calls and RT loading	p159
Chapter 8.10	Controller's equipment	p162
Section 9	Weather	p166
Chapter 9.1	Wind	p167
Chapter 9.2	Visibility	p169
Chapter 9.3	Cloud	p173
Chapter 9.4	ATIS and validity of weather reports	p175
Chapter 9.5	Runway surface condition	p176
Section 10	Emergencies	p178
Chapter 10.1	Categories of emergencies	p179
Chapter 10.2	Radio failure	p181
Chapter 10.3	Radar failure	p186
Chapter 10.4	Emergency descent	p187
Bibliography		p191

Abbreviations

aal	Above Aerodrome Level
AIP	Aeronautical Information Publication
amsl	Above Mean Sea Level
ANO	Air Navigation Order
ATC	Air Traffic Control
ATIS	Automatic Terminal Information Service
ATPL	Airline Transport Pilot Licence
ATSOCAS	Air Traffic Services Outside Controlled Airspace
CAA	Civil Aviation Authority
CAP	Civil Aviation Publication
CAS	Controlled Airspace
CRM	Cockpit Resource Management
CTOT	Calculated Take-Off Time
DA/H	Decision Altitude/Height
DME	Distance Measuring Equipment
EAT	Expected Approach Time
EOBT	Estimated Off Blocks Time
ETA	Estimated Time of Arrival
FAF	Final Approach Fix
FISO	Flight Information Service Officer
FL	Flight Level
FMS	Flight Management System
FPS	Flight Progress Strip
ft	Feet
G/A	General Aviation
IAF	Initial Approach Fix
IAS	Indicated Air Speed
ICAO	International Civil Aviation Organisation
IFR	Instrument Flight Rules
ILS	Instrument Landing System
IMC	Instrument Meteorological Conditions
IRVR	Instrumented Runway Visual Range
kg	Kilogramme
km	Kilometre
kts	Knots
LARS	Lower Airspace Radar Service
LVP	Low Visibility Procedure
m	Metre
MATS	Manual of Air Traffic Services
mb	Millibars
MDA/H	Minimum Descent Altitude/Height
Met	Meteorological
MET VIS	Meteorological Visibility
METAR	Meteorological Aerodrome Report
MHz	Mega Hertz
mins	Minutes
MORA	Minimum Off-Route Altitude
MSA	Minimum Sector Altitude

NDB	Non-Directional Beacon
nm	Nautical Mile
NOTAM	Notice to Airmen
Ops	Operations
PAPI	Precision Approach Path Indicator
PPL	Private Pilot Licence
QFE	Altimeter sub-scale setting to obtain height
QNH	Altimeter sub-scale setting to obtain elevation
RA	Resolution Advisory
RCS	Radar Control Service
RT	Radiotelephony
RVR	Runway Visual Range
RVSM	Reduced Vertical Separation Minima
secs	Seconds
SID	Standard Instrument Departure
SLP	Speed Limit Point
SMR	Surface Movement Radar
SOP	Standard Operating Procedure
SSR	Secondary Surveillance Radar
STAR	Standard Instrument Arrival Route
SVFR	Special VFR
TA	Traffic Advisory
TAF	Terminal Aerodrome Forecast
TCAS	Traffic Alert and Collision Avoidance System
Tels	Telecommunications
UHF	Ultra High Frequency
UK	United Kingdom
VDF	VHF Direction Finding
VFR	Visual Flight Rules
VHF	Very High Frequency
VMC	Visual Meteorological Conditions
VOR	VHF Omni-directional Range
VRP	Visual Reporting Point
"Hg	Inches of Mercury

Specific terms

Below is a list of terms that have been identified as having specific meanings. It is explained in the relevant chapters that it is important for pilots to be (pedantically) aware of the use of the exact terms and phrases as they have specific meanings. Pilots who are not aware of the exact use of such phraseology and the associated specific meanings will not therefore have a full understanding of the clearance they are in receipt of, or be fully aware of the environment they are operating in. As some of the terms listed below have lengthy definitions, which are explained in depth in the relevant chapters, rather than repeat the definitions below, the chapter reference is given to direct the reader to the location of the full explanation.

Term	Chapter
Separation	2.1, 6.1
Traffic information	2.2, 2.4, 2.6, 3.4
Traffic avoidance advice	2.3, 2.5
Essential traffic information	6.6
Avoiding action	6.5
Caution wake turbulence. The recommended distance is	3.8, 8.6
Visual approach	6.16
Visual separation	6.4
Reduced separation in the vicinity of aerodromes	6.4
Immediate take-off	1.14
Intermediate departure	8.6
Intersection departure	8.6
After the landing/departing [aircraft type] cleared to land	1.15
Land after	1.15
Band-boxed	8.10
Freecall	4.8
Handover	4.8
Identification	5.6
Validation	5.7
Verification	5.8
Release	6.3
Delay not determined	6.13
Expected approach time	6.13
No traffic delay expected	6.13
Request level change en-route	10.2

Runway-in-use		8.4
CAVOK		9.3
Cloud base		3.7, 9.3
Cloud ceiling		3.7, 9.3
Visibility		9.2
Prevailing visibility		9.2
MET VIS		9.2
RVR		9.2
Surface wind		9.1
Damp	(runway surface)	9.5
Wet	(runway surface)	9.5
Water patches	(runway surface)	9.5
Flooded	(runway surface)	9.5

Symbols

Below is a list of symbols, some of which are standard symbols controllers use to write on FPS's, that may aid pilots to quickly write down the clearances given to them by ATC.

A	Altitude
FL	Flight level
I	IFR
V	VFR
N	North
E	East
S	South
W	West
RH	Runway heading
SA	Straight ahead
SQ	Squawk
SL	Slot
CE	Clearance expires
RLCE	Request level change en-route
◿↗	Cleared to leave controlled airspace
△↙	Cleared to enter controlled airspace
───	Not above (when the line is above the text). Not below (when the line is below the text).

Classification of airspace table

Class	Flight rules	Requirements	ATC service
A	IFR only	ATC clearance before entry. Comply with ATC instructions.	Separate all aircraft from each other.
B	IFR and VFR	ATC clearance before entry. Comply with ATC instructions.	Separate all aircraft from each other.
C	IFR and VFR	ATC clearance before entry. Comply with ATC instructions.	Separate IFR flights from other IFR and VFR flights. Separate VFR flights from IFR flights. Pass traffic information to VFR flights on other VFR flights and give traffic avoidance advice if requested.
D	IFR and VFR	ATC clearance before entry. Comply with ATC instructions.	Separate IFR flights from other IFR flights. Pass traffic information to IFR flights on VFR flights and give traffic avoidance advice if requested. Pass traffic information to VFR flights on IFR flights and other VFR flights.
E	IFR and VFR	IFR flights to obtain ATC clearance before entry and comply with ATC instructions. VFR flights do not require clearance.	Separate IFR flights from other IFR flights. Pass traffic information, as far as practicable, to IFR flights on VFR flights. VFR flights in contact are to be given traffic information as far as practicable.
F	IFR and VFR	Participating IFR flights are expected to comply with ATC instructions.	Separate participating IFR flights from each other.
G	IFR and VFR	None.	None.

VMC table

The pilot of an aircraft is responsible for determining whether or not the met conditions permit flight in accordance with visual flight rules. The criteria for determining visual met conditions are given in the table below.

Note: For fixed wing and helicopter flights taking off or landing at aerodromes within Class C or D airspace the reported met visibility at the aerodrome shall be taken to be the flight visibility.

Aircraft position	Distance from cloud	Flight visibility
At and above FL100: Class C, D, E, F and G airspace	1500m horizontally 1000ft vertically	8km
Below FL100: Class C, D, E, F and G airspace	1500m horizontally 1000ft vertically	5km
Alternatively, at or below 3000ft amsl: Class F and G airspace *For aircraft, other than helicopters, flying at 140kts IAS or less:*	Clear of cloud and with the surface in sight.	5km
Class C, D and E airspace	Clear of cloud and with the surface in sight.	5km
Class F and G airspace *For helicopters:*	Clear of cloud and with the surface in sight.	1500m
Class C, D and E airspace	Clear of cloud and with the surface in sight.	1500m
Class F and G airspace	Clear of cloud, with the surface in sight and at a speed which, having regard to the visibility, is reasonable.	1500m

MATS Part 1, MATS Part 2 and CAP 413

Many references are made in this book to MATS Part 1, MATS Part 2 and CAP 413. For those of you that are not familiar with them, it is therefore worth explaining what they are.

'MATS' is an abbreviation for the 'Manual of Air Traffic Services'. This manual is separated into two separate manuals – MATS Part 1 and MATS Part 2.

MATS Part 1 details all the procedures, practices, rules, phraseology, etc. that controllers are to use and is legally binding. During initial training, controllers must therefore learn MATS Part 1 inside out.

MATS Part 2 is specific to each ATC unit and details specific procedures to use at each controlling position i.e. at each sector, each approach controllers position, each tower position, etc. These procedures may be in addition to, or supersede, those given in MATS Part 1. For example, MATS Part 1 may specify a minimum radar separation of 5nm, but MATS Part 2 allows this to be reduced to 3nm for approach controllers at a certain aerodrome. MATS Part 2 details everything relevant to that controlling position, and so includes such things as airspace diagrams of that sector, lighting available on runways and taxiways at that airport, agreements between sectors of the levels aircraft are to be at before transferring to the next sector, etc. During training at a particular position, controllers must therefore learn MATS Part 2 inside out before being licensed to work at that position.

This essentially means that MATS Part 1 details how to do the job of a controller in general, and MATS Part 2 details how to control at each individual position at each airport or centre. It also means that there is only one MATS Part 1 but many MATS Part 2 as each MATS Part 2 is specific to each ATC unit. To distinguish them they are called '[Unit name] MATS Part 2', for example, 'Heathrow MATS Part 2'.

Should you wish to reference MATS Part 1 it can be obtained from the CAA either as a paper copy or via the internet from the CAA's website. MATS Part 1 and 2 must also be kept, by law, at each ATC unit and so are available at all ATC towers and centres should you visit them.

CAP 413 is the radiotelephony (RT) manual published by the CAA. It details RT phraseology and procedures for use by those with an RT licence. Pilots will be more familiar with CAP 413 as it is usually used during initial pilot training.

Section 1   RT discipline and phraseology

As stated in the introduction, the intention of this book is not to preach how to say "fower" instead of "four". However, having a sound knowledge of correct phraseology and maintaining a good RT discipline are some of the foundations of understanding ATC. This is due to the fact that controllers are taught such standard phraseology and practices thoroughly during their initial training, therefore any transmissions made to pilots are based on the actual definitions of such phraseology and practices. This section is therefore intended as helpful advice rather than a lecture.

It is a fact that speaking clearly and using standard words and phrases greatly improves the RT, resulting in less misunderstanding, less need for repeating things, and consequently less congestion of the frequency. However, RT discipline goes much further than that with an awareness of a concept that even many professional pilots find it difficult to grasp. The concept is basically to listen to the exact words transmitted on the RT and not to assume anything.

It is quite difficult to write down on paper and really needs to be demonstrated live whilst flying. But try to imagine a lawyer in court, they will take any words or sentences literally as they are given without putting them into context or assuming things. For example, you are 100% sure that your friend went to the shop today because earlier he said he was "going" to the shop. However, he may have later decided that he could not be bothered, but you are still left with the mental picture and are 100% sure he went because he said he was "going to the shop".

This basically centres on the fact that communication is only about 7% verbal, the rest we pick up from external clues. This is discussed in more detail in 'Human Performance and Limitations' lessons during ground school for pilot training. When speaking on the RT we only have the verbal parts. When being given important info by ATC we are therefore missing 93% of the clues our minds are used to having. It can therefore (and has done in the past) prove a real problem if you do not take the words and phrases heard on the RT literally and exactly as they are given. Everyone makes their own mental pictures and assumptions, but it cannot be stressed enough how much of an advantage it is if you can treat every transmission without any bias.

To begin, the first chapter defines some of the more commonly misunderstood standard words, and explains how these can be used advantageously in RT transmissions where often one word can replace a whole bumbling sentence, therefore making the transmission much more efficient and clear.

Chapter 1.1   Standard words

The following are standard phraseology definitions as given in CAP 413.

<u>Affirm</u>   Definition: Yes.

Note that this word used to be 'affirmative' but was changed a number of years ago to 'affirm' due to the fact that 'negative' also ends with the sound "ative". Pilots often mis-hearing the word would then incorrectly assume it to be the one they wanted or were expecting.

<u>Roger</u>   Definition: I have received all your last transmission.

'Roger' only has the meaning as defined above. It is important that pilots fully understand this one and only meaning because the problem lies with RT in the real world where, for some reason, many pilots use the word 'roger' as a reply to an instruction that either requires 'affirm', 'negative', or a full read back as the answer.

'Roger' does not mean 'yes'. Neither does it mean 'no'. It solely means: 'I have received all your last transmission'. CAP 413 includes the reminder that it should not be used to reply where a direct answer of affirm or negative is required.

A practical example is: The controller instructs "remain east of the runway due departing traffic". The pilot replies "roger" instead of reading back the clearance as is required by law. At the fourth time of asking the controller changes his RT tactics slightly by saying "confirm you are remaining east of the runway", but the pilot still replies "roger" instead of "affirm".

<u>Wilco</u>   Definition: I understand your message and will comply with it.

This word is used as it is an abbreviation of the phrase 'will comply'. Depending on the instruction given by ATC it is often more correct to use 'wilco' as the reply rather than 'affirm' (which simply means yes) or 'roger' (which means you have received the transmission, but has no implication that you will comply with it).

<u>Confirm</u>   Definition: I request verification of …

This single word can be used for clarity rather than saying "did you ask me to…", or "did you say…" etc. For example: "Confirm climb to altitude 3000ft". However, see 'say again' as explained on the following page.

Say again
Definition: Repeat all, or the following part of your last transmission.

'Say again' is much more efficient and clearer than uttering something like "I'm sorry, what was that again?"

Most people only tend to use 'say again' when they have missed the whole transmission and will use 'confirm…' if they think they have heard correctly but want to check it. There are no rules about this, it is purely at the choice of the individual, but it is true to say that using 'say again' is more likely to be the safer option even when 'confirm…' would have sufficed. This is because when 'say again' is used the controller must repeat the whole message again and the pilot must acknowledge it. But, when 'confirm…' is used the controller can simply reply with 'affirm', but he may have mis-heard an incorrect read back from the pilot which now gives an undesirable situation.

Monitor
Definition: Listen out on [frequency].

For those new to flying this may seem a strange concept to understand at first. It is used when the controller you are being transferred to is busy. It is therefore a method of reducing RT loading by removing the need for pilots to transmit a check in call.

The two relevant controllers will have a method whereby the one you have been transferred to knows that you are on his frequency and he will also have details of the clearances the last controller gave you (e.g. A holding point to taxi to, or a heading and altitude to fly). When ready, the new controller will then call you.

Upon hearing an instruction "[callsign] monitor [frequency]," the correct response is therefore to reply "monitor [frequency] [callsign]", dial up the new frequency, and listen carefully to that frequency but do not transmit on it.

Request
Definition: I should like to know… or, I wish to obtain…

If you would like to ask ATC to do something then say "request" instead of saying "can we…", or "if you're not too busy is it possible to…". For example: "Request climb to altitude 5000ft", or "request to orbit in present position".

Chapter 1.2   Read backs

When controllers pass instructions or information to pilots, pilots are often unsure about what needs to be read back and in which format. This can lead to long winded replies when virtually nothing needed to be read back, and sometimes results in virtual nonsense when the pilot is a bit hesitant and makes a bit of a hash of it all. Such unsure-ness is understandable for those that are new to RT. Talking on the RT is very much like learning a new language, unfortunately, it is very rarely explained practically. This chapter explains how simple it is to reply to ATC and just what exactly is required in the reply. It is recommended that experienced and professional pilots also read this chapter as, being human, most of us forget things as the years go by.

When ATC make a transmission to a pilot there are 3 types of reply that the pilot can make to ATC. That, pure and simply, is it. Whenever ATC talk to you, rather than mumbling back hesitantly some vague approximation of the sentences that ATC said, all you have to do is to think which one of the 3 types of replies is suited to ATC's transmission. The 3 types of reply are:

        Type 1.   Full mandatory read back
        Type 2.   Answer to a question
        Type 3.   Standard word reply

1. <u>Full mandatory read back</u>

CAP 413 states that the messages listed below are to be read back in full by the pilot:

1. Taxi instructions
2. Level instructions
3. Heading instructions
4. Speed instructions
5. Airways, route and approach clearances
6. Runway-in-use
7. Clearance to enter, land on, take-off on, backtrack, cross, or hold short of an active runway
8. SSR operating instructions
9. Altimeter settings and Transition levels
10. VDF information
11. Frequency changes
12. Type of radar service

Having said that read backs are easy because there are only 3 types to remember, you are now probably thinking that this is far from the truth as a list has just been given of 12 things to remember! However, I shall simplify this into a more common sense way of thinking, as explained in the following pages.

From the list, numbers 1, 2, 3, 4, 5 and 7 are all movement related instructions. Therefore, any instruction to move in any direction - either forward, backward, left, right or vertically, whether on the ground or in the air (including the 'condition' if it is a conditional clearance – see chapter 1.13 for further explanation) requires a full mandatory read back. For example:

"Taxi hold G2"
"Cleared to leave the control zone to the east"
"Route direct GOW VOR"
"Cross runway 06"

So, having put numbers 1 to 5 and 7 from the list under one title (i.e. movement related instructions), how is the rest of the list remembered? Well, numbers 8, 9 and 11 you will be reading back from the first week of being a pilot without realising you are doing it. Every time ATC gives you an SSR instruction (usually squawk code or squawk IDENT), an altimeter setting, or a frequency change, you will be reading it back as if it is second nature. But now you know that it is a mandatory requirement.

So how do we remember numbers 6, 10 and 12 from the list? Well, unfortunately, I have no magic answer to this. However, pilots in general have a habit of repeating the runway number whenever ATC mention it (just like they do with QNH and squawk codes). So hopefully you will do the same now that you know that reading back the runway-in-use is mandatory. Note, however, that the 'runway-in-use' is different to just a runway number. 'Runway-in-use' actually has a defined meaning and is explained in chapter 8.4.

As for VDF information, should you ever need it then hopefully you will remember your emergency training as a trainee pilot and that you always read back the VDF information.

Finally we come to 'Type of radar service'. This is the most commonly forgot mandatory read back and pilots often do not get the hint even when asked by ATC a second or third time to confirm the new type of radar service! Again I have no magic formula to remember this by, but maybe you can remember the fact that everyone else forgets it and so you are going to be different and actually remember it! For those of you that are trainee pilots, you are more likely to be in an environment where you will be changing the type of radar service relatively often (compared to airline type flying) and will therefore hear the type of radar service being stated to you by ATC more often. If you can remember to read back the radar service from the start of your flying training then it should stay with you as a good habit.

It is worth noting that CAP 413 states:

> If a read back is not received the pilot will be asked to do so.

Also, MATS Part 1 states:

> Errors in a read back must be corrected by the controller until the pilot gives an accurate read back.

This is why a pilot that is unaware of what transmissions require a full mandatory read back will appear to be hassled by ATC. By law, the controller must obtain a full read back and therefore will (apparently) keep hassling the pilot until he gets it. It is also worth noting that this policy of the controller having to monitor read backs is not a legal requirement in all countries. Therefore, when flying in countries other than the UK do not get into the habit whereby if you are not 100% sure of what the controller transmitted to you, you read back what you thought you heard, thinking that if it is incorrect the controller will correct you. Where controllers are not legally required to monitor read backs they will, in general, not pay attention to any replies by pilots. This may seem to be an undesirable practice, but the fact remains that it is legal and is therefore a possible pitfall.

This consequently reinforces the fact that, where ever you are, if you are unsure of what the controller transmitted to you, the best practice is to use the phrase 'confirm…' or, even better, 'say again'. Using 'say again' removes all doubt as it forces the controller to repeat the whole transmission again

2. <u>Answer to a question</u>

This is relatively simple. If ATC ask you a question then there is nothing complicated about the reply, just simply give the answer. The trick comes with how to keep the answer concise.

If the question simply requires either yes or no then just reply with 'affirm' or 'negative' as appropriate. The question does not need to be included in the reply. For example:

>"G-AB are you Mode C equipped?"
>Just reply: "Affirm G-AB".
>You do not need to say: "Affirm we are Mode C equipped G-AB".

Or, "G-AB are you presently orbiting over the lake?"
>Just reply: "Affirm G-AB".
>You do not need to say: "Affirm we are orbiting over the lake G-AB".

If the question requires you to give information, then just give that information. For example:

Question	Reply
"G-AB report P.O.B.".	"4 P.O.B. G-AB".
"G-AB report aircraft type".	"PA28 G-AB".
"G-AB report your routeing after Lincoln".	"Routeing Lincoln, Scunthorpe, Humber Bridge G-AB".

And if you do not have the required information at that precise moment, then reply "standby" and give the information later. For example:

The controller asks: "G-AB report estimate at POL".
Your initial reply is: "Standby G-AB".
Then when you have the estimate, reply: "G-AB estimates POL time 1134".

3. <u>Standard word reply</u>

All other transmissions, i.e. those that do not require a full mandatory read back or an answer to a question, can be answered with one of the two 'standard words' - 'roger' and 'wilco'. This may seem too simple to be true, but rest assured it does work.

Simply put, any information transmitted to you (which is not a question or does not require a full mandatory read back) can be answered with 'roger'. Remember 'roger' does not mean 'yes', but means 'I have received all your last transmission'. If this information is an instruction to report something in the future (the important thing here is the fact that it is in the future), then 'wilco' is a more appropriate answer.

The following are examples of information being transmitted (which is not a question or does not require a full mandatory read back). These can therefore be answered with 'roger':

- "Traffic information a PA28, one o'clock, five miles, opposite direction".
- Any weather information (excluding altimeter settings) e.g. "surface wind is…" or "cloud base is…".

Below are examples of instructions to report something in the future. All these can therefore be answered with 'wilco':

- "Report downwind/ base leg/ final"
- "Report overhead [a place or a navaid]"
- "Report visual with [an aircraft or a place]"
- "Report taking up the hold at [hold name]"
- "Report beacon inbound/outbound"

Note from the previous page that the word 'report' is also often used to ask a question, for example, "report P.O.B." or "report aircraft type". However, it is obvious that such a phrase is a question and can be answered immediately with the required information e.g. "4 P.O.B." or "PA28".

Using the word 'report' in an instruction to report something in the future means that the report can only be given when the condition is met in the future, therefore the initial response can only be "wilco". For example: "G-AB report in the overhead", the initial response can only be "wilco G-AB", then when eventually in the overhead report "G-AB in the overhead".

Compound read backs

In some cases a transmission from ATC will require you to reply with a full mandatory read back, an answer to a question, and the word 'roger' or 'wilco' all in the same transmission. But do not despair! As long as you know the practicality of it, as has been described in this chapter, then in a very short space of time you will be able to quickly break down each of ATC's transmissions into Types 1, 2 and 3 so that you can formulate a clear and concise compound read back (just like fluently speaking a foreign language). Below are some examples of compound read backs:

Instruction: "G-AB taxi hold D1, QNH 1004, report ready for departure".
Correct reply: "Taxi hold D1, QNH 1004, wilco G-AB".

The taxi instruction and the QNH both require a full mandatory read back, but the request to report ready can be answered with 'wilco'.

Instruction: "G-AB join left base runway 23, surface wind 200°, 7 knots, QNH 1012, report base".
Correct reply: "Join left base runway 23, QNH 1012, wilco G-AB".

The routeing instruction and QNH both require a full mandatory read back, but the request to report base can be answered with 'wilco'. Note, however, that the surface wind has not been acknowledged with the word 'roger'.

In general, if a transmission solely consists of information, then acknowledge the transmission with the word 'roger'. But if a transmission consists of information and other details, then reply as is appropriate to the individual parts of the transmission but without "roger"-ing any pieces of information!

It is worth emphasising that pilots must at all times listen to the exact words and phrases used by ATC and fully understand what those exact words and phrases mean. For example:

"Report taking up the hold".
This is simple enough and is replied with "wilco".

But: "Hold at [navaid], report taking up the hold".
This requires the reply "hold at [navaid], wilco" because it is a routeing instruction and a request to report something in the future.

Read back misconceptions

Pilots often have common misconceptions. They are like bad rumours as everyone seems to think they are true! Read backs are no exception to this, so below is the truth about some of them.

1. As explained in this chapter, weather does not need to be read back at all (except for altimeter settings).

2. Pilots are not required to report taking up the hold unless specifically requested to do so by the controller.

3. When ATC inform a pilot that he is identified there is no requirement for the pilot to read back that he is identified.

Note that the initial instruction to squawk IDENT must be read back as this requires a full mandatory read back (as it is an SSR operating instruction). But when ATC subsequently informs the pilot that he is identified, this does not need to be read back as most pilots believe it does. So, the correct dialogue should be:

Controller:	"G-AB squawk IDENT".
Pilot:	"IDENT G-AB".
Controller:	"G-AB identified".
Pilot:	"Roger G-AB".

Chapter 1.3   Can you?

The first example of maintaining a good RT discipline is on the subject of being asked a question. ATC may ask if you can do something. If ATC say, for example: "Are you able to push-back in the next 5 minutes", then it is unlikely that anything serious will result from this as it is obvious that ATC is only asking a question and have not given a clearance to push-back. Similarly, if ATC say: "Can you see the Seneca orbiting at the end of downwind leg", you will reply either yes or no and nothing further will happen - there is no confusion from the question that you may have been cleared to move anywhere or do anything - it was simply a transmission asking if you can see something.

Now take the example where ATC say: "Can you climb to altitude 5000ft". Whilst you are sat down reading this book, drinking a cup of tea and having a nice couple of biscuits, (taking into account that you have been prompted by the previous paragraph) you are still thinking: 'So what? ATC have only asked a question', and you will reply yes or no and that will be the end of it as you continue with your day. However, put yourself into the following situation, which, unfortunately, is the real world, and remember this example the next time it happens to you when you are flying:

> You are flying along as per usual. ATC say: "Can you climb to altitude 5000ft", and you reply "affirm". Then there is an eerie silence. No reply from ATC, no "roger" or anything. And the silence continues a little longer. Then, because humans are human and not machines, the seeds of doubt start creeping into your mind and you start assuming things. It may only have been 5 seconds since ATC talked to you, but when it is an eerie silence 5 seconds seems like 5 minutes. You are thinking to yourself: 'Well, he asked us to climb. Did he clear us to climb? Well he obviously wants us to or he would not have asked, so it is obviously what he meant' you correctly assume to yourself. So that is what you do, you climb to 5000ft as we all would, but now you are thinking that ATC may make some quick remark because you were a little slow in initiating the climb.

> Ten seconds later you suddenly get avoiding action barked at you by ATC with, in time, the subsequent telling off from ATC for climbing without being instructed to do so. However, you being the strong minded pilot are 100% sure that you were instructed to do so and so you tell ATC that. But ATC says you were not. But you say you were and you know you were, just like you know for a fact that your friend went to the shop! (See section 1).

This example may seem a little far fetched, but if you have not yet faced the situation where ATC ask you if you can climb or descend but then do not reply to your answer, you will come across it at some point in the future. The usual occurrences of this are when the controller is unsure if the aircraft is able to make the level in question due to either a) the level is close to the maximum cruising level for that aircraft type, or b) the level must be made relatively quickly, for example: "Can you make [level] in [number] minutes/miles".

On occasions I find myself in similar situations, and even though I know there should be no need to ask, I often do not feel comfortable until I have resolved the situation for my own peace of mind beyond all reasonable doubt by asking "confirm maintain [present status] or cleared to [change as per the question]" even though I know a clearance was never given - just a question asked. It all comes back to what was stated in section 1 – take each transmission literally and do not assume anything. When ATC say "are you able to climb to altitude 5000ft" there are no words in that sentence that give any indication what so ever that you have a clearance to climb to 5000ft. It is only because there is a silent pause, and then we assume that ATC asked because they wanted us to do it, and then we assume that if we do not start climbing now that ATC will tell us off for not complying with their instruction, that we convince ourselves that what was only a question was actually an instruction to do something.

There are endless examples of questions that ATC may ask you, but it is a fundamental point that if ATC say "can you …", or "are you able to …", then this is not a clearance to do anything. If you are in doubt then ask e.g. "confirm maintain altitude or cleared to climb?"

The example of being asked to climb (or descend) is probably the most common and obviously a dangerous example of misinterpreting a question for a clearance. So, as it is common, here is a bit more information, this time from ATC's perspective:

> The more astute or strong minded of pilots are probably thinking that ATC had a major part in this incident because they did not resolve what is obviously an ambiguous transmission by saying, for example, "maintain altitude 4000ft, call you back", or even just saying "standby". Well, there are always two sides to every story. But what is important is that we prevent it from happening again no matter who is more to blame, and this chapter is intended to do just that.
>
> From the ATC perspective, what usually happens on these occasions is that the controller sees an opportunity for you to climb (or descend) but this requires either a) you to commence it in the next few seconds due to other traffic, or b) other traffic to be climbed or descended along with you.
>
> So, the controller asks if you can climb (or descend) and, in case a) during the couple of seconds it takes you to reply, the controller decides that the climb (or descent) should not be undertaken, and because he never actually gave you a clearance to climb (or descend) then he gives no further reply. In case b) the other relevant traffic is under the control of another controller, so your controller is co-ordinating on the phone with the other controller to enable both aircraft to manoeuvre. Of course, whilst he is doing this, the RT is eerily silent and the seeds of doubt start to appear in your mind and you assume that the controller meant for you to climb (or descend).

So now you see the eerie silence was not actually an eerie silence at all, it was just you assuming so. Of course on some occasions when this occurs, and the astute pilot then attempts to make 100% sure by asking "confirm maintain altitude 4000ft", the controller will have, in that short space of time, decided on what to do or completed the co-ordination and will reply with "climb to altitude 5000ft". Which then puts the pilot in the wrong mindset for the next time he faces this situation as he is now thinking: 'Well he must have cleared us to climb in the first transmission after all!'

Remember also that the word "roger" does not mean yes. So, should ATC ask if you can do something and you reply "affirm" and ATC then immediately replies "roger", this is still not a clearance to do anything. It is likely, as described above, that the controller is in the process of planning something and is just acknowledging your "affirm" by saying 'I have received all your last transmission'.

As said earlier there are endless examples of questions that ATC may ask you. The more common of those that can be misinterpreted and pose a significant threat to air safety are those asking if you can:
- climb or descend.
- turn.
- enter or cross a runway.

You may be struggling to think of questions that involve being able to cross a runway, but it may be as bizarre as:

"Are you able to enter via [an intermediate holding point] backtrack and 180° at the far end to line up runway 26".

You may justify your assumption with even more confidence if ATC use words like 'expedite' or 'immediate'.

I may have exhausted the example of climbing and descending by now, but consider when ATC say: "Can you expedite a climb to FL120". Again in the two seconds it takes you to say "affirm" the controller thinks to himself: 'Actually that's not going to work, he's much safer staying where he is until the other traffic has past'. And, again, the controller does not reply because he did not clear you to climb in the first place. But you are now thinking: 'Crikey, he asked us to expedite and I haven't done anything yet'. So you go for the throttles and initiate a climb.

Similarly, you are at the holding point with landing traffic relatively close in when ATC say: "Can you expedite line up and take an immediate departure". In the two seconds it takes you to say "affirm" the controller decides that it would not actually work. But in the next couple of seconds you think: 'Crikey, he wanted us to get a shift on and that traffic is getting close now'. So off you go onto the runway at quite a pace (and maybe even in the ensuing rush begin the take-off roll even though you were not cleared to take-off either). Should you be wondering what phraseology to use to resolve this situation, the phrase "confirm line up or hold position" will suffice.

Hopefully this chapter has highlighted how easy it is to misinterpret transmissions and assume things. To be fore warned is to be fore armed, so I hope this will help you to be very vigilant throughout your flying career. The next chapter highlights another example.

Chapter 1.4   Go ahead

Controllers may be heard to use the phrase 'go ahead'. This phrase has only one meaning, that being 'pass your message'. Pilots must understand that this is all that it means, it never means go ahead in the sense that you may move ahead, whether on the ground or in the air.

You may think that its meaning is obvious, however, it has on a number of occasions been misunderstood with near fatal consequences. For example: A pilot requests to cross a runway, the controller only hears the callsign and does not hear the message and so says "[callsign] go ahead". So the pilot does, he goes ahead and crosses the active runway.

You may think that as a back up the controller will see the infringement or hear the pilots read back and therefore take immediate action. However, incidents often happen through a combination of reasons. In the example above there would be no correction if the pilot with his poor RT did not read back what he thought was a clearance to cross the runway, there was fog at the airport, and the controller did not have ground movement radar so was unable to see the aircrafts position.

Similarly, take the example where: A pilot requests to enter a certain airspace. The controller does not hear the transmission. The pilot then transmits his callsign in the tone of a question just to get the controllers attention e.g. "Radar, [callsign]". The controller hears this transmission and so replies "[callsign] go ahead". Again, the pilot thinks he has a clearance to go ahead i.e. enter the airspace, so he does, and because he has poor RT he does not read back the clearance.

For these very reasons, in the UK the phrase 'go ahead' has been removed from phraseology and is replaced with 'pass your message'. However, most other countries still use 'go ahead'.

It should be noted that no matter where in the world you hear the phrase 'go ahead', even if a UK controller happens to use it, the fact still remains that it never means move ahead – its sole meaning is pass your message.

Chapter 1.5   Line up and wait

Controllers often give aircraft that are waiting to depart permission to enter the runway and line up but without giving permission to take-off. This can be for a variety of reasons, but a very common reason is that there is a vehicle or aircraft on the runway. Therefore take-off clearance cannot be given until that vehicle or aircraft is clear of the runway, however it is still safe (and expeditious) for the departing aircraft to line up on the runway in the meantime.

The standard phraseology used for this in many countries is 'line up and hold'. There have been actual occurrences, however, where controllers have issued the instruction "[callsign] line up and hold runway [number]" but the pilot thought the controller said "line up and go". Having thought he heard "line up and go" the pilot (not having a thorough knowledge of RT principles) mistook this as a clearance to take-off and consequently did take-off.

In the less serious of these occurrences the result was that the aircraft got airborne without having a clearance to do so. However, in the more serious cases the aircraft took off whilst other vehicles or aircraft were still on the runway. You may think on these occasions that the pilots should simply have looked down the runway first before taking off. However, at night aircraft can very easily disappear even with all the aircraft lights switched on, and many runways have humps in them which can completely hide aircraft further along the runway (even with a 60ft tall tail!).

For this very reason, in the UK the phrase 'line up and hold' has been removed from phraseology and is replaced with 'line up and wait'.

It should be noted that no matter where in the world you hear the instruction 'line up and hold', or think you heard 'line up and go', even if a UK controller happens to use it, the fact still remains that:

a)   'line up and go' does not exist as an instruction, and
b)   the only instruction that allows a pilot to take-off is 'cleared for take-off'.

Chapter 1.6   Take-off clearance

With the exception that Flight Information Service Officers (FISO's) cannot "clear" aircraft to take-off and will therefore use the phrase 'take-off at your discretion', it may seem completely obvious that you cannot take-off without take-off clearance. However, there have been many occurrences in the past where pilots have done just that, and there will unfortunately be many in the future.

Although every pilot throughout the world knows they are not allowed to take-off without take-off clearance, many of these incidents occur, again, due to pilots assuming things when certain situations give that feel or mindset.

One such example is that from the previous chapter where pilots thought they heard "line up and go" and mistook it for a clearance to take-off. Each one of those pilots when asked otherwise would know that they are not cleared to take-off without the instruction "cleared for take-off", however, in those particular situations when they thought they heard "line up and go" it just made sense in their minds that they could take-off. Maybe they were not being as vigilant as they should, maybe this was because they were less alert due to tiredness, or maybe they were in a rush so whilst in the mindset of 'we need to get airborne as quickly as possible' the misinterpretation was easily made.

It can also happen where ATC have not made any transmissions at all on the subject of taking-off, but because you are in such a rush you blast along the taxiway, rush through the pre-departure/take-off checks which you just happen to complete as you approach the holding point, and then because you are in the mindset of getting airborne as quickly as possible you automatically enter the runway and commence the take-off. Maybe not only have you not been given take-off clearance, but you may even not have received a departure clearance i.e. cleared to leave the control zone VFR, or a radar heading, etc.

So again the advice is to remain vigilant, listen carefully to the exact words and phrases used, and don't assume things. However, because we are human and do get into mindsets at times, maybe putting the principle of take-off clearance in a different way will help trigger alarm bells in your head. Try to think of take-off clearance in the following way, no other way, just this single fact:

Never ever take-off unless you have heard the phrase "cleared for take-off" (with your callsign obviously!).

This may seem the same as the fact that you cannot take-off without take-off clearance, and indeed it is. But if you can get into the habit where every time you reach for the throttle levers to start the take-off you think to yourself: 'Have I heard the words cleared for take-off', it may prove a more obvious and effective way of preventing un-cleared take-offs. And if you get into this (good) habit, habits stick and so you will do it every time.

Another piece of information that may be helpful is that the word "take-off" only occurs twice in standard phraseology. The two phrases being:

  'Cleared for take-off', and
  'Hold position. Cancel take-off, I say again cancel take-off, acknowledge'.

If the controller is using the phrase to cancel your take-off, then he must have already given you the phrase of 'cleared for take-off'. So, with that exception, and to put this into blatantly obvious terms, the only time you should ever hear a controller use the word "take-off" is in the phrase 'cleared for take-off'.

Now, having said that, should ATC use the word "take-off" in another way for some reason, for example, "awaiting your take-off clearance", or "after take-off maintain altitude 3000ft", please do not lose all rationale and assume that you have take-off clearance because the controller said the word "take-off"! The one and only overriding factor is that you never take-off without the instruction "cleared for take-off".

In a common sense approach to try and prevent runway incursions and un-cleared take-offs, controllers in the UK are required to repeat/include the instruction to "hold position" if they are giving departure instructions to aircraft that are either at the runway holding point or lined up on the runway. This UK requirement has been brought in due to previous incidents. In these incidents aircraft had been holding at the runway holding point or lined up on the runway ready for departure. The controller then either gave departure clearance or revised the departure clearance, for example, "cleared to leave the control zone VFR", or "after departure fly runway heading maintain altitude 3000ft". Even though the instruction "cleared for take-off" had not been given, the receiving and phrasing of the departure clearance whilst at the holding point or lined up on the runway was enough to give the pilot the wrong mindset and mistake it as a clearance to take-off.

In these circumstances, UK controllers will therefore begin any such departure clearance with the words "hold position". In other countries however, there is no requirement for controllers to include the words "hold position" in such circumstances, so this is another example of why you should remember that you must not take-off until you receive the instruction "cleared for take-off".

If the instruction to hold position is included by ATC in the departure clearance (or any other transmission), pilots are to include it in their read back as it is a mandatory read back – with reference to chapter 1.2 it is a movement related instruction.

It is also worth mentioning, with reference to the earlier paragraph, that as the word "take-off" only occurs twice in standard phraseology, when controllers issue departure instructions they should use the word "departure" and not "take-off". For example, they should say "after departure maintain altitude 3000ft," not "after take-off maintain altitude 3000ft". It is therefore recommended that pilots do the same.

As an additional piece of advice, always treat runways as live, and as such never enter them or do anything on them unless specifically instructed to do so by ATC. The authorities are trying to increase awareness about runway incursions due to an increase in runway incursions during recent times and unfortunately some fatal accidents. So, to wrap up the subject of take-off clearance and of entering the runway (with reference to the previous chapter) hopefully you will get into the habit of doing the following two things:

1. Whenever crossing a holding point or entering a runway, use it as a trigger to think: 'Have we be given clearance to enter' (i.e. from the instructions "enter runway", "cross runway", or "line up").
2. Whenever starting the take-off think: 'Have I heard "cleared for take-off".'

Chapter 1.7 Crossing runways

Continuing from the last two chapters concerning lining up and taking off from runways, pilots can often be misled into thinking they have a clearance to cross a runway when actually they have not.

This is a bit of a contentious point as in some countries a clearance to taxi to a holding point beyond a runway does not require an instruction to cross runways along that route – being cleared to that holding point implies a clearance all the way to it. So, for example, if ATC say "taxi hold V1 via taxiways E and V" and this route crosses runway 26, then there is no requirement to include an instruction to cross runway 26.

Note however that the previous paragraph stated 'in some countries'. In other countries a clearance must be given to cross any runway, whether active or not. So, from the previous example, the clearance would become "taxi hold V1 via taxiways E and V, cross runway 26".

This now leaves you in the quandary of having to find out what procedures are in use in each country. However, you cannot fail to agree that receiving a clearance to cross each runway, whether active or not, is much safer than implying that a clearance has been given. So, in the interests of safety, and using some common sense, it is recommended that pilots get into the (good) habit of always treating all runways, whether active or not, as live and of going by the rule that you must have a specific clearance to cross a runway even if cleared to a point beyond the runway.

It may be the case that if you are given a clearance that implies that you are cleared to cross a runway, and you subsequently ask for specific confirmation e.g. "confirm cleared to cross runway 26", the controller may reply in a very stern and annoyed tone of voice as if you should know better. But in this case rest assured that the controller should know better than to treat such a safety related issue with such contempt.

In the interests of safety and for your own piece of mind, no matter where in the world you are, it is recommended that you always get specific clearance to cross a runway, whether active or not. This very advice is highlighted in the UK CAA's literature on preventing runway incursions.

Confusion may also exist when instructed to follow other traffic. Again, different countries have different policies, but it is recommended that you use common sense and the safe rule that an instruction to follow other traffic never automatically includes a clearance to enter or cross a runway – each aircraft requires a specific instruction to enter or cross a runway, whether active or not. If you are unsure then ask for specific confirmation. This very advice is also highlighted in the UK CAA's literature on preventing runway incursions.

Confusion or misinterpretation may also exist with regards to the use of the two standard phrases as follows:

> An ICAO standard phrase is 'taxi to holding position'. Its meaning is to taxi to the holding point, holding short of the runway.

> However, some countries use a non-ICAO phrase of 'taxi into position and hold'. The meaning given to this is to line up on the runway and wait.

It can be seen that due to the similar words used in these two phrases, but the phrases having very different meanings, that an incorrect action could be taken, and unfortunately runway incursions have occurred in the past due to the misunderstandings associated with this.

Again, the only way to prevent runway incursions of this nature (i.e. those attributed to phraseology) is for pilots to always use the rule that they never enter or cross a runway without a specific clearance to do so. If this means that the controller becomes annoyed at a pilot requesting such clarification, or that the traffic flow is delayed as it takes a while for such a pilot to be able to transmit on a busy frequency, then so be it. Runway incursions are a very serious matter and this is one of the few ways that can prevent them.

Chapter 1.8   Crossing red stop bars

It is obvious to state that aircraft should not cross red stop bars, just like it was obvious to state that you should not take-off without take-off clearance. However, pilots often do cross red stop bars, and again it is usually due to the pilot's perception of the situation.

In the cases I refer to, the pilots have been given clearance by ATC to cross the holding point to which the red stop bar was lit. So you may be thinking that as the pilot had clearance to cross where the stop bar was (it just so happened that the stop bar remained lit instead of being extinguished) that there is no problem. However, this is exactly where the problem lies.

In 99% of these occurrences the pilot had the correct clearance and so there was not a problem. The usual reason that the stop bars remain lit when cleared to cross them is that the controller simply forgets to press the button to extinguish them! But the problem is that the holding point name is never mentioned when being given a clearance to cross it i.e. if, for example, you are holding at V1 (i.e. you are already at V1) and ATC instruct you to line up and wait, it is not standard phraseology to say "[callsign] line up and wait via V1". The standard phraseology is simply "[callsign] line up and wait". Similarly, your reply is simply "line up and wait [callsign]" without identifying the holding point. So, although you think that you have clearance to cross where the stop bar remains lit, if the controller has mistaken you as being at another holding point (and therefore extinguishes the stop bar at that holding point instead) then you do not have clearance to cross the red stop bar. Consequently, as the holding point is not identified in the clearance or read back, the only defence is if the pilot refuses to cross a red stop bar whilst ever it remains lit.

In the remaining 1% of occurrences the stop bars remained lit because the aircraft was actually at a different position to which the controller thought it was. This was because either the controller cleared the aircraft to an incorrect position and did not notice the mistake, or the pilot took a wrong turning and neither the controller nor the pilot realised the mistake. There are many reasons why controllers may not realise these mistakes, but at night it can be surprisingly very difficult to see aircraft even with their lights switched on, and in reduced visibility the aircraft can be out of sight of the controller. In both cases if the controller does not have Surface Movement Radar (SMR) available then he has no way of monitoring aircrafts positions himself – he must rely on accurate reports from pilots as to which taxiways or holding points they are at. Unfortunately, in a high percentage of these cases the result of crossing the red stop bars was serious.

In exceptional cases stop bars do become faulty and remain lit even when commanded off by the controller, and sometimes they will even flash on and off! But in the interests of safety and common sense it is recommended that pilots get into the (good) habit of using the following one rule for stop bars:

> Never cross red stop bars unless a clear, specific and unambiguous clearance has been given to cross the red stop bars.

It is worth illustrating in real terms what a clear, specific and unambiguous clearance actually is in this case. For those of you that are learning to fly from smaller airports or possibly grass airfields, you may not be familiar with the following example. But for those of you that are learning to fly from larger airports or those that intend to fly as a career, the following example will become very familiar. The most common scenario is as follows:

You are either at a standstill holding at a holding point with the red stop bar lit, or are just reaching the holding point you have been cleared to with the red stop bar lit, when ATC give you a clearance to cross the holding point i.e. either "taxi ...", or "line up and wait" (again without identifying the holding point). The stop bar remains lit however, so those of you that have good airmanship query the lit stop bar with ATC rather than crossing it whilst lit. However, although your intention is good, the query often takes the form of you saying "stop bar still lit," and that is your entire transmission. No mention of a callsign, and no mention of which holding point you are at. The entire transmission consists of just 4 words – "stop bar still lit".

In most cases the controller will then extinguish the red stop bar having simply forgot to do so when issuing your clearance to cross the holding point. However, it is a possibility that the controller may extinguish the wrong stop bar and it just so happens that you are at that same (wrong) stop bar. For example:

> You are at G1 but the controller thinks that you are at V1. When instructed to "line up and wait" you query the lit stop bar by saying "stop bar still lit". The controller then realising he has forgot to extinguish the stop bar goes to do so but mistakenly presses the button for G1. With the stop bar at G1 now extinguished you enter the runway at G1 but the controller still thinks you are entering at V1.

You are probably thinking that this is an extreme chain of mishaps. But accidents often happen due to a long chain of events (called the error chain) where in each event an error went undetected – error chains are discussed in depth in CRM courses. As such circumstances will result in a runway incursion, serious consequences can result. So although you think that this extreme chain of mishaps is unlikely to happen, if you can reduce the chances of it happening even further by taking literally one second to include the holding point name and your callsign when saying "stop bar still lit", then safety is maintained by using this seemingly pedantic (but expeditious) practise.

So, in the interests of safety, to get a clear, specific and unambiguous clearance to cross a holding point when the stop bar remains lit, it is recommended that you include your callsign and the holding point to which stop bar you are referring to in your initial query. That way it gives the controller two extra pieces of vital information that can trigger the controller into checking that everything is as it should be i.e. correct aircraft at the correct holding point. So rather than saying "stop bar still lit", say, for example, "stop bar still lit at G1, G-AB".

To further ensure that this piece of good airmanship actually works it is necessary for pilots to accurately report the taxiways and holding points they are at. With reference to the earlier paragraph, in some cases the only method the controller has of monitoring the position of aircraft is by accurate reports from pilots. Practically speaking, what is meant by this is that although you may now be in the (good) habit of including your callsign and holding point in your transmissions, if for example you are cleared to V1 and consequently taxi until reaching the red stop bar at the holding point, do not just automatically say "stop bar still lit at V1, G-AB" – because you are again assuming that you have got to where ATC told you to go! It is important that you read the signage to check that you are where you think you should be (especially at night or in reduced visibility) as you may have inadvertently taxied to G1 for example.

Fatal accidents have occurred in the past where part of the error chain was that the pilots taxied along incorrect taxiways and holding points without reading the signage and consequently either did not report the mistake to ATC, or reported that they were where they thought they should be rather than their actual position as per the signage.

Another important point to make is that if you are at a holding point, ATC have not made a transmission to you, but the stop bar suddenly extinguishes, do not just assume that you may cross the holding point. With reference to chapter 1.6 remember the rule: Whenever crossing a holding point to enter a runway, use it as a trigger to think: 'Have we been given clearance to enter?' You should never cross a holding point or runway without a specific clearance. With reference to earlier paragraphs in this chapter, a likely explanation of why your stop bar suddenly extinguished could be that the controller was clearing another aircraft across a holding point but pressed the button to extinguish the wrong stop bar – the wrong stop bar being the one at the holding point that you are at.

It is likely, due to the wording used in this chapter, that the mental picture you have in your mind with regards to crossing red stop bars is solely a picture of crossing red stop bars coincident with a runway. Whilst this is where the majority of such stop bar related incidents occur, it is a fact that red stop bars are present at other points along taxiways. It is still possible to have a severe incident or accident if crossing a red stop bar at these other points on taxiways, so it is necessary to treat all lit stop bars with the same caution, not just those coincident with a runway.

The advice of not crossing red stop bars is highlighted in the UK CAA's literature on preventing runway incursions and a recent analysis showed that 20% of runway incursions involved pilots crossing red stop bars. This subject is treated with such seriousness that some authorities intend to adopt a policy whereby if a stop bar remains lit due to malfunction, it may only be crossed with the assistance of a 'follow me' vehicle.

Chapter 1.9   The take-off roll

Once take-off clearance has been given it is human nature for pilots to become completely absorbed in concentrating on the aircraft during the take-off roll and initial climb-out. Whilst this phase of flight does require a high degree of care and attention the concentration on the aircraft itself should not be to such an extent that other vital clues are cut off. To this I refer to two main aspects:

1. Keep a look out of the window as a final defence to enable you to take action should something infringe the runway or initial climb-out path.
2. Keep a good listening watch on the RT as a final defence to enable you to take action should traffic be inadvertently cleared onto the runway, or should ATC instruct you to abandon the take-off.

During the take-off roll pilots often block out the radio from their hearing without realising it because they are so absorbed in concentrating on the aircraft. Incidents have happened where ATC have instructed an aircraft to abandon its take-off (with more than one transmission) but the pilots did not hear it – in the sense that the sound entered their ears, but the brain could not acknowledge it because of being completely focused on the aircraft. The subject of becoming 'tunnel visioned' when workload increases is covered in CRM courses.

It is therefore another (good) habit to be able to remain vigilant and to listen to the RT during the take-off roll. It is also worth noting the standard phraseology used for abandoning take-off and the correct reply required by the pilot. CAP 413 gives the correct standard phraseology as follows:

a) When an aircraft is stationary and it is necessary to cancel the take-off clearance:

    The instruction shall be: "[callsign] hold position, cancel take-off, I say again cancel take-off, acknowledge".
    The reply shall be: "Holding [callsign]".

b) When an aircraft has commenced the take-off roll and it is necessary to abandon the take-off:

    The instruction shall be: "[callsign] stop immediately I say again [callsign] stop immediately acknowledge".
    The reply shall be: "Stopping [callsign]".

Chapter 1.10   Altitude, Height and Flight Level

It is a requirement that the appropriate word 'altitude', 'height' or 'flight level' is included in any transmission relating to a level.

In practice pilots and controllers will always include the words 'flight level' when referring to a flight level. This is because there is no other option - without the words 'flight level' all that remains are numbers e.g. 180 or 90. However, the words 'altitude' and 'height' are often omitted from transmissions. This is because the word 'feet' is still included, so the meaning of the number can still be grasped by the listener, for example, "request 3000ft". Whilst this often occurs, it is not recommended or correct, and the word 'altitude' or 'height' should always be included to completely remove any possibility of ambiguity or mistake, for example, "request altitude 3000ft".

Another point that is often forgotten with regards to levels is the incorrect use or omission of the word 'to'. By this I refer to the following standard phraseology convention that is given in CAP 413:

 a) The word 'to' is to be omitted from messages relating to flight levels.
 b) The word 'to' followed immediately by the word 'altitude' or 'height' shall be included in messages relating to an aircrafts climb or descent to an altitude or height.

It may be argued that the omission or inclusion of the word 'to' when referring to flight levels is unlikely to result in a reduction in safety. But there is a convention so it should be adhered to. There is, however, an important reason why the word 'to' should be included when referring to climb or descent to an altitude or height. This reason may again seem very far fetched, but the convention was brought in due to actual incidents that have occurred. The incidents occurred due to a misunderstanding of the phraseology used, as illustrated in the following example:

G-AB is maintaining altitude 6000ft. ATC instruct "G-AB descend 2000ft". The pilot replies "descend 2000ft G-AB" and then he does just that, he descends 2000 feet worth of altitude i.e. he descends by 2000ft which results in him levelling off and maintaining an altitude of 4000ft!

This example may seem pedantic and unlikely, but it has happened on a number of occasions, which is why the new convention has been implemented. The correct phraseology is now therefore:

Controller: "G-AB descend to altitude 2000ft".
Pilot: "Descend to altitude 2000ft G-AB".

You will now undoubtedly notice when flying in the future that ATC are very strict and exact when using the word 'to' with reference to levels, and as such pilots should do the same. As a further practical point, should a controller omit the word 'to' when instructing to climb or descend to an altitude or height, e.g. "G-AB climb 3000ft", then this is a slip of the tongue – it never means (in this example) climb by 3000 feet worth of altitude. In such a case, to obtain a correct clearance, the pilot should reply "confirm climb to altitude 3000ft G-AB" so the controller now has to reply to your question and confirm the correct clearance.

Chapter 1.11   Millibars

There is a standard phraseology convention for the use of the word 'millibars'. This convention is given in CAP 413 and is as follows:

> The word 'millibar' shall be appended to figures when transmitting a pressure setting below 1000mb.

This may seem another minor and pedantic point, but the reason it is used is because of misunderstandings that led to previous incidents. The incidents arose because some countries use inches of mercury to measure pressure rather than millibars. When the pressure in inches of mercury is spoken on the RT it is often abbreviated by both pilots and ATC, so for example, a QFE of 29.87"Hg is often said as "QFE 987". The misunderstandings and incidents then occur when a pilot who is used to dealing with pressure in inches of mercury operates in an environment where millibars are used. The controller then passes the pressure as, for example, "QFE 987" implying millibars, but the pilot sets the altimeter to 29.87"Hg.

The opposite also applies where a controller gives the abbreviated pressure implying inches of mercury, but the pilot sets the altimeter using millibars.

You may argue that for a pilot using a UK callsign flying in UK airspace, it is obvious that he will only use millibars. However, that pilot may have done his training abroad where inches of mercury are used (e.g. USA), or he may be a foreign pilot flying for a UK airline, or … etc, etc. So using the convention every time removes the possibility of ambiguity or confusion.

You will now undoubtedly notice when flying in the future that ATC are very strict on using the word 'millibars' when the pressure is 999mb or less, and as such ATC expect pilots to do the same.

Chapter 1.12　　　　Abbreviating callsigns

The question is often asked (more so by trainee pilots) of just exactly what are the rules about abbreviating callsigns. Can pilots abbreviate their callsign when they like, or do ATC have to do it first?

The rules about this are very simple. They are given in CAP 413 and are as follows:

1. When establishing communication an aircraft shall use the full callsigns of both stations.

2. After satisfactory communication has been established and provided that no confusion is likely to occur, the ground station may abbreviate callsigns. A pilot may only abbreviate the callsign of his aircraft if it has first been abbreviated by the ground station.

Chapter 1.13   Conditional clearances

When the term 'conditional clearance' is mentioned, those new to RT often get into a bit of a fluster as it sounds very technical and they do not really know what to do with them or how they should be phrased correctly. In reality, conditional clearances are very simple and can be taught with ease. There are only a few rules that govern conditional clearances, but it is necessary that these rules are remembered, as well as the reason why the rules are used.

So what is a conditional clearance? Simply, it is a clearance that only becomes valid once a certain condition is fulfilled. Hence the name! As an example, the following is a conditional clearance:

"G-AB, after the landing 737, line up and wait".

In the example, the clearance is to line up and wait, but the clearance only applies after the condition is met i.e. after the landing 737.
So that is conditional clearances, simple! Another example is:

"G-AB, after the departing A320, route north remaining east of the airfield".

So now you know what a conditional clearance is. But it is important that you also understand the rules that govern conditional clearances. The first rule is given in CAP 413 and is as follows:

> A conditional clearance shall be given in the following order:
>
> 1. Callsign.
> 2. The condition.
> 3. Identification of subject of the condition.
> 4. The instruction.

The reason why it is important to realise why it must be given in that order is because without the order, the clearance could be given as, for example:

"G-AB, line up and wait, after the landing 737".

In this case, should the transmission be clipped, the pilot then receives the clearance of "G-AB, line up and wait". The consequences of this would be very serious, which is why ATC are very strict on using the correct order.

It is also worthy of noting two points with regards to the read back of conditional clearances by pilots. These being:

- Conditional clearances will always require a mandatory read back. With reference to the list of full mandatory read backs in chapter 1.2, although the list does not state 'conditional clearances', any clearance of a 'conditional' nature will always be a message type from that list.
- Pilots should similarly always use the convention when reading back a conditional clearance.

For example, the read back would be:

"After the landing 737, line up and wait, G-AB".

As further understanding of conditional clearances it is worthy of noting the following two rules that ATC apply when issuing conditional clearances. These are also given in CAP 413:

- Conditional phrases will not be used for movements affecting the active runway except when the aircraft or vehicles concerned are seen by the controller and pilot.
- Conditional clearances are to relate to one movement only and, in the case of landing traffic, this must be the first aircraft on approach.

Conditional clearances are used because they allow an expeditious traffic flow to be maintained i.e. the pilot is given the clearance in advance so that when the condition is met he can act upon it immediately. However, to maintain the utmost safety the above rules apply whereby the clearance must only relate to one movement, and for those affecting the runway the subject must already be visible and, if it is landing traffic, it can only be the first aircraft on approach.

Chapter 1.14   Immediate take-off

In general, pilots taxi aircraft at a slow to medium pace, and when lined up on the runway may even bring the aircraft to a halt and hold it on the brakes before commencing the take-off roll. But in some circumstances it is necessary for the departing aircraft to commence the take-off roll as quickly as possible, within the realms of safety obviously. The usual reason for this is due to the proximity of inbound traffic.

In such circumstances ATC will use the phrase 'cleared for immediate take-off'. Although it is obvious in general terms what this phrase means, it does actually have a specific definition. Controllers expect pilots to operate within the confines of this definition when accepting an immediate take-off clearance, so it is necessary that pilots know what this definition is. CAP 413 gives the definition of 'cleared for immediate take-off', this being:

> When given the instruction 'cleared for immediate take-off' the pilot is expected to:
>
> a)   If at the holding point: taxi immediately onto the runway and commence take-off without stopping the aircraft.
> b)   If lined up on the runway: take-off without delay.

It is important that pilots adhere to this definition when cleared for an immediate take-off. If unable to operate within the confines of its definition, then simply reply "unable to depart immediate". This is greatly preferred by ATC rather than stopping on the runway or generally being sluggish, as this all too often results in a go-around.

Chapter 1.15   Landing clearance

The subject of landing clearance may seem very simple, aircraft are not allowed to land until ATC give the instruction 'cleared to land', and to be able to give this instruction the runway must be clear of all other traffic and obstacles. Whilst this is true, the subject of landing clearance does not end there.

There are actually three types of landing clearance, and the main problem is that there are some crucial legalities incorporated in them. This therefore requires a thorough understanding of the subject, but unfortunately it is usually only briefly covered during pilot training. As a result, when ATC (who are taught the subject thoroughly) issue such clearances, pilots will read back the clearance and think they know what is happening by the nature of the words used in the clearance. Unfortunately they are often completely unaware of the responsibilities and legalities that they have brought upon themselves by accepting such clearances!

This chapter therefore intends to give a thorough understanding of landing clearances. Like many other aspects of ATC and RT in this book, once taught correctly it is relatively simple, but the first couple of times you read through it, it may seem very complex. To that end some points may be repeated, but that is purely in an attempt to emphasise where the responsibilities and legalities lie so that you have a thorough understanding.

The three types of landing clearance are:

    a)   'Cleared to land'
    b)   'Land after the [aircraft type]'
    c)   'After the landing/departing [aircraft type] cleared to land'

The first points to note about landing clearances are to do with phraseology. The standard phraseology for the clearances is exactly as given above. Therefore pilots must listen carefully to the actual words used by ATC when giving landing clearance because:

- Clearances 'a' and 'c' both use the words 'cleared to land', but clearance 'c' has the condition of 'after the landing/departing'.
- In clearance 'c' the condition of 'after the landing/departing' must be put before the words 'cleared to land'.
- Clearance 'b' does not (importantly) have the word 'cleared' in it. If it did then it could be confused for being clearance 'c' with the words re-arranged e.g. 'cleared to land after the [aircraft type]'.
- As this is standard phraseology, pilots are to use it correctly in the read back.

Land after

To understand the responsibilities and legalities associated with landing clearances let us start at the beginning. MATS Part 1 and CAP 413 state:

> A landing aircraft may be permitted to touchdown before a preceding landing aircraft which has landed is clear of the runway provided that:
>
> a) The runway is long enough to allow safe separation between the two aircraft and there is no evidence to indicate that braking may be adversely affected.
> b) It is during daylight hours.
> c) The controller is satisfied that the landing aircraft will be able to see the preceding aircraft which has landed clearly and continuously until it is clear of the runway.
> d) The pilot of the following aircraft is warned. Responsibility for ensuring adequate separation rests with the pilot of the following aircraft.
>
> In such circumstances ATC will provide this warning by giving the instruction:
> '[callsign] land after the [aircraft type]'.

Note (importantly) that the above procedure is stated for use for a landing aircraft behind a preceding landing aircraft. It cannot, therefore, be used for a landing aircraft behind a departing aircraft.

It is the controller's responsibility to decide that conditions 'a', 'b' and 'c' are met before giving the 'land after' instruction. The important thing for pilots to note is the last condition given in 'd', that being:

> 'Responsibility for ensuring adequate separation rests with the pilot of the following aircraft'.

This is very important for pilots to know as it has serious consequences with regards to the legalities of the change in responsibility for the provision of adequate separation. Pilots are very often unaware of this. The following is an explanation in more practical terms:

When ATC issues the instruction 'cleared to land' it is the controller that is responsible for ensuring that adequate separation exists between the landing aircraft and the preceding aircraft. With reference to the earlier paragraph, it is deemed that the definition of 'adequate separation' is that the landing aircraft must not touchdown before all other aircraft are clear of the runway.

Whilst it is a fact that the pilot is always responsible for the safe conduct of his aircraft, whilst under the control of ATC the pilot puts a certain amount of trust in the controller as the controller is legally responsible for the provision of 'adequate separation'. So this means that even when a landing situation appears to become "a little tight", the pilot (trusting the judgement of the controller who is legally responsible for the provision of adequate separation) is unlikely to initiate a go-around unless he feels that the controller has obviously misjudged the situation to the point that the safety of the aircraft is now coming under question.

Now take the case when a 'land after' instruction is given. A 'land after' instruction is usually given because the controller judges that it will be unlikely that he will be able to give a 'cleared to land' instruction i.e. the landing aircraft will touchdown or be within a few seconds of touching down before the preceding aircraft is clear of the runway. So the controller gives a 'land after' instruction to the pilot of the landing aircraft, which now means that legally the responsibility for the provision of adequate separation rests with that pilot.

The danger is that a pilot who is unaware of this change of responsibility is still (as usual) placing his trust in the controller's judgment, thinking that the controller is still responsible for giving a go-around instruction should the situation become "too tight".

If then, for example, the preceding aircraft suddenly came to a halt on the runway (for whatever reason) or missed a turn off and consequently continued along the runway now at a slow taxi speed (to vacate at a turn off further along the runway), the unsuspecting pilot may continue to land and touchdown thinking that everything is within limits because the controller would instruct him to go-around if it was "too tight". The reality of the situation is that the controller has legally passed the responsibility and judgment for the provision of adequate separation to the pilot, after which, the situation became "too tight" but the unsuspecting pilot (not having been given a go-around instruction) continues with the landing and is at risk of collision after the touchdown.

It is therefore necessary when accepting a 'land after' instruction to continue to observe the subject aircraft so that you the pilot can initiate a go-around should the subject aircraft do something unexpected like stop or miss a turn off (because ATC will not issue a go-around instruction).

If after accepting a 'land after' instruction you decide that the distance between the aircraft is becoming too close for comfort then you are well within your rights to go-around. Even if the subject aircraft has not done anything unusual, you may just feel that on this occasion you would rather err on the safe side and do not want to "push it", so a go-around is the sensible option.

You may be wondering why use a 'land after' instruction as its purpose seems to be to allow a tight situation to continue. The reasons it is used are twofold:

Firstly, with a 'cleared to land' instruction there is no leeway. Until all other aircraft are clear of the runway the landing aircraft cannot be allowed to touchdown. Taking this to the extreme, think of an airport with a hugely long runway e.g. Heathrow. If the only landing clearance available was 'cleared to land' then, for example, a Jetstream or Fokker 50 (i.e. an aircraft requiring a relatively very short piece of tarmac to land on) could not be allowed to land whilst another aircraft was about to vacate at the very far end at the last exit even though the distance between the two aircraft is around five times the landing distance required by the landing aircraft.

Taking it to the other extreme, if the distance between the two aircraft became obviously too close then ATC would instruct the landing aircraft to go-around rather then giving a 'land after' instruction.

So, a 'land after' instruction allows an aircraft to land when otherwise ATC could not allow it to do so. But as most situations lie between the two extremes it is necessary for the pilot to be responsible for judging whether the distance between the aircraft is sufficient as only the pilot knows what is appropriate for his aircraft in that non-standard situation.

Secondly, there are many occasions where a 'cleared to land' instruction can be given but only at the "last minute" i.e. at the point that the preceding aircraft becomes clear of the runway the landing aircraft will be within a few seconds of touching down. So, by being able to give a 'land after' instruction, giving this early allows the aircraft to land should someone transmit on the RT in those few seconds, whereas otherwise the pilot would have to initiate a go-around having not received a 'cleared to land' instruction.

Being able to do this is very useful for a controller, even more so at airfields where the runway controller also controls ground movement and departure clearance. In such cases pilots often make long transmissions with regards to start up and departure clearance, which can involve the aircraft type, position on the apron, intended departure route, requested altitude, etc. With reference to the above example, in such a case a 'land after' instruction can often prevent a go-around.

A final point to note is that condition 'a' states that the runway must be long enough to allow safe separation. Due to this it may be stated in MATS Part 2 that a 'land after' instruction cannot be given. So in such tight situations pilots should not automatically expect to be given a 'land after' clearance, nor should they pre-empt or question controllers by saying "we can accept a land after". If a 'land after' clearance is a viable and appropriate option then the controller will use it, and if it is not then he will not!

<u>After the landing/departing cleared to land</u>

MATS Part 1 states:

> Unless specific procedures have been approved by the Authority, a landing aircraft shall not be permitted to cross the beginning of the runway on its final approach until a preceding aircraft, departing from the same runway, is airborne.

Recall also that MATS Part 1 and CAP 413 also state:

> A landing aircraft may be permitted to touchdown before a preceding landing aircraft which has landed is clear of the runway provided that:
>
> a)   The runway is long enough to allow safe separation between the two aircraft and there is no evidence to indicate that braking may be adversely affected.
> b)   It is during daylight hours.
> c)   The controller is satisfied that the landing aircraft will be able to see the preceding aircraft which has landed clearly and continuously until it is clear of the runway.
> d)   The pilot of the following aircraft is warned. Responsibility for ensuring adequate separation rests with the pilot of the following aircraft.

Note that the first statement relates to a landing aircraft following a departing aircraft. The second statement relates to a landing aircraft following a preceding landing aircraft.

The previous paragraphs on the subject of the 'land after' instruction explained that this procedure enabled what would otherwise be a mandatory go-around to be prevented by transferring the responsibility for the provision of adequate separation from the controller to the pilot.

The Authority has, however, deemed it appropriate that in some of the above cases, where a 'cleared to land' instruction cannot be given, the controller can still retain the responsibility for the provision of adequate separation. In such a case it is therefore not necessary to give a 'land after' instruction. However, the controller is legally unable to give a 'cleared to land' instruction, so a third type of landing clearance is used. That being:

'After the landing/departing [aircraft type] cleared to land'.

You may be thinking, why not just use the 'land after' procedure instead of complicating things further. The reason it is used is that its definition assures the pilot that ATC are still responsible for the provision of adequate separation even though another aircraft is still on the runway at the time the landing instruction is given. Its use is therefore intended to enable high amounts of runway utilisation to be maintained by preventing associated go-arounds. The procedure is consequently only used at major airports that have a high traffic demand and a sufficiently long runway.

You will now want to know in what cases does this procedure apply. The Authority looks at each individual airport. As stated previously, due to the intention of the procedure, the airport must have a high traffic demand and a sufficiently long runway. When its use is approved there are a number of conditions that apply when using the procedure. As it is airport specific, the approval and its associated conditions are therefore stipulated in MATS Part 2 and also, for the pilot's reference, in the aerodrome charts or booklets. For those of you that are in the early stages of pilot training, you may not be familiar with aerodrome charts and booklets yet as they are usually covered in IFR training. It is worth noting that the approval and conditions are given in the aerodrome charts or booklets but not in NOTAM's, as NOTAM's are basically for temporary information.

The final part of this subject is to explain what conditions are associated with the use of this procedure. The following is a general example of the conditions that apply. I stress that these are generic, as previously stated they are specific to, and different at, each airport, so the example given should not be learned verbatim. For the actual conditions and figures read the notes in the appropriate aerodrome charts. Controllers must commit the conditions and figures to memory (from MATS Part 2) before being licensed to work at the specific airport.

The generic conditions are:

- At the time the aircraft crosses the threshold, the previous landing/departing aircraft must be at least 2000m from the threshold.
- If both aircraft are propeller driven the above distance can be reduced to 1500m.
- There is no evidence to indicate that braking may be adversely affected.
- It is during daylight.
- The controller is able to see both aircraft continuously.

In such circumstances ATC will issue the instruction:
    '[callsign] after the landing/departing [aircraft type] cleared to land'.

Note that the above conditions do not include the statement 'responsibility for ensuring adequate separation rests with the pilot of the following aircraft', as is included in the conditions for a 'land after' instruction. This is because when a 'after the landing/departing [aircraft type] cleared to land' instruction is given, such responsibility remains with the controller.

Also note that some airports may not have approval to use this procedure, so in such a "tight" situation pilots should not automatically expect to be given this instruction.

Chapter 1.16   Touch and go

The following two points may seem obvious, but it is worth stating just to make sure that no confusion exists:

> If ATC clear you for a touch and go then you must do exactly that i.e. touch down, continue to roll, and get airborne again. You are not cleared to land and remain on the ground.

> If ATC clear you to land (using one of the three landing clearances) then you must land and not execute a touch and go.

Using practical examples on this subject, should you request a touch and go and ATC replies "cleared to land", do not read back "cleared to land" but assume that you may execute a touch and go - you must land. There will be a valid reason that ATC require you to land, one example is traffic blocking the climb-out, and if you would like a brief explanation of why your touch and go has been refused then simply ask the controller.

This is also important if, for example, you are expecting to be given a late touch and go clearance but at the last minute the controller actually gives you a "land after" or a "after the landing/departing [aircraft type] cleared to land" instruction. With reference to the previous chapter on the definitions of such, the likely reason why this has occurred is that the distance between your aircraft and the preceding aircraft has become such that the controller judges it unsafe for you to touchdown, continue rolling at high speed and then accelerate (i.e. execute a touch and go) towards an aircraft that may not have cleared the runway or has not yet become airborne.

Similarly, if you request and are given touch and go clearance, but then realise that you actually meant to ask for landing clearance, then make the transmission: "Correction, request full stop landing". This is likely to happen on the last circuit of a series of touch and goes where you have got into the habit of saying "request touch and go" and consequently did so again on the final circuit rather than requesting a full stop landing.

If you accept a touch and go clearance but subsequently execute a full stop landing, this could result in an aircraft behind you having to go around. This is because during a touch and go the aircraft continues rolling at high speed and then becomes airborne again relatively quickly. This usually takes less time than for the same aircraft to roll along the runway slowly and vacate, especially if the turn off is a little further along the runway.

With that in mind, if a controller has cleared you for a touch and go he may have traffic relatively close behind you in order to maximise runway utilisation based on your expected (small) runway occupancy time. So, when you actually execute a full stop landing, the traffic close behind you has to go around. It may also be that due to your position on the runway (with regards to distance from the landing threshold) a 'land after' or a 'after the landing [aircraft type] cleared to land' instruction cannot be given, so a go-around is the only option.

Chapter 1.17   Low approaches

Pilots may sometimes wish to fly (relatively) low above the runway and then climb away, rather than landing or executing a touch and go. If a pilot wishes to make a low approach he can request it by saying "request low approach".

A point to note about this is that if ATC reply "cleared low approach runway [designation]" without giving a minimum height restriction, then it is the pilot who may decide just exactly how low he wishes to fly above the runway.

MATS Part 1 states:

> The runway-in-use shall be kept clear of aircraft and vehicles if an approaching aircraft is likely to descend below 400ft above the threshold elevation.

ATC may therefore restrict your low approach request to a certain height above the threshold elevation. If this restriction is due to traffic on the runway then the minimum height you can be cleared to descend to is 400ft. The standard phraseology for this clearance is:

> "Cleared low approach runway [designation] not below [number] feet above threshold elevation".

Note that the restriction is above threshold elevation, i.e. height not an altitude. So beware if your altimeter is set to QNH. You should, however, listen carefully to the instruction given by ATC just in case the controller happens to give the restriction as an altitude and not height above threshold elevation, for example, "not below altitude [number] feet".

Common examples of why traffic may be occupying the runway are:

- Aircraft backtracking, crossing or lining up on the runway.
- Vehicles working on the runway or commencing a runway inspection.

In such circumstances it may be more appropriate and expeditious to allow an aircraft to conduct a low approach, but with a minimum height restriction, rather than attempt to clear the traffic from the runway.

Section 2   Preventing airborne collisions

This section is intended to enlighten pilots with what they need to know about how ATC control traffic with respect to preventing airborne collisions. There are, however, a few terms that are fundamental to the control of air traffic. Pilots must know the definitions and have a good practical understanding of these terms in order to fully understand how ATC control traffic with respect to preventing airborne collisions.

These terms are: 'Traffic information', 'Separation', and associated with these are 'Traffic avoidance advice' and the 'Classification of airspace table'. From here on, whenever these terms are used, they should be thought of as given by their exact definitions rather than as a general term.

Chapter 2.1   Separation

Pilots know in general what 'separation' is. In general terms 'separation' is when ATC keep aircraft a certain distance apart e.g. 5nm horizontally or 1000ft vertically.

To give the full meaning: 'separation' (or 'standard separation' as it may also be referred to) is when aircraft are kept apart by a prescribed minimum. If aircraft are kept apart by this prescribed minimum then they are said to be 'separated'.

Not all controllers use radar, so if a controller does not have a radar screen then he obviously cannot look at it to see if aircraft are separated. Consequently there are a few methods that ATC use to ensure that aircraft are separated and remain separated (e.g. reports over different navigation beacons) and therefore there may be a different prescribed minimum associated to each method.

So the distance aircraft have to be apart in order to be classed as separated is dependent on which method ATC are using to separate the aircraft.

An in depth explanation of the different methods used to separate aircraft and their prescribed minimum is only necessary in the discussion of IFR and SVFR flights, and so such an explanation can be found in the IFR and SVFR sections.

What is required at this stage is that pilots understand the meaning of 'separation', that being: aircraft are considered to be separated when ATC keep the aircraft apart by a prescribed minimum.

Although separation has different methods and minimums, in order to help visualise the meaning of separation, if you prefer to think of it as a radar controller using 5nm horizontally or 1000ft vertically then this is fine at this stage.

Chapter 2.2   Traffic information

Pilots know in general what 'traffic information' is. In general terms 'traffic information' is when ATC give you information on traffic that may be relevant to you due to the proximity of such traffic.

The actual definition of 'traffic information' is:

> Information issued by a controller to alert a pilot or controller to other known or observed air traffic which may be in proximity to the position or intended route of flight.

It is very important that pilots note that when traffic information is given, effectively what happens is that the responsibility for preventing collisions is transferred from the controller to the pilot. It is therefore a very dangerous trap for an unsuspecting pilot who is unaware of its meaning. This is explained in depth in chapter 2.4.

Traffic information is given in one of two forms. If the controller has radar available then the added benefits of radar will be used in giving the traffic information i.e. the bearing from the aircraft in terms of clock position, the distance from the aircraft and the relative direction compared to the aircraft (e.g. opposite direction) will be given as well as the level of the traffic if available.

If the controller does not have radar available i.e. during a procedural service or when the tower controller gives traffic information just prior to departure, the traffic information is given in a more basic and generic format i.e. the relevant part of the route of the traffic is given (e.g. routeing east to west, or, routeing Tamworth to Lichfield) but the clock position, distance and relative direction cannot be given as the controller does not have an exact view of the situation without a radar "picture".

Chapter 2.3 Traffic avoidance advice

At first you may think that 'traffic information' and 'traffic avoidance advice' are the same thing, however, they are not. The definition of traffic information is given in chapter 2.2. The definition of traffic avoidance advice is:

> Advice specifying manoeuvres to assist a pilot to avoid a collision.

This may seem very similar to traffic information, but in practical terms the difference is that with traffic information the controller will simply give you information on where the other traffic is and what it is doing but will not give you any advice on how to avoid it. Traffic avoidance advice is when the controller gives you a manoeuvre to execute (e.g. a heading to turn onto) in order to avoid the other traffic. Note, however, that 'traffic avoidance advice' is not the same as 'avoiding action'. Avoiding action is explained in chapter 6.5.

It can be seen from chapter 2.5 (where traffic avoidance advice is explained in more depth) that traffic avoidance advice follows on from traffic information if the pilot believes he may be at risk of collision.

Chapter 2.4   Methods used by ATC to prevent collisions

The purpose of ATC is to prevent collisions between aircraft whilst expediting and maintaining an orderly flow of traffic. If asked how do ATC prevent collisions, most people will probably say that it is done by separating aircraft. However, as explained in the previous pages, separation has a defined meaning. So the subject of preventing collisions is a little more involved than simply separating everything.

The answer to the question of how do ATC prevent collisions is found in the 'classification of airspace table'. For the benefit of those new to flying, the table requires some explaining in order to be fully understood, and this is also why the terms separation, traffic information and traffic avoidance advice were explained in the previous pages.

The classification of airspace table is given in the glossary. The correct way to read the table, with respect to preventing collisions, is very simple and has only 3 steps. The 3 steps are:

1. In the column 'Class' locate the appropriate class of airspace.
2. Move along the row for that class of airspace to the column 'ATC service'.
3. The resulting box gives the method that ATC use to prevent collisions.

By reading through the column 'ATC service' a few times there are two important factors that should become apparent and must be understood:

1. The 'ATC service' only relates to how collisions are prevented i.e. no other topics are present in that column.
2. In the column there are only two terms used with respect to preventing collisions, these being 'separate' and 'pass traffic information'.

It is this second point that pilots must note, as this is a fundamental principle of preventing collisions. To put this into more obvious terms:

> ATC prevent collisions by using one of two methods – they will either separate traffic or they will pass traffic information to the pilots.

What this means in reality is that if you are being separated then the controller will get on with it without telling you that he is doing it i.e. he will issue instructions to aircraft (e.g. headings and levels) in order to keep aircraft separated, but he will not give you information on the position of proximate traffic, nor will he say on the RT that you are being separated. So the controller will always be manoeuvring aircraft so that collisions do not occur, and consequently the pilot does not have to look out of the window to resolve any conflicts (because that is what the controller is doing).

However, it is a very different case if the method ATC are using to prevent collisions is by passing traffic information. With reference to the classification of airspace table, the term used in the column 'ATC service' is 'pass traffic information', so once it is passed you are then under the 'see and avoid' principle. So effectively what happens is that when traffic information is given, the responsibility for preventing collisions is transferred from the controller to the pilot. This fundamental principle must therefore be fully understood by pilots. So once traffic information is given it is therefore up to you the pilot (and the pilot of the other aircraft) to see and avoid each other, ATC will not manoeuvre you around any conflicts. It is also worth noting that traffic information need only be given once (to both the relevant aircraft) for the controller to fulfil his legal obligation in preventing the collision, so do not expect regular traffic information updates, you should only expect to be given traffic information once.

Although on some occasions, if the controller is not too busy and is being helpful, you may receive traffic information more than once, the reason why you will generally not be given it more than once, other than there is no legal obligation to, is as follows:

Once the controller has given traffic information to both aircraft he knows that they are responsible for preventing a collision between themselves and they will do so by using the 'see and avoid' principle. If the controller does not have radar then he does not have an exact "view" on the aircrafts relevant positions, and so he cannot give any exact updates or avoiding manoeuvres. When flying under the 'see and avoid' principle it is possible for aircraft to get very close together without the pilots considering it as dangerous, for example, if one aircraft crosses half a mile behind another aircraft, that half a mile can seem like plenty of space between the aircraft and not unsafe at all. But to a controller looking at his radar screen it may be impossible to tell at the time the aircraft cross whether they have collided or not i.e. the blips may all but merge.

So, once traffic information has been given, although the radar may portray a possible collision, the pilots are actually visual with each other and manoeuvring visually around each other at a relatively close distance under the 'see and avoid' principle.

It is also a fact that when the controller is busy, only having to give traffic information once by law actually helps the controller to keep up with the traffic demands, or to put it another way, for a certain class of airspace it allows the controller to handle more traffic than he otherwise would. This is because if legally the controller had to keep updating traffic information and possibly give avoiding manoeuvres, he would have less time to concentrate on other blips and talk to those pilots i.e. controllers only have a certain amount of mental capacity, so if they have to focus more on each piece of traffic then they cannot control as many movements as they otherwise would. And the reason why it is not a legal requirement for the controller to keep updating the traffic information is because the pilots are now seeing and avoiding each other, so there is no need to keep intervening, just let the pilots get on with it.

Here is a quick summary of the pertinent points from this chapter:

- ATC prevent collisions by either separating aircraft or passing traffic information.
- When traffic information is given the responsibility for preventing collisions is transferred from the controller to the pilot.
- Traffic information only has to be passed once.

Chapter 2.5   Understanding the classification of airspace table

Refer to the classification of airspace table given in the glossary. The table has already been mentioned in the previous chapter with respect to preventing collisions. In this chapter however it is explained in full.

<u>Controlled and Uncontrolled airspace</u>

In the table, look at the columns entitled 'Class' and 'Requirements' and notice the following points:

- In Class A, B, C and D airspace the requirement is for all aircraft to have ATC clearance before entry into the airspace and to subsequently comply with ATC instructions whilst in the airspace.
- In Class E airspace the previous is true but only for IFR flights. VFR flights do not require clearance.
- In Class F airspace aircraft do not require a clearance to enter the airspace. With respect to complying with ATC instructions, the words used are 'participating IFR' and 'expected'.
- In Class G airspace aircraft do not require a clearance to enter the airspace nor do they have to comply with ATC instructions.

What this means in real terms is that, with the exception of VFR flights in Class E airspace, all aircraft in Class A to E airspace must be under the control of ATC. Therefore Classes A to E are called 'Controlled airspace' and as such ATC provide a 'Control service'. Note that no other airspace other than Class A to E are called controlled airspace.

Class F and G airspace are not under the control of ATC and so are called 'Uncontrolled airspace'.

Class F airspace is also called 'Advisory airspace'.

As an additional note, an ATC service may be provided in Class F and G airspace, but this is not a 'Control service' due to the fact that the airspace is not under the control of ATC i.e. it is uncontrolled airspace. This may sound confusing but is explained in section 4.

Who decides whether to separate aircraft or pass traffic information

This now brings us back to the subject of collision avoidance as was discussed in the previous chapter. With reference to the classification of airspace table, as Classes A to E are 'controlled' by ATC, then it makes sense that the minimum they must do is to prevent collisions between all aircraft in that airspace i.e. the minimum 'ATC service' is to separate or pass traffic information. The exception to this being VFR flights in Class E airspace as previously noted.

As Class G airspace is uncontrolled, then it follows that there is no minimum service that ATC have to provide.

Similar is true for Class F airspace with the exception of IFR flights that 'participate' in the advisory service.

So to the question of: who decides whether the aircraft should be separated or given traffic information. It can now be seen from the table that it is not up to the controller to decide what he wants to do with each aircraft, it is decided by two factors and nothing else. Those being:

- The class of airspace, and
- The flight rules that both aircraft are operating under.

So, for example, if a controller is controlling in Class C airspace, he must separate IFR flights from IFR and VFR flights, separate VFR flights from IFR flights, but if two VFR flights are in conflict he only has to pass traffic information.

This is another fundamental principle that pilots should be aware of.

Note from the table that in controlled airspace IFR flights are always separated from each other. This, again, makes sense as if you are IFR then you can/will be in conditions that preclude flight with visual references (e.g. being in cloud) and therefore neither of you can see and avoid each other if given traffic information.

Conflict between IFR and VFR flights

In Class D airspace if an IFR and a VFR flight are in conflict the controller is only required to give traffic information to the aircraft. It may seem strange that an IFR flight (that may be in cloud) is given traffic information. But it is important to remember that the pilot flying VFR must remain a minimum distance from cloud in order to be classed as VFR (see the 'VMC table' given in the glossary). As such, should the conflicting IFR traffic be in cloud, then the two aircraft should not be in danger of colliding due to the fact that the VFR flight is keeping that minimum distance from cloud.

Traffic avoidance advice

It can be seen from the classification of airspace table that traffic avoidance advice follows on from traffic information i.e. in practical terms, if after being given traffic information the pilot cannot see the conflicting traffic and consequently thinks he may be at risk of collision, he can request traffic avoidance advice. Note that the traffic avoidance advice must be requested and is not given automatically.

Note from the table, however, that the controller is not always legally obliged to give traffic avoidance advice when requested after traffic information, so do not fall into the trap of thinking that you always have it as a back up to avoid conflicting traffic.

The table shows that the legal requirement to give traffic avoidance advice only applies to VFR flights in Class C airspace, and IFR flights in Class D airspace. It does not apply to VFR flights in Class D and E airspace or IFR flights in Class E airspace.

Chapter 2.6 Misconceptions about traffic information and collision prevention

The list below should help to clear up some common misunderstandings with regards to traffic information and collision prevention. It also summarises some of the main points in the previous chapters of this section.

- Traffic information only has to be given once (to each aircraft), further updates are not required by law.

- When traffic information is given, the responsibility for preventing collisions is transferred from the controller to the pilot.

- The decision of whether to separate or give traffic information to the aircraft is governed purely by the class of airspace and the flight rules of the aircraft concerned (IFR or VFR).
  Note that it does not therefore depend on aircraft size. For example, if it is necessary to give traffic information to a Cessna 152 and a 747, the 747 does not automatically have any right of way or priority because it is much bigger. Both pilots should act accordingly to prevent a collision.

- If just prior to take-off clearance you are given traffic information, you are not given any extra protection just because you are about to commence a critical stage of flight i.e. the take-off roll and initial climb-out. You are still required to abide by the 'see and avoid' principle, as you would be if given traffic information during any other stage of flight. Chapter 3.4 explains this in more detail.

Section 3   Control of VFR flights

This section explains the methods ATC use to control VFR traffic and why these methods are used. Note that this section is concerned with ATC 'controlling' VFR traffic i.e. it relates to the 'control service' given in Class B, C, D and E 'controlled airspace'.

For information on how traffic is handled outside controlled airspace see section 4.

The paragraphs below are taken from MATS Part 1 and are an explanation of the philosophy used to control VFR flights:

> Notwithstanding that VFR flights in Class E controlled airspace may operate without reference to ATC, it can be expected that the majority of flights will communicate with ATC and can be expected to comply with the instructions issued. These instructions may comprise routeing instructions, visual holding instructions and level instructions in order to establish a safe, orderly and expeditious flow of traffic and to provide for the effective management of overall ATC workload.
>
> For example, routeing instructions may be issued which will reduce or eliminate points of conflict with other flights, such as final approach tracks and circuit areas, with a consequent reduction in the workload associated with passing extensive traffic information. Visual Reference Points (VRP's) may be established to assist in the definition of frequently utilised routes and the avoidance of instrument approach and departure tracks.
>
> When issuing instructions to VFR flights controllers should be aware of the over-riding requirement for the pilot to remain in VMC, to avoid obstacles and to remain within the privileges of his licence.

Chapter 3.1   VFR routeing instructions

Most people are familiar with the image of a controller sat in front of the radar screen giving heading instructions, for example, "Funjet 163 turn left heading 240°". However, with VFR flights a different principle must be applied.

In order to fly VFR the pilot must remain within the limits of VMC applicable to the class of airspace i.e. he must remain a certain horizontal and vertical distance from cloud and have a minimum in flight visibility. The 'VMC table' is given in the glossary for reference. If controllers gave specific heading instructions to VFR flights and it was a legal requirement for the pilot to comply with the instruction i.e. turn onto and maintain the heading, it could result in the VFR flight flying into an area where the VMC minima cannot be upheld, for example, flying into cloud or into an area of mist. There would be many consequences of this, the most dangerous of which is the fact that most VFR/PPL pilots are not trained to fly in IMC and so could very easily lose control of the aircraft.

It is therefore impractical/impossible to give, in general, VFR flights specific heading instructions. But ATC still need to control VFR flights and so will still need to give them instructions regarding the horizontal plain i.e. the route. VFR routeing instructions are therefore always given as cardinal points of the compass, or with respect to geographical locations that the pilot can visually identify (i.e. see out of the window), for example:

"Route north east"
"Cleared on track Stapleford"
"Left turn out, cleared to leave the control zone via ECCUP"

Such instructions therefore control the flight in the sense that it restricts the general direction, but, as no specific heading is given it allows the pilot the freedom to manoeuvre as required to remain VMC (e.g. avoiding clouds) whilst proceeding in that general direction.

Another consideration is that in order to remain within the privileges of the licence, the VFR pilot may also have to manoeuvre whilst proceeding in the general direction of the clearance in order to avoid an obstacle e.g. a tall mast, or to fly around an area in which he could not land clear of in the event of an engine failure.

Finally, it is also worth mentioning that one of the reasons of allowing VFR flight is to give the pilot as much freedom as possible within reason. Therefore, whilst proceeding in the general direction of the clearance, it allows you to do a bit of sight seeing whilst on your jolly jaunt!

To clear up any confusion that may still exist, when ATC give a VFR routeing instruction including a compass point or route to a geographical location, it does not imply that the exact heading to that location or compass point must be maintained. The pilot is allowed to manoeuvre, within reason, whilst proceeding in that general direction.

So, for example, if the controller wanted the aircraft to maintain a westerly heading, he would have to use the word 'heading' in the instruction i.e. "heading 270°", not "route west" as would be used for a VFR clearance. Similarly, to instruct the pilot to maintain the specific heading he would have to say "route direct Stapleford, maintain the heading when on track", not "cleared on track Stapleford", as would be used for a VFR clearance.

The term 'within reason' is used in the previous paragraphs with respect to manoeuvring whilst proceeding in the general direction of the clearance. Although there are no set limits to remain 'within reason', if you decide whilst routeing in the cleared direction to turn by 90° and fly in that direction for a bit, the controller will obviously assume after a while that you are either lost or incompetent as you are not complying with the clearance. The controller will then intervene as necessary. Also, should you decide to orbit for a while, for example, to look at a building or a lake, this is unlikely to be a problem whilst there is no conflicting traffic. But should some conflicting traffic appear, the controller may ask you how long you intend to remain there or may even instruct you to move if necessary.

It may be necessary on some occasions to instruct a VFR flight to fly a specific heading. These occasions do not occur often due to the factors given previously in this chapter, but it is possible. For such occasions the following is stated in MATS Part 1:

> Radar controllers in particular should exercise extreme caution in radar vectoring VFR flights – a geographical routeing is preferable. Prior to radar vectoring the controller must establish with the pilot the need to report if headings issued are not acceptable due to the requirement to remain VMC, avoid obstacles, and comply with the low flying rules. Controllers should be aware that pilots of some VFR flights may not be sufficiently experienced to comply accurately with radar headings, or to recover to visual navigation after radar vectoring.

Chapter 3.2　　　　　　VFR level instructions

Most people are familiar with the image of controllers giving level instructions, for example, "Funjet 163 climb to altitude 5000ft". Similar to that explained in the previous chapter for VFR routeing instructions, the pilot of a VFR flight may need to climb or descend in order to remain VMC, remain within the privileges of his licence, or simply to enjoy the relative freedom of VFR flying. VFR level instructions therefore use the same principle as that described in the previous chapter for VFR routeing instructions i.e. they do not specify an exact level to be maintained. There is in general, therefore, only one term used when giving VFR level instructions, this term being 'not above'. For example:

"Route north east, not above Flight Level 50"
"Cleared on track Stapleford, not above altitude 2500ft"

When a controller gives a 'not above' instruction he writes it on the FPS as a 'not above' instruction rather than a climb, descend, or maintain a level instruction. It is not necessary therefore, for pilots to request/inform the controller that they are changing levels – you can climb and descend as much as you like so long as you do not go above the 'not above' restriction. The benefits of the 'not above' instruction are that it reduces RT workload for the controller as well as giving the pilot a certain amount of freedom. It is necessary, of course, to request climb if the pilot wishes to go above the 'not above' restriction.

It is important to realise that as a 'not above' instruction has a very different meaning to a climb, descend, or maintain a level instruction, the term 'not above' must be included appropriately in the pilots read back. Should a pilot omit the term 'not above' from the read back or replace it with the word 'climb', 'descend', or 'maintain', the controller will ask the pilot to read back the clearance correctly to confirm the pilot has fully understood the clearance. It is also entirely reasonable, and good practice, for pilots to request a 'not above' level when requesting a VFR clearance from ATC, for example, "request to enter the zone routeing east not above altitude 3000ft".

ATC may on some occasions instruct a VFR flight to maintain a specific level. Again, similar to VFR routeing instructions, they do not very often, but it is possible. An example of why it may be necessary to give a VFR flight a 'maintain' a level instruction is given in Chapter 3.5. It is important therefore that you listen to the exact term used when a controller gives a VFR level instruction. Should you ask for or expect to be given a 'not above' level instruction, but the controller actually gives you a 'maintain' a level instruction, you must read back and understand that you are to 'maintain' the assigned level and do not have the freedom associated with a 'not above' clearance.

As a final note to clear up any confusion, if ATC give a VFR flight a specific heading to fly or a specific level to maintain, they can give one or the other without having to give both, for example, "route east, maintain altitude 3000ft" or "fly heading 310°, not above altitude 2500ft". Similarly, the instructing of a heading or level to be maintained does not automatically imply that the other must be maintained. So, for example, if you were cleared on track Stapleford not above altitude 3500ft and the controller later instructed you to maintain altitude 3500ft, it does not imply that you must automatically maintain that direct heading to Stapleford. Nor would it have automatically meant that you must maintain altitude 3500ft if the controller had instead instructed you to continue the present heading.

Chapter 3.3 VFR departure clearance

For a trainee or low hour pilot, reading back clearances is often difficult as the brain is not yet fluent in the format of such clearances and neither does it have much experience of RT. There are many occasions when professional pilots stumble over the RT when trying to remember what it was that ATC said five seconds ago, including myself! There are, however, some techniques that can help pilots become more fluent at this a little quicker and easier than would otherwise be possible. This chapter details departure clearances in particular, as departure clearances usually contain more information than other clearances and therefore there is a higher probability of getting something wrong. IFR departure clearances are detailed later in chapter 6.10.

The first point to note is that departure clearances are normally given in a set format. Once the pilot is familiar with the format it becomes much easier to recall the details when giving a read back. A VFR departure clearance is normally given in the following format:

1. Initial route
2. Level
3. Flight rules
4. Squawk

For example: "Cleared to leave the control zone to the east, not above altitude 2000ft, VFR, squawk 2102".

Note that the route and level instructions are normally given in the form as explained in the previous two chapters for a VFR flight i.e. a general direction and a 'not above' instruction.

The second point to note is that writing the clearance down makes it much easier to read back as you can read it whilst speaking rather than having to instantly remember it. The tricky part is how to write down the many words that the controller says (like in the example above) in the three seconds it takes the motor mouth to say them! To write down all the information in such a short space of time would require the pilot to be good at shorthand. So that is what you should do. Not necessarily go to night school to learn shorthand, but devise a set of symbols that quickly abbreviate the more common words/terms that ATC use in clearances.

It may be a little time consuming to devise your own set of symbols, however, the glossary lists some of the standard symbols that ATC use to write on the FPS's as well as some other symbols that maybe useful to pilots. Obviously there is no legal requirement for pilots to use those exact symbols, but the list is there should you find it helpful, and the symbols can be applied to any clearances, not just departure clearance.

Using the standard symbols list, the clearance given in the previous example would be written as:

        ⊿↗   E $\overline{2A}$ V   SQ2102

Chapter 3.4 Traffic information on departure

Although this chapter is included in the VFR section, due to the fact that it concerns traffic information the details apply as equally to IFR flights as they do to VFR flights. For example, as given in the classification of airspace table, in Class D airspace VFR flights are to be given traffic information on IFR flights, and IFR flights are to be given traffic information on VFR flights.

As stated previously in chapter 2.6, if just prior to take-off clearance you are given traffic information, you are still required to abide by the 'see and avoid' principle as you would be if given traffic information during any other stage of flight. The more common examples of this are when an aircraft is or is expected to cross through the climb-out, and when an aircraft is orbiting or hovering next to the climb-out. For example:

"Traffic information, a Cherokee north west of the airfield routeing south through the climb-out, not above altitude 2000ft", or

"Traffic information, a helicopter in your 11 o'clock, one mile, holding south of the climb-out at 1000ft".

In such circumstances, the technicalities of being given traffic information have been explained in previous chapters, and you should now be aware of the airmanship responsibilities required during the take-off roll and initial climb-out. There is, however, another similar example where, due to the perception of the situation by the pilot, he may forget that the responsibility for collision avoidance has been transferred after being given traffic information. This situation occurs when an aircraft that is about to depart is given traffic information on an aircraft that has just departed, for example:

You are lining up on the runway as the previous departing aircraft gets airborne. Within a couple of seconds of that aircraft getting airborne the controller says: "Traffic information, the departing Cessna 152 is turning left after departure, cleared for take-off".

Because the controller has given you traffic information the change of responsibility for collision avoidance still occurs as it would during any other stage of flight. Therefore, it is up to you, not the controller, to give yourself sufficient space behind the departing aircraft before commencing take-off. You should not just roll automatically because the controller cleared you for take-off.

On many occasions the previous departing aircraft is of the same speed or faster than the aircraft that is about to depart, so there is not a problem with regards to spacing, although the pilot that is about to depart must still understand that he is responsible for collision avoidance. The problem arises when the aircraft that is about to depart is faster/much faster than the previous departing aircraft, for example, a jet following a Cessna 152.

When two aircraft are departing, the earliest the second aircraft can be cleared for take-off is when the first aircraft becomes airborne i.e. its wheels leave the runway. The controller also has to consider wake turbulence spacing and, if the aircraft are to be separated, the appropriate amount of minutes required for the separation. If, however, the aircraft do not require separating (therefore only traffic information is required) and there is no wake turbulence spacing, then the controller can legally clear the fast aircraft for take-off as soon as the slow aircraft becomes airborne. This may seem an odd situation and, should it happen to you, it may look as if the controller has obviously made a mistake when he clears you for take-off whilst a much slower aircraft will be blocking the climb-out for a while. But remember it is allowable because traffic information has been given, so it is now up to you to decide, in the interests of collision avoidance, when you have sufficient space behind the previous departing aircraft and consequently commence the take-off roll. Remember that this does not only apply to VFR flights, but also to IFR flights depending on the class of airspace.

Often the controller will wait for the slower aircraft to become established in the climb-out first before giving the second aircraft take-off clearance. But the controller is allowed, should he choose to do so, to give take-off clearance as soon as the first aircraft becomes airborne. On these occasions it is usual for the pilot of the second aircraft to either wait for the slower aircraft to make its initial turn before commencing the take-off roll, or give the slower aircraft a few seconds after being airborne before commencing the take-off roll with the intention of making an early turn himself.

Chapter 3.5 Additional instructions after traffic information

When it is required to give traffic information to aircraft then, as previously explained, no further action is required by the controller with respect to collision prevention. But in some situations the controller may give additional instructions which ensure that the controller maintains a safe, orderly and expeditious flow of traffic whilst providing a control service. These additional instructions are given due to either:

a) They are an extra precaution that decreases the probability of a pilot that is unfamiliar with the area or, to be blunt, an incompetent pilot from causing an incident.
b) Because the controller has the best overall picture of the situation, and due to his experience he can judge aircraft speeds and tracks very accurately and therefore the controller can provide the most efficient solution.

To give a practical understanding of this, consider the following situation:

An aircraft is departing from runway 09 whilst another aircraft is routeing northbound 2nm east of the airfield i.e. to cross through the climb-out, and traffic information has been given to both aircraft.

If the flight paths of the two aircraft were such that at the time the northbound aircraft crossed the climb-out the departing aircraft would be very close to that crossing aircraft (and flying towards it), an unfamiliar or incompetent pilot may not judge the situation appropriately after being given traffic information. This may therefore result in the aircraft having to make evasive manoeuvres. To prevent such a situation occurring, the controller may therefore give traffic information to the crossing aircraft, followed by the instruction "hold south of the climb-out, route north behind the departing [aircraft type]".

If, however, the crossing aircraft had been instructed to hold until the departing aircraft had passed, but the pilot of the crossing aircraft is very cautious, he may wait a relatively long time after the departing aircraft has passed before crossing the climb-out. This results in either the next departing aircraft having to be delayed, or the crossing aircraft being delayed, as the controller has to instruct it to orbit again and wait for the next departing aircraft to pass before crossing the climb-out. At a busy airport this can produce serious capacity problems. In such a situation, once the departing aircraft has passed, the controller using his experience and judgement may give the instruction "route northbound now, further traffic to depart".

Many of the situations where additional instructions are given after traffic information, occur close to the airport where controllers have to maintain a constant flow of inbound and outbound IFR flights, whilst trying to integrate VFR flights that wish to cross the final approach, initial climb-out, or cross overhead the airport.

When an aircraft wishes to cross overhead the airport whilst there is departing traffic, the crossing aircraft will usually be instructed to either route directly over the departure threshold or to route to the approach side of the departure threshold, for example, "route north, pass directly over the 09 threshold", or "route north, remain west of the 09 threshold at all times".

By routeing aircraft over the departure threshold e.g. the 09 threshold when aircraft are departing from runway 09, the crossing and departing aircraft will not come into conflict due to the fact that the departing aircraft commences its take-off roll at the 09 threshold and consequently will not become airborne until further along the runway towards the 27 threshold.

In such cases, if the controller says "departure threshold" make sure you identify the correct threshold, because if you do not think about it you may fly over the threshold at the wrong end of the runway and therefore be in conflict with the departing aircraft as it gets airborne. If the controller actually specifies the threshold numbers, for example, "09 threshold", the numbers are painted on the runway in very large figures for you to look at, so you should be able to identify it should you have any doubt!

When an aircraft wishes to cross overhead the airport or through the initial climb-out whilst there is arriving traffic or departing traffic with a relatively low stop altitude, the crossing aircraft may be instructed to cross but maintain a specific altitude (rather than being given a 'not above' clearance). This altitude would be such that it provides a precautionary vertical separation from the departing aircraft or from the arriving aircraft should that aircraft have to go-around, rather than relying on the pilots to see and avoid each other as per the traffic information principle. This therefore allows the crossing aircraft to continue its flight without being delayed, and can therefore also be of benefit to the controller in a busy traffic environment. For example, if the go-around stop altitude is 2000ft, then the crossing aircraft could be instructed to maintain 3000ft whilst crossing. If, however, the go-around stop altitude was 3000ft, but the cloud base was around 4000ft and the crossing aircraft was VFR, the aircraft on approach could be instructed to maintain 2000ft in the event of a missed approach and the crossing aircraft allowed to cross maintaining 3000ft.

Again it is important to listen to the exact clearance given by ATC. For example, you may already be operating on a clearance of not above altitude 3000ft, the controller later clearing you to route through the climb-out maintaining altitude 3000ft. You must therefore listen and understand that you are now to maintain the given altitude and are not operating on a 'not above' clearance as you previously were, even though the numbers that are given may be the same e.g. 3000ft.

Chapter 3.6   Visual reporting points

Pilots will become familiar with visual reporting points (VRP's) during initial navigation training. As VRP's are points that pilots need to identify visually, then it will be of no surprise to find that VRP's are chosen individually as relatively large features that stand out from their surroundings. Below are excerpts taken from MATS Part 1 that detail why VRP's are established and how controllers use them:

> VRP's are established to assist ATC in routeing VFR traffic and at the same time integrate it with IFR flights. VRP's are established for some aerodromes outside controlled airspace which have instrument approach procedures in order to assist ATC in routeing VFR traffic clear of the instrument traffic.
>
> Where VRP's are established outside controlled airspace controllers should avoid concentrating traffic over VRP's and should not instruct aircraft to hold over those VRP's. This does not apply to VRP's established within controlled airspace where a known traffic environment exists.

Note from the above that two philosophies are used with regards to VRP's, one for use with VRP's that are within controlled airspace where all the traffic is known to and in contact with ATC, and the other for use with VRP's that are outside controlled airspace where not all the traffic is known to or in contact with ATC.

The philosophies are different because within controlled airspace, due to the fact that all the traffic is known to ATC, the controller is 'controlling' the entire traffic within that airspace and is doing so to prevent collisions. It is therefore possible to use the VRP's as an easily identifiable point for VFR pilots to route over in the interests of either keeping an orderly traffic flow in general, or to integrate VFR flights with IFR flights i.e. sequencing for the approach.

However, outside controlled airspace not all the traffic is known to ATC, so the controller is not 'controlling' the entire traffic within that airspace and therefore cannot guarantee to prevent all possible collisions. As such, if controllers routed or held VFR traffic over VRP's outside of controlled airspace, they would actually be increasing the likelihood of a collision due to the fact that unknown VFR traffic is also very likely to route over the VRP's, using the VRP's as a navigation point or general sight seeing feature - as the VRP's are by nature easily identifiable and stand out from their surroundings.

Therefore, outside of controlled airspace, controllers use VRP's as points for VFR traffic to keep away from, in general, keeping the traffic away from IFR traffic that is on an instrument approach and therefore requires some degree of priority.

Examples of such controlling are:

   a)   A departure clearance where the controller specifies a VRP to route via i.e. fly directly over (within reason), in order to leave controlled airspace, for example, "cleared to leave the control zone via ECCUP, not above altitude 2000ft, VFR, squawk 3613".

b) Advice from the controller that the aircraft should remain away from a VRP i.e. do not fly directly over it, in order to keep the aircraft away from the instrument approach area, for example, "remain north of [name] reservoir due arriving instrument traffic".

When VFR flights are cleared to enter a control zone, the standard procedure for that airport may be for ATC to route the aircraft via VRP's near the edge of the zone boundary. When more than one aircraft is being routed inbound via a VRP it may therefore be necessary to give traffic information to those aircraft. Sometimes there can be quite a few aircraft all wishing to route via the VRP at the same time, for example, at busy training schools where everyone is coming back to land from the training area at the same time.

The question that pilots often wonder on these occasions is: should ATC prioritise the inbound order, as there are obviously a number of aircraft fighting for the same piece of airspace and all wanting to get home before the others? The simple answer to this is no. Again it is due to the principle of traffic information. If the controller is required to give traffic information to the aircraft rather than separate them, then provided traffic information is given to all relevant aircraft, the controller has fulfilled his obligation. So yet again it is up to the pilots to see and avoid each other, and that includes giving way as necessary to fit into the inbound stream via the VRP.

It may also be the case that you obtain your clearance to enter the zone via a VRP after hearing another aircraft being given the same clearance, but you know that you are closer to the VRP than the other aircraft is i.e. you receive your clearance second, but will actually be first to reach the VRP. If this is the case you do not automatically need to wait for the other aircraft to enter via the VRP first just because you received your clearance second. Again, under the principle of traffic information, so long as you see and avoid, and give way where necessary, you may enter the zone via the VRP when you wish.

In such circumstances the controller does not automatically assume that the aircraft will enter the zone via the VRP in the order of who received their clearance first. The controller knows that he has given traffic information, and therefore also knows that it is up to the pilots to produce their own inbound order via the VRP. What happens in practise is that if the controller has radar, he will put the FPS's into the order that emerges as he sees each aircraft pass over the VRP. If the controller does not have radar, then he will instruct each aircraft to make a certain position report, for example, overhead the VRP or downwind, and he will then put the FPS's into the order that emerges as the aircraft make the position reports.

Chapter 3.7   Refusing VFR flights due to weather

The pilot is responsible for determining whether the met conditions permit flight in accordance with visual flight rules. The VMC table given in the glossary gives the criteria for determining visual met conditions with respect to the class of airspace. Note that it is the pilot that is responsible for determining this. There are occasions, however, when controllers cannot allow pilots to operate as a VFR flight due to the met conditions. Those occasions are actually specified by law and have been stipulated as a precaution against inexperienced or incompetent pilots. The rules for this are given below as written in MATS Part 1:

> ATC shall advise pilots of aircraft intending to operate under VFR, to or from aerodromes in Class D airspace, if the reported met conditions at those aerodromes reduces below the following minima:
>
> - Aircraft other than helicopters: Visibility 5000m and/or cloud ceiling 1500ft.
> - Helicopters: Visibility 1500m
>
> ATC will then request the pilot to specify the type of clearance required and if necessary, obtain SVFR or IFR clearance from approach control.
>
> Additionally, ATC shall not issue any further VFR clearances to aircraft wishing to operate under VFR to or from such aerodromes within Class D airspace when the reported met conditions at those aerodromes are below the minima stated above.
>
> When the reported visibility consists of two values, the lower of the two values shall be used when determining whether to implement the procedures above.

Whilst the above statement of the rules is very precise and legally correct, it is worth dissecting and explaining in detail so that every aspect of the rules is fully understood.

Visibility

Note that the visibility to be used is as per the 'reported met conditions at those aerodromes'. The pilot cannot, therefore, use the in flight visibility for this purpose. Neither can the pilot use his determination of the visibility at the aerodrome, it must be the 'reported' met visibility i.e. the visibility at the aerodrome as reported by the official met observer, which is subsequently transmitted on the ATIS. This fact is included in the VMC table as the 'Note'.

Cloud

The term used with regards to cloud is 'cloud ceiling'. The definition of cloud ceiling is: 'The height above the aerodrome of the lowest part of any cloud that is sufficient to obscure more than one half of the sky'.

Note that this provides for a different set of circumstances than if the term 'cloud base' was used. The definition of cloud base being: 'The height above the aerodrome of the base of any cloud'.

Aircraft wishing to enter controlled airspace

In the statement 'ATC shall not issue any further VFR clearances ...', the use of the word 'shall' in the phrase 'ATC shall not' is legally binding, and means that ATC will not issue any further VFR clearances to aircraft wishing to operate to or from such aerodromes i.e. the controller is not allowed to use his judgement and issue further clearances if he thinks it is appropriate. Once the limit is reached (i.e. once below the stated minima) he cannot legally issue further VFR clearances for operations to or from such aerodromes.

Also, because the term used with regards to the minima is 'below' and is legally binding, again controllers will be very strict with this. So, if the reported met visibility is, for example, exactly 5000m, then operations will continue as such. It is only when it becomes less than the minima that the operations will change.

The third paragraph of the rules continues to say '... wishing to operate under VFR to or from such aerodromes'. An aircraft wishing to depart VFR from an aerodrome within Class D airspace will therefore not be allowed to get airborne VFR. An aircraft already airborne and (importantly) outside controlled airspace will not be allowed to enter the airspace VFR in order to land, but (obviously) the aircraft is allowed to remain flying VFR. This is due to the premise that whilst inside the control zone it is the reported met visibility at the aerodrome that is relevant to taking off and landing. Whilst airborne, however, the pilot is the only relevant person who can determine the met conditions in his location with respect to the visual flight rules, and therefore ATC cannot tell the pilot what to do with respect to this.

This now leaves the question of what about aircraft that are already airborne and (importantly) inside controlled airspace.

Aircraft airborne and inside controlled airspace

The first paragraph of the rules states '... intending to operate under VFR, to or from aerodromes ...'. It has already been explained that the third paragraph of the rules refuses VFR clearance to aircraft either outside controlled airspace intending to enter, or inside the control zone intending to take-off. Therefore, the first paragraph relates to aircraft already airborne and inside controlled airspace.

The use of the terms 'ATC shall advise ... if the reported ...', and subsequently 'ATC will then request the pilot to specify the type of clearance required and if necessary, obtain SVFR or IFR clearance' therefore provide a specific course of action with respect to VFR flights already airborne and within controlled airspace. This course of action is that ATC will inform the VFR flights of the relevant met conditions and then ask the pilot what clearance he would like. The important thing to understand from this is that for VFR flights already airborne and within controlled airspace, nowhere in the rules does it state that the controller can refuse the pilot to continue VFR. The controller must ask the pilot to specify the type of clearance required, but if the pilot wishes to remain VFR then he can elect to do so and the controller must allow it. This is therefore different to the case of pilots wishing to depart VFR or enter controlled airspace VFR in order to land, as in those cases ATC must refuse the VFR clearance. This may appear to be a contradiction in policy, but there is a good reason for it. The relevance of the figures stated as the minima are obviously due to the VMC minima for VFR flight, as can be seen in the VMC table. Due to the fact that it is the reported met conditions at the aerodrome that are relevant for the purpose of taking off and landing, it makes sense for the controller to refuse new VFR clearances for the purpose of taking off and landing when the met conditions at the aerodrome are below the VMC minima. Once airborne inside controlled airspace however, the pilot is given the benefit of deciding whether the met conditions allow him to continue VFR (even though the met conditions at the aerodrome may be below VMC minima) and therefore ATC cannot refuse a pilot to continue VFR.

The VMC table shows that in certain circumstances pilots must remain 1000ft vertically from cloud in order to remain VFR. The relevance of the 1500ft cloud ceiling stated in the procedures in this chapter is so that pilots can remain 1000ft vertically from cloud (i.e. within the VMC minima) and at the same time obey the '500ft rule'.

Recall also that the cloud ceiling refers to cloud covering more than one half of the sky (i.e. 5 oktas or more). In such cases there could be cloud well below the ceiling of 1500ft, in fact, by definition, up to 4 oktas of it. This, therefore, could make a flight under VFR very difficult, and in some locations impossible. Consequently, when ATC give this reminder, pilots should realise that the weather could already be very dire.

Chapter 3.8   VFR approach

When VFR flights are in the aerodrome circuit and other traffic is already on the final approach, if the aircraft do not require separating then traffic information will be given as necessary to allow the aircraft in the circuit to position behind the aircraft on final approach. On such occasions it is therefore up to the pilot to decide what is a safe and appropriate distance for him to be behind the preceding aircraft. ATC will not intervene on this matter, and if a go-around occurs due to insufficient distance between the two aircraft then it is the pilot who is at fault, as he was responsible for the spacing.

Usually the controller will give the traffic information when the circuit aircraft is downwind and will include the instruction 'report base'. The fact that traffic information has been given, and the instruction to report base has also been given, means that the circuit aircraft is cleared to fly the base leg when the pilot decides it is safe to do so with respect to the traffic on final approach.

On some occasions, however, the controller will give what may be confused to be an instruction to report base, but what the controller actually says is "report ready to turn base". This is not a clearance to fly the base leg, but is an instruction to report when you are ready to make the turn onto base leg. Therefore, care must be taken to listen to the exact instruction that ATC have given.

Due to the fact that traffic information has been given, all the controller then has to do by law is to let the pilot turn base when the pilot decides it is safe and appropriate to do so. However, on some occasions the controller yet again has the best overall picture of the situation as well as the experience of judging aircraft speeds and spacing. So, in order to provide the most efficient solution, this is why the controller may use the instruction 'report ready to turn base'. When the pilot subsequently reports ready for base leg the controller will then know whether it is more appropriate to allow the aircraft to turn base at that time or if it should be delayed, for example, by orbiting or extending downwind.

In the examples above, if there is also a requirement for wake turbulence separation, then this information will be given along with traffic information. The standard phrase for controllers to use in these situations is:

   'Caution wake turbulence. The recommended distance is [number] miles'.

This is explained further in chapter 8.6 and it means that the pilot is now responsible for ensuring that this distance between the aircraft is applied. The only legal obligation that ATC have on this matter is to inform the pilot of the recommended distance i.e. the controller will not give instructions to provide the wake turbulence separation. The controller may still, however, ask you to report ready to turn base so that the traffic situation is managed appropriately.

Section 4   Types of air traffic service

There are different types of air traffic services that can be given to pilots. In general terms there are two types of service that can be given by ATC. These are:

- Control Service
- Flight Information Service

If an aircraft is inside controlled airspace then it must, by definition, be given a 'control service'. Consequently a control service cannot, by definition, be given outside controlled airspace.

According to ICAO rules, in general terms, individual states are responsible for establishing their own services that will be provided outside controlled airspace. Services outside controlled airspace are grouped under the generic term 'Flight Information Services', however, as individual states are responsible for establishing their own such services, the names and specific details of such services may differ between countries.

In the UK the services available outside controlled airspace are: Basic Service, Traffic Service, Deconfliction Service and Procedural Service. Therefore, this gives an amendment to the first paragraph of this section and means that in the UK there are five different types of service that can be given by ATC. These are:

- Control Service
- Basic Service
- Traffic Service
- Deconfliction Service
- Procedural Service

A Basic Service, Traffic Service, Deconfliction Service or Procedural Service are given outside controlled airspace and cannot be given inside controlled airspace.

With reference to the classification of airspace table (given in the glossary) and chapter 2.5, recall that Class A to E airspace is controlled airspace and Class F and G airspace is uncontrolled airspace. Therefore in Class A to E airspace (with the exception of VFR flights in Class E airspace) a control service must be given. Whilst in Class F and G airspace a Basic Service, Traffic Service, Deconfliction Service or Procedural Service can be given.

Note that as Class F and G airspace are uncontrolled airspace, pilots can choose not to receive a service at all if they wish i.e. it is not mandatory to select a Basic Service, Traffic Service, Deconfliction Service or Procedural Service.

Chapter 4.1   Control Service

A control service can be either:

- a) An Aerodrome control service
- b) An Approach control service, with or without radar
- c) An Area control service, with or without radar

As these are all control services then the 'type' of service being given is the same i.e. a control service. To put this another way, there are no differences in the services with respect to legalities or responsibilities - they are all control services - but are provided by either an aerodrome controller, an approach controller or an area controller. Therefore, in countries that conform to ICAO practices, when a control service is provided this 'type' of service means that ATC will provide the appropriate separation and traffic information to IFR and VFR flights as dictated by the classification of airspace table.

So when a controller informs you that you are receiving a '[name] control service' the prefix name as such is not important, it is the words 'control service' that are important. This is different to a Basic Service, Traffic Service, Deconfliction Service or Procedural Service as these different names relate to a different 'type' of service, each therefore having different legalities and responsibilities.

When an approach or area service is provided without the use of radar this is referred to as a 'procedural' service. The word 'procedural' is not usually used on the RT however. In contrast, when a control service is being provided with the aid of radar the prefix 'radar' is often used instead of 'approach' or 'area' i.e. the controller may say 'radar control service'.

Further to this, if you are flying VFR or SVFR and the controller informs you that you are under a radar control service (RCS), you should not be confused into thinking that the controller will start giving you vectors like an IFR flight. It simply means that because you are in controlled airspace then a control service is provided and to do this the controller is using information provided by radar. But because you are VFR or SVFR the controller will still use the principles applicable to controlling VFR or SVFR flights as explained in sections 3 and 7.

Note that when then term 'procedural' (with lower case letters) is used in this book it refers to the generic fact that the service is a non-radar service. However, when the term 'Procedural Service' is used (with capital initial letters) it solely refers to the Procedural Service described in chapter 4.6 and therefore refers to the procedures and meanings that are unique to that type of (flight information) service.

Chapter 4.2   Flight Information Services

The definition of a Flight Information Service is: 'A non-radar service that gives information useful for the safe and efficient conduct of flight'.

Note that this service is a non-radar service. There is not an exhaustive list of the information that the controller must give under this service. It is therefore left to the judgement of the controller to decide what information is useful to each flight for its safe and efficient conduct. In general, such information would be information about weather, changes of serviceability of facilities (e.g. navaids or runways) and information concerning collision hazards with other aircraft (e.g. traffic information).

The controller may attempt to identify on the radar screen an aircraft in receipt of a Flight Information Service for monitoring and co-ordination purposes only. It is important to note that such identification does not imply that a radar service is being given or that the controller will continuously monitor the aircraft.

It follows that whilst in receipt of a Flight Information Service, as this is a non-radar service, information concerning collision hazards with other aircraft may be generic rather than being given using the clock code. This information will only highlight a potential collision hazard to the pilot (i.e. as per traffic information) and no avoiding manoeuvres or instructions will be given. Furthermore, when the controller does not have a radar "picture" he therefore does not have a view of all traffic and consequently cannot give information on aircraft that are not in radio contact. This is of particular significance to the Basic Service and Procedural Service given outside controlled airspace.

Due to the fact that individual states are responsible for establishing their own (flight information) services that will be provided outside controlled airspace, some countries may solely provide the basic Flight Information Service as defined and explained above, whereas other countries may give varying (increased) levels of service. In the UK, as previously stated, the flight information services that are available are the Basic Service, Traffic Service, Deconfliction Service and Procedural Service, and these are designed so that each of the services builds on the provisions of the Basic Service.

The UK flight information services i.e. the Basic Service, Traffic Service, Deconfliction Service and Procedural Service, are explained individually in the remaining chapters of this section. The details given in the remainder of this chapter apply equally to, and are fundamental principles of, all the UK flight information services and so should be remembered when reading the remaining chapters of this section. Such details of the UK flight information services in this section are taken from CAP 774. It is important to note that CAP 774 is the authoritative source and should therefore be used as such for current procedures and should also be checked frequently in order to be aware of any future changes. The procedures detailed in MATS Part 1 are taken directly from CAP 774 to ensure commonality.

Are you being given a service?

When pilots outside controlled airspace make the initial call to ATC and request a service they often wrongly assume that they are being given a service when in reality no service is being given at all. The way this usually happens is that on your initial call you give all your relevant details and request, for example, a Traffic Service. The controller then replies:

"[callsign] roger, squawk [number]".

It must be understood that until the controller informs you of the service you are being given with the exact words i.e. "Basic Service", "Traffic Service", "Deconfliction Service" or "Procedural Service" then you are not being given any service at all. Recall from chapter 1.1 that the use of the word 'roger' in the above example does not imply that a service is being given. Also recall from chapter 1.2 that when the controller does inform you of the service you are being given, you are required to give a read back of that service so that no doubt exists between yourself and the controller.

The reason why controllers often only reply (initially) with the word 'roger' and a squawk code is because the controller must/chooses to identify your aircraft on the radar screen first before providing you with the service. There is therefore a time delay between issuing you with a squawk code and the controller informing you that a service has commenced. As explained later in this chapter, the controller may be busy with traffic that is already being given a service, so this can result in a long delay between you receiving a squawk code and your service commencing.

Similarly, pilots often assume that they are being given a service outside controlled airspace when the controller informs them that they are identified. Again this is not the case. The identification procedure does not imply that a service is being given. As stated above, until the controller informs you of the service you are being given with the exact words, you are not being given any service at all.

Refusing a service

Recall from earlier in this section that outside controlled airspace pilots can elect not to receive any service due to the fact that it is uncontrolled airspace. However, this also means that if a pilot requests a service, the controller has no obligation to provide that service or any other service, therefore the controller can refuse to provide the pilot with anything at all!

Should a controller refuse to provide a service there must be a valid reason for it. Controllers are to endeavour to provide the service requested, but there are many reasons why it may not be possible to provide that service. These reasons are basically due to the amount of remaining capacity the controller has, or in general terms, how busy the controller is. This, however, is not simply a case of how much the controller is talking on the radio.

The different types of service available each require the controller to work in different ways and provide different things to the pilot, as can be seen in the following chapters. Each service therefore has different demands on the controllers capacity, both mental i.e. thinking time, and physical i.e. talking on the RT and co-ordinating with other controllers. It therefore follows that it is not simply a case of how many aircraft the controller is working or how much he is talking on the RT that limits the controller's capacity, but also the permutations of what types of service are being given.

In some locations controllers will be providing a service to portions of both controlled and uncontrolled airspace at the same time. In such circumstances controllers will, due to best practice, give priority to aircraft within controlled airspace. This therefore can be one reason to refuse a service to an aircraft outside controlled airspace.

If the controller is near to capacity and an additional aircraft requests a service that has a high capacity demand, the controller may decline to give that service but offer to give a service that has a lesser capacity demand, therefore not overloading the controller e.g. the pilot asks for a Deconfliction Service but the controller offers a Traffic Service.

The issue of capacity can also mean that when a pilot outside controlled airspace requests to enter controlled airspace, he is told to remain outside controlled airspace. In this case the aircraft is not further encroaching the controllers capacity as it is either not receiving a service at all or is on a lesser demanding service than a control service.

Reduced Traffic Information/Limiting a service due to equipment

There can be occasions when controllers are unable to give traffic information or are only able to give it at a late stage. On these occasions the term 'reduced traffic information' is used and the reason for the reduction will also be stated. MATS Part 1 states that reduced traffic information should be given when:

   a) A high workload situation exists.
   b) A high traffic density exists.
   c) The aircraft is operating near to the lateral or vertical limits of radar cover, close to a radar overhead, or close to permanent echoes or weather clutter.
   d) The service is being provided using secondary radar only.

From the list it can be seen that the controller has limited information on traffic relevant to you because such traffic would be either outside of the radar beam coverage or inside an area of dense returns e.g. permanent echoes, weather, or high traffic density. The controller therefore cannot see any radar returns (i.e. traffic relevant to you) in these areas and consequently may only be able to give you late or even no warning at all of traffic in or emerging from such areas.

Due to the fact that radar waves travel in straight lines, although you may not be at an extreme distance from the radar head, if there is a hill or obstacle close to your line of sight to the radar head, you could still be at the edge of radar cover (either laterally or vertically). In such cases this could therefore mean late or no warning of traffic from above or below.

It is worth noting that a service can be considered to be limited when only secondary radar (SSR) is available (i.e. when primary returns are not available to the controller). Although controllers generally want all the information given by secondary radar, the advantage of also having primary returns is that absolutely everything can be seen. Controllers can therefore take appropriate action against aircraft, balloons, (spaceships!) etc. that appear and are not squawking whether outside controlled airspace or infringing controlled airspace. It is also worth noting however, that even when primary radar is available there are certain objects (generally gliders, hang gliders and parachutes) that on occasions may not show on the radar screen due to their structure giving a weak or no return.

Controllers may give reduced traffic information due to controller workload. It must be understood that when a controller gives a service it must be provided fully or not at all i.e. the controller cannot give a "half-hearted" service. So, for example, if a controller is reaching capacity and two additional aircraft ask for a Traffic Service, the controller cannot tell the pilots that they are being given a Traffic Service but then not scan those aircraft as often as he would normally. However, it is permissible to provide the flight information services with reduced traffic information due to controller workload. As stated, in such situations the service is still being provided as per its definition, but the use of the phrase 'reduced traffic information due to controller workload' refers to the fact that any such traffic information may be given at a late stage.

To complete the understanding of reduced traffic information it must be remembered that, as detailed later in this chapter, when receiving any of the flight information services (in any country) the pilot is always responsible for his own collision avoidance. Therefore the reduction in the provision of traffic information by the controller is not incorrect or a poor practice as it is always the case that the pilot is responsible for his own collision avoidance when receiving any of the flight information services. Note that this still applies even when the definition of such a flight information service states that the controller will issue instructions/manoeuvres to resolve potential collisions.

Collision avoidance

When receiving any of the flight information services the pilot is always responsible for his own collision avoidance. This fundamental principle must always be remembered and therefore applies equally to the Basic Service, Traffic Service, Deconfliction Service and Procedural Service, even when the definition of such a flight information service states that the controller will provide traffic information or issue instructions/manoeuvres to resolve potential collisions.

Terrain clearance

When receiving any of the flight information services the pilot is always responsible for his own terrain clearance. This fundamental principle must always be remembered and therefore applies equally to the Basic Service, Traffic Service, Deconfliction Service and Procedural Service, even when the definition of such a flight information service states that the controller will issue heading and/or level instructions to pilots.

Standard application of service

Pilots must be aware that controllers are required to provide the flight information services as per their definition, but not to provide anything extra, for example, if the controller is not required to provide headings and/or levels to avoid collisions then he should not routinely provide such headings and/or levels. The rationale of this is that if controllers were to provide additional information, pilots may have the mindset that such additional information will always be given, and therefore the actual definition and application of the flight information services will become confused. As such, it is worth noting that although it may be thought that any extra information where appropriate can only be of benefit to pilots, when controllers (pedantically) provide such services as per their definition, if the pilot requires any extra information then simply request an upgrade to the appropriate service.

LARS

The term 'LARS' is an abbreviation of the Lower Airspace Radar Service and is simply a generic term for the Basic Service, Traffic Service and Deconfliction Service i.e. it is not another type of service to add to those previously listed in this section. The Lower Airspace Radar Service is therefore available in certain locations outside controlled airspace, and in general the boundaries of the locations are due to the boundaries of adequate radar coverage.

ATSOCAS

The term 'ATSOCAS' is an abbreviation for Air Traffic Services Outside Controlled Airspace. This term is often used by controllers (although not over the RT as it is not a standard phraseology term) but is not often used by pilots. ATSOCAS is therefore simply a generic term for the Basic Service, Traffic Service, Deconfliction Service and Procedural Service (recall from earlier in this section that these are the only services available outside controlled airspace).

Chapter 4.3   Basic Service

Recall that the basic principles described in chapter 4.2 are included in the Basic Service.

<u>The service</u>

A Basic Service can be provided by a controller or a FISO. In doing so a FISO will not use radar in the provision of the service. A controller (i.e. not a FISO) may use radar if he so wishes to aid in his duties, however, the Basic Service is still fundamentally a non-radar service and will be provided as per that definition. Consequently, if a controller identifies an aircraft in receipt of a Basic Service, pilots must not assume that the aircraft will be radar monitored. Note that FISO's can only provide a Basic Service and cannot, therefore, provide a Traffic Service, Deconfliction Service or Procedural Service. In general awareness of this, note that FISO callsigns have the suffix 'information', for example, 'London Information'.

When providing a Basic Service the controller or FISO will give information useful for the safe and efficient conduct of flight. In general, such information will be information about weather, changes of serviceability of facilities (e.g. navaids or runways) and general information concerning the traffic environment. Note that the phrase 'general information concerning the traffic environment' means just that i.e. specific traffic information relating to individual aircraft is not provided, but general information such as an area of glider activity may be given.

When providing a Basic Service controllers are not required (at any time) to give traffic information. On initial contact the controller or FISO may give generic traffic information as explained in the previous paragraph. Note that in addition to it not being a requirement to give traffic information, if generic traffic information is given, it is not a requirement to update such information. If a pilot wishes, at any time, to be given specific traffic information i.e. relating to specific aircraft that may constitute a collision hazard, then the pilot should request a Traffic Service or a Deconfliction Service.

A Basic Service therefore has the lowest capacity demand on a controller of all the air traffic services. This is due to the fact that the controller is not required to continuously monitor the aircraft or give instructions, and can consequently just give general information.

<u>Flight rules</u>

A Basic Service can be provided to aircraft whether IFR or VFR, IMC or VMC.

Collision avoidance

When in receipt of a Basic Service the pilot is always responsible for his own collision avoidance.

Terrain clearance

When in receipt of a Basic Service the pilot is always responsible for his own terrain clearance. Note that due to the nature of the service, a Basic Service may be given below any ATC terrain safe levels.

Pilot initiated changes

When providing a Basic Service the controller may ask the pilot to maintain a level, level band or route if thought necessary due to the traffic environment. Note that due to the nature of the service the pilot is not required to accept any such requests. However, if the pilot agrees to any such course of action requested by the controller, the pilot is then required to inform the controller before deviating from such agreement i.e. before changing from the agreed level or route.

Chapter 4.4   Traffic Service

Recall that the basic principles described in chapter 4.2 are included in the Traffic Service.

The service

A Traffic Service contains the information of a Basic Service but with radar derived traffic information to assist pilots in visually acquiring and avoiding that traffic. This is therefore a radar service and consequently the aircraft must be radar identified and radar monitored by the controller. Recall, however, that the act of identification does not imply that a service has commenced.

Traffic information will be given to aircraft in receipt of a Traffic Service when the controller judges that such traffic will pass within 3nm and 3000ft. The information should be given before the traffic is within 5nm so that the pilot has sufficient time to visually acquire the traffic and manoeuvre as necessary. Note that under the definition of a Traffic Service the controller will not issue any deconfliction advice i.e. traffic information will be given but instructions to resolve such conflicts will not be given. Therefore, if a pilot wishes to be given deconfliction advice i.e. a turn or change of level to avoid the traffic, then the pilot should request a Deconfliction Service. In such circumstances the controller will endeavour to provide a Deconfliction Service as soon as possible, but pilots should be aware that this may not be immediately possible due to controller workload.

When providing a Traffic Service the controller may issue headings or levels for planning or sequencing purposes. However, due to the definition of a Traffic Service, such headings or levels will not be issued solely for the purpose of resolving conflicts.

Flight rules

A Traffic Service can be provided to aircraft whether IFR or VFR, IMC or VMC. Note that if a controller gives a heading or level that would require flight in IMC, a pilot who is not qualified to fly in IMC shall inform the controller and request alternative action.

Collision avoidance

When in receipt of a Traffic Service the pilot is always responsible for his own collision avoidance. This always applies whether traffic information has been given or not, and also applies when headings or levels have been given for planning or sequencing purposes.

Terrain clearance

When in receipt of a Traffic Service the pilot is always responsible for his own terrain clearance. This still applies when headings or levels have been given for planning or sequencing purposes. A Traffic Service may be given below any ATC terrain safe levels. When a pilot requests descent below the ATC terrain safe level the controller will issue the reminder "[callsign], taking your own terrain clearance, descent approved".

When providing a Traffic Service controllers shall only instigate headings when the aircraft is at or above ATC terrain safe levels. However, if pilots request a heading whilst below the ATC terrain safe level this may be provided as long as the controller reminds the pilot that he remains responsible for terrain clearance.

Pilot initiated changes

When in receipt of a Traffic Service the pilot will be flying on his own navigation (unless he has accepted a heading or level at the request of the controller for planning or sequencing purposes). However, whilst flying under own navigation, pilots shall not change the level, level band or route without advising the controller as the controller may have co-ordinated the flight with other aircraft or controllers.

When providing a Traffic Service the controller may ask the pilot to maintain a level, level band, heading or route if thought necessary due to the traffic environment. Note that due to the nature of the service the pilot is not required to accept any such requests. However, if the pilot agrees to any such course of action requested by the controller, the pilot is then required to inform the controller before deviating from such agreement i.e. before changing from the agreed level, level band, heading or route.

Chapter 4.5   Deconfliction Service

Recall that the basic principles described in chapter 4.2 are included in the Deconfliction Service.

<u>The service</u>

The Deconfliction Service is an enhancement of the Traffic Service. It is a radar service and consequently the aircraft must be radar identified and radar monitored by the controller. Recall, however, that the act of identification does not imply that a service has commenced.

When providing a Deconfliction Service the controller will give traffic information and issue heading and level instructions aimed at achieving the required deconfliction distances given below against all observed traffic. As the service is a flight information service and not a control service, pilots are not required to comply with any such instructions. However, due to the nature of the service, pilots are expected to comply with such instructions. If a pilot chooses not to follow such instructions he must inform the controller, the pilot then becomes responsible for initiating any manoeuvres necessary to avoid conflicts. As such instructions are not mandatory they are, in legal terms, 'advice' rather than 'instructions'. However, due to the nature of the service they will be issued in the form of instructions.

As the Deconfliction Service is a service given outside controlled airspace, in the event of a sudden appearance of unknown traffic or when unknown traffic make unpredictable manoeuvres, the first transmission that the controller makes with respect to that conflicting traffic may be in the form of avoiding action. This will be followed by information on that traffic.

When providing a Deconfliction Service the controller may also issue heading or level instructions for planning or sequencing reasons.

For participating aircraft on an advisory route (Class F airspace) a Deconfliction Service shall be provided unless the aircraft is below radar coverage or below the ATC terrain safe level. In such cases a Procedural Service shall be provided.

The deconfliction distances to be applied are:

    5nm laterally or 3000ft vertically against un-coordinated traffic.
    3nm laterally or 1000ft vertically against co-ordinated traffic.

Flight rules

A Deconfliction Service can be provided to aircraft whether IFR or VFR, IMC or VMC. Note, however, when providing a Deconfliction Service, controllers will issue heading and level instructions and expect pilots to comply with those instructions. As such instructions could require flight in IMC, a pilot who is not qualified to fly in IMC should think practically before requesting a Deconfliction Service i.e. only request a Deconfliction Service when it is guaranteed that the flight can remain in VMC.

Collision avoidance

When in receipt of a Deconfliction Service the pilot is always responsible for his own collision avoidance. This always applies whether headings or levels, or deconfliction instructions have been given or not.

Terrain clearance

When in receipt of a Deconfliction Service the pilot is always responsible for his own terrain clearance. However, due to the nature of the service, a Deconfliction Service will only be given to aircraft operating at or above the ATC terrain safe level and, additionally, to aircraft during departure whilst climbing to the ATC terrain safe level, and to aircraft following an instrument approach procedure.

If a pilot in receipt of a Deconfliction Service wishes to descend below the ATC terrain safe level, the controller therefore cannot continue to provide a Deconfliction Service. In such circumstances a Traffic Service or a Basic Service can be provided.

Pilot initiated changes

When in receipt of a Deconfliction Service, due to the nature of the service, if the pilot is flying on his own navigation he shall not change his level or heading without advising the controller.

When providing a Deconfliction Service the controller will expect pilots to comply with any level or heading instructions, although such instructions are not mandatory. Due to the nature of the service, if pilots are unable to comply, or wish to deviate from such instructions, they must advise the controller.

Chapter 4.6   Procedural Service

Recall that the basic principles described in chapter 4.2 are included in the Procedural Service.

<u>The service</u>

The Procedural Service is, as its name suggests, a non-radar service. However, note that a Procedural Service will only be provided by a controller, and therefore not a FISO.

Flights in receipt of a Procedural Service will be procedurally separated from other flights in receipt of a Procedural Service. The separation minima to be applied, unless otherwise stated in MATS Part 2, is as per the procedural separation minima described in chapter 6.1. When possible the vertical separation minima of 1000ft will be used in preference to the horizontal procedural separation minima. When levels are given in accordance with the quadrantal rule, 500ft vertical separation will be given.

The controller shall provide traffic information if it is considered that a confliction may exist. Note, however, that as the service is a procedural (non-radar) service such traffic information can only be given on known aircraft, i.e. aircraft that are either in communication with the controller or whose details have been passed by another controller.

As the Procedural Service is a flight information service and not a control service, pilots are not required to comply with any instructions issued by the controller. However, due to the nature of the service, pilots are expected to comply with such instructions. If a pilot chooses not to follow such instructions he must inform the controller. As such instructions are not mandatory they are, in legal terms, 'advice' rather than 'instructions'. However, due to the nature of the service they will be issued in the form of instructions. Note that as the service is of a procedural nature, the instructions issued may be in the form of radials, tracks, levels or time restrictions at relevant positions/navaids.

Controllers may issue a squawk to aircraft in receipt of a Procedural Service so that other radar controllers are aware that the aircraft is in a receipt of a service from that controller as dictated by the individual squawk (see chapter 5.1 for further explanation). In such cases, pilots must remember that they are not in receipt of a radar service and neither will they be radar monitored.

<u>Flight rules</u>

A Procedural Service can be provided to aircraft whether IFR or VFR, IMC or VMC. When providing a Procedural Service, if the controller's instructions require flight in IMC, a pilot who is not qualified to fly in IMC shall inform the controller and request alternative action.

Collision avoidance

When in receipt of a Procedural Service the pilot is always responsible for his own collision avoidance. This always applies, including when the controller issues instructions in the provision of the service.

Terrain clearance

When in receipt of a Procedural Service the pilot is always responsible for his own terrain clearance. However, due to the nature of the service, the levels allocated in accordance with a published procedure or advisory route will ensure terrain clearance.

Pilot initiated changes

When in receipt of a Procedural Service, due to the nature of the service, the pilot is expected to comply with ATC instructions. If the pilot does not wish to comply with such instructions he must advise the controller.

Chapter 4.7   Summary of services

- In the UK there are five types of service.
- Inside controlled airspace a control service must be given.
- Outside controlled airspace the available services in the UK are the Basic Service, Traffic Service, Deconfliction Service and Procedural Service.
- Outside controlled airspace a service is not provided until the controller states the service using the exact words.
- The type of service provided requires a mandatory read back from the pilot.
- Being identified does not imply that a service is being given.
- When receiving a Basic Service and identified, this does not imply the controller will continuously monitor the aircraft on radar. Also, any information given will be generic.

	Resolving conflicts	Pilot initiated changes
Basic Service	Generic traffic information. No manoeuvres offered.	If agree to ATC instructions, inform before deviating.
Traffic Service	Traffic information. No manoeuvres offered.	No deviations without informing ATC, even if on own navigation.
Deconfliction Service	Traffic information and manoeuvres given.	No deviations without informing ATC, even if on own navigation.
Procedural Service	Separate aircraft on a Procedural Service from other aircraft on a Procedural Service. Traffic information given on known aircraft.	No deviations without informing ATC.

When in receipt of a Basic Service, Traffic Service, Deconfliction Service or Procedural Service the following equally apply:

- Flight rules: Available IFR or VFR, IMC or VMC.
- Collision avoidance: Pilot always responsible for collision avoidance.
- Terrain clearance: Pilot always responsible for terrain clearance.

Chapter 4.8   Handover and Freecall

In ATC the term 'Handover' has a specific meaning. It is the process that occurs in order to transfer all the relevant details of the flight from one controller to another.

When aircraft pass from one controller to the next in controlled airspace the accepting controller will always have the relevant details of the flight before the aircraft is transferred to him. The term handover is therefore not used on the RT for flights in controlled airspace. However, in uncontrolled airspace there is no requirement for adjacent controllers to pass information between them about their traffic. Once the aircraft is leaving the controller's area of responsibility he can simply inform the pilot that the service is now terminated and leave the pilot to decide whether or not to contact the next relevant frequency. However, should the controller decide (through necessity or simply to be helpful) to co-ordinate the flight's details with the next controller, then a handover will occur and it is here where controllers are often heard to use the phrase "[callsign] contact [station, frequency] on handover".

The term 'handover' is not actually a standard phraseology term. The only such standard phraseology terms are 'contact' and 'freecall' and these are defined in CAP 413 as:

'Contact' - Establish radio contact with [unit], your details have been passed.
'Freecall' - Call [unit], your details have not been passed.

When in uncontrolled airspace and the controller informs you to contact a frequency, the use of the term 'contact' therefore means, by definition, that a handover has occurred. However, controllers often use the term 'handover' on the RT to make it obvious to the pilot that a handover has occurred. Note that if a handover has occurred, when the pilot is transferred to the next controller he only has to check in and does not have to follow up with the flight details i.e. departure airfield, aircraft type, squawk, intended route etc.

As previously stated, when in uncontrolled airspace, once the aircraft is leaving the controllers area of responsibility the controller is only required to inform the pilot that the service is now terminated and leave the pilot to decide whether or not to contact the next relevant frequency. Consequently, there is no requirement for the controller to inform the pilot of the next relevant frequency, but in the interests of best practice controllers will often pass the frequency using the phrase "[callsign] freecall [station, frequency]". Note that in this case there is no requirement for the pilot to call that frequency, but if the pilot does decide to, the controller will not have any details of the flight as a handover has not occurred.

Section 5   Principles of how to use the radar

This section is included to give pilots a better understanding of how controllers do their job and the certain things they must do by law when using the radar. It is not intended as a guide to teach pilots how to be a radar controller, and the parts of this section that may seem rather detailed are there purely to give a good understanding of the parts of a radar controller's job that are relevant to pilots.

Modern radar screens show three main pieces of information about an aircraft. These are as follows:

The first is the actual 'blip' which is the primary radar return and is usually shown as either a large dot or as a '+' sign.

The second is the secondary response of the Mode A 4-digit code. The actual position of the aircraft as dictated by the secondary response is usually shown as either a circle or as a 'X' sign. This therefore allows both the primary and secondary returns to be seen at the same time even though they are in the same place, for example, they will be shown as either a circle with a dot in the middle or as an asterix. Next to the secondary blip are the four numbers of the Mode A 4-digit code. Where code/callsign conversion is used the actual callsign of the aircraft will be displayed instead of the Mode A 4-digit code (see chapter 5.2 for further explanation.)

The third is the level readout of the Mode C secondary response. This level is shown next to the blip as either an altitude or flight level (see chapter 5.3 for explanation of how and when the two are given). The usual convention is for altitudes to be shown in multiples of hundreds of feet with the letter 'A' at the end, for example, an altitude of 600ft is shown as '06A' and an altitude of 3500ft is shown as '35A'. Flight levels are also shown in multiples of hundreds of feet but have no letters associated with them, for example, flight level 210 is shown as '210'. When the aircraft is climbing or descending an arrow is also shown in front of the level readout pointing in the appropriate direction, for example, '↑23A' or '↓184'.

With the introduction of new technologies such as Mode S transponders, the information available to the controller via his display will be greatly increased. This will provide more information on the aircraft's current flight path, information from the aircraft's FMC, and details of what the pilot has set in the (autopilot) mode control panel windows. This will therefore enable controllers to view future predictions of the aircraft's flight path, as well as linking to safety systems such as conflict alert and level bust alert.

Chapter 5.1   Issuing aircraft with a squawk code

When a controller gives an aircraft a squawk code it is not a figure picked at random by the controller, but is assigned according to the 'code allocation plan'. The code allocation plan lists squawk codes in groups and the list is split into two sections as follows:

a)   Domestic codes which are assigned to aircraft flying within the area of responsibility of the assigning ATC unit.
b)   ORCAM codes which are assigned to aircraft to be retained beyond the area of responsibility of the assigning ATC unit when the flight is to remain within controlled airspace.

This means that for domestic codes the controller can only give squawk codes within the group assigned to his unit e.g. Thames may use 7050 to 7067. Domestic codes are generally used by general aviation (G/A) type flights that freecall the local ATC unit for each portion of the flight and mainly remain outside controlled airspace. When the pilot makes his initial call the controller will pick a squawk code from the group assigned to his unit making sure that no other aircraft under his control is using that code and will write the code on the aircraft's FPS. If the initial call is to a tower controller, as will be the case for departing aircraft, the tower controller cannot assign squawk codes – this must be done by a radar controller. Therefore, the radar controller will assign and include the squawk code in the departure clearance when the tower controller requests the departure clearance from the radar controller. The tower controller can then issue the departure clearance, including the squawk code, to the pilot.

Note that each code can only be assigned to one aircraft, so if a controller has all the codes in his group assigned to aircraft then any subsequent aircraft cannot be given a code. However, it is more likely in reality that the controller will be at the limit of capacity with regards to the number of aircraft under his control before he runs out of codes.

An advantage of having the domestic codes assigned to ATC units in groups is that controllers know which groups of codes are assigned to their unit and any adjacent units. Should an aircraft displaying the code of an adjacent unit be operating in the vicinity of another controller's airspace or infringe his airspace, the controller knows instantly which unit to telephone in order to gain the required information or co-ordinate appropriate action rather than having to make time consuming multiple enquiries.

Due to the fact that domestic codes can only be retained within the area of responsibility of the assigning ATC unit, when the aircraft subsequently leaves the controller's area of responsibility the controller will either:

a)   Instruct the aircraft to squawk 7000 and contact the next frequency, upon which the new controller may assign a code allocated to his unit, or
b)   Co-ordinate with the next controller via the telephone. This will include a new squawk code as dictated by the next controller, and the present controller will then instruct the aircraft to squawk this new code and contact the next frequency.

When ORCAM codes are assigned the codes are picked automatically by the master computer. As such, the squawk code is already included on the FPS when it is printed. As stated, the ORCAM codes are used in order to be retained when talking to subsequent controllers rather than having to continually re-select new codes. ORCAM codes are therefore used by airline type flights which will pass through many controllers during the flight, some for only a short space of time, but only for those portions of the flight that remain within controlled airspace. This means that any flights (i.e. not just G/A flights, but large airliners also) that depart from an airport outside of controlled airspace will initially be given a domestic code and then at some point whilst airborne before entering controlled airspace be instructed to change squawk (to an ORCAM code). The reverse will happen when exiting controlled airspace during arrival to airports outside of controlled airspace.

Chapter 5.2   Code/callsign conversion

When a transponder transmits a Mode A 4-digit squawk code the four figures are displayed on the radar screen next to the aircraft's blip. To enable controllers to work more efficiently however, it is ideal to have the aircraft's callsign displayed on the radar screen next to its blip. To do this the 4-digit squawk code and the aircraft's callsign are input to the radar processing computer. The radar display will then show the aircraft's callsign instead of its 4-digit squawk code.

The inputting of the squawk code and callsign is not done at each controlling position. This is done at the master computer so that all the radar screens show the aircraft's callsign automatically without the controllers having to use their time and capacity in doing this themselves for every aircraft.

As a general rule, code/callsign conversion is used for flights issued with an ORCAM code. Flights issued with domestic codes, whether operating inside or outside controlled airspace, will not have their callsign shown on the radar screen.

Chapter 5.3 Displaying altitude or flight level

The levels that aircraft fly at are either altitudes or flight levels, therefore the radar screen must be capable of showing whether an aircraft is flying at an altitude (i.e. with QNH set) or at a flight level (i.e. with 1013mb set). This situation would be problematic if altitudes and flight levels were to be mixed up and not displayed correctly to the controller. Therefore this is taken care of automatically by the computers that process the radar information.

To describe how this is done would require a long in depth technical explanation. I shall not attempt to give such a description, but it basically requires the QNH and transition altitude to be input to the radar processing computer. The relevant points that are useful for pilots to note are that when an aircraft is at or below the transition altitude its Mode C response will always be shown on the radar screen as an altitude. When the aircraft is above the transition altitude its Mode C response will always be shown on the radar screen as a flight level.

The Mode C readout shown on the radar screen is (importantly) entirely independent of the subscale setting the pilot has set on his altimeter (again an explanation would require a long technical description). So, should a pilot have finger trouble and select a wrong subscale setting, the controller will still see the aircraft's actual altitude or flight level and be able to challenge the pilot.

It also follows that if an aircraft is below the transition altitude and is cleared to climb to a flight level, if the pilot selects 1013mb whilst below the transition altitude (which is an approved procedure) the controller will still see the aircraft's altitude whilst it is below the transition altitude even though the pilot is seeing flight levels on his altimeter (and vice versa when descending). This can have consequences when reporting the passing 'level' on departure, as explained in chapter 5.8.

Chapter 5.4   Radar maps

To aid radar controllers in doing their job radar screens have maps that can be superimposed onto them. These maps are usually outlines of rivers, coastlines and airspace boundaries, and pinpoints of navaids, waypoints, aerodromes and significant obstacles. It is usual to be able to select each of these on or off at the touch of a button. It is not usual to be able to select roads or towns, however, controllers that handle VFR traffic get to know with experience where many of these are on their radar screens.

Note the use of the words 'outlines' and 'pinpoints' as they are exactly that i.e. there are no shades, detailed diagrams and more importantly no labels of names or altitudes etc. This means that anyone who is not familiar with a sector when viewing its radar screen will see a mass of squiggly lines, dots and straight lines but with no labels identifying them. It may seem odd that these are not labelled, especially when some (e.g. airspace boundaries) are necessary for the controller to be able to do his job. However, each of these are learnt by controllers during their training on each sector, and controllers will become fluent in their meanings and altitudes before they are licensed to operate that sector. Part of the licensing test includes a verbal exam that includes a test of the knowledge of such radar maps.

Chapter 5.5   Actions before providing a radar service

Before a controller provides a radar service he must either:

a)   Identify the aircraft himself, or
b)   Have had the identity of the aircraft transferred from another controller.

To put this in other words, the aircraft must be identified to the radar controller before he can do anything with it. The reason for this is so that the controller has confirmed that the blip on the screen is the one he thinks it is and also that it is shown in the correct place. It is therefore a method in the interests of safety to ensure the controller is not giving instructions to the wrong blip, or to the correct blip that is shown on the radar screen in the wrong place due to technical problems.

The minimum a controller must do before providing a radar service is therefore to identify the aircraft. If the controller then wants to use the Mode A information associated with the blip, this must also be checked for correctness before it can be used - this process is called 'Validation'. If the controller then wants to use the Mode C information associated with the blip, this must also be checked for correctness before it can be used - this process is called 'Verification'.

It is stipulated in MATS Part 1 that an aircraft must be identified before it is validated, and it must be identified and validated before it is verified. In the majority of cases when you as a pilot make initial contact with a radar controller, the controller will therefore identify, then validate, then verify your radar response before providing you with a service.

Chapters 5.6 'Identification', 5.7 'Validation' and 5.8 'Verification' explain these terms in more depth.

Chapter 5.6   Identification

As stated previously the radar controller must identify the aircraft before he can do anything with that aircraft. The process of identification confirms to the controller that he has the correct blip and that his radar screen is showing the blip in the correct location. There are only a few certain ways that controllers can, by law, identify aircraft. If using primary radar there are three different ways to identify aircraft, the controller only having to choose one of these methods to identify an aircraft. If using secondary radar there are three different ways to identify aircraft, all of which are different to those used with primary radar and, again, the controller only has to choose one of these methods to identify an aircraft. The identification methods are:

Primary radar:
- a) Turn method
- b) Departure method
- c) Position report method

Secondary radar:
- a) Selecting a new squawk method
- b) Recognising a previously selected squawk method
- c) Squawk IDENT method

An explanation of each of the identification methods would be lengthy, and such in depth knowledge is not vital for pilots. There are some points worthy of note to pilots however.

Recall that primary radar only shows a blip on the radar screen and no additional information. The identification methods used with primary radar therefore involve correlating the blip to either a turn as instructed by the controller, or to a specific position i.e. departing from an airfield or at the position of the position report. The practicalities of this are that any instructions issued for reasons of primary radar identification must be correctly acknowledged and actioned by the pilot in order for the identification to be within legal tolerances. So, should pilots make identification turns incorrectly or with a delay after the instruction, or make incorrect or inaccurate position reports, the controller may legally have to issue further instructions to attempt to identify the aircraft again.

Secondary radar has additional information as given by the Mode A 4-digit code and the IDENT feature. This information can therefore be used for identification by secondary radar.

When an aircraft is identified by recognising a previously selected squawk MATS Part 1 states:

> An aircraft may be identified by recognising a validated 4-digit code or callsign if code/callsign conversion is used which has been previously assigned to an aircraft.

Adjacent sectors therefore usually have written agreements between them stating that aircraft transferred to them have been validated unless otherwise informed by that controller. This means that controllers do not have to make any transmissions to the pilot for reasons of identification. This instruction-less method of identification is therefore an efficient method and can lead to the situation (usually for flights remaining within controlled airspace) where every radar controller for that flight is able to perform this efficient method of identification.

Informing the pilot that he is identified

Pilots will be familiar with the practise whereby they are informed by the controller that they are identified. However, not every identification requires a confirming transmission to be given to the pilot. The occasions when pilots are to be informed they are identified are given in MATS Part 1. Some of those occasions also require the controller to pass to the pilot the position of the aircraft (i.e. as seen on the radar screen). The details of when such identification and position information are to be passed to pilots are determined by the identification method and the class of airspace. This usually means that when an aircraft is identified inside controlled airspace the pilot does not need to be informed, but when identified outside controlled airspace the pilot will be informed. An in depth explanation of such is not vital for pilots, but what is worthy of noting is that the following situations usually occur:

- Flights that remain inside controlled airspace for the whole of the flight will not usually be informed when they have been identified.
- When an aircraft is outside controlled airspace the pilot will always be informed when he has been identified.
- When a flight passes from uncontrolled airspace into controlled airspace and at the same time is transferred to another controller (due to that airspace boundary) the pilot will not usually be informed that he is identified upon entering the controlled airspace.
- When a flight passes from controlled airspace into uncontrolled airspace and at the same time is transferred to another controller, the pilot will be informed that he is identified when outside controlled airspace.

Recall from chapter 4.2 that the act of identification does not imply that a service is being provided by the controller.

Recall from chapter 1.2 that when an aircraft crosses the boundary between controlled and uncontrolled airspace the controller must inform the pilot of the change of service and the pilot is required to give a read back.

It is also a legal requirement for controllers to inform pilots whenever radar identification is lost. When able, the controller must then undertake the process of radar identification for such aircraft i.e. the controller cannot assume that the aircraft can be considered to have remained being identified.

Chapter 5.7   Validation

In ATC the term 'validation', when used in the context of the radar, has a specific meaning. Pilots will, in general, know what 'identification' is but be unaware of what 'validation' is or that it even exists.

In simple terms validation is a check that the Mode A 4-digit code, or callsign if code/callsign conversion is used, displayed next to the aircraft's blip is the correct code or callsign.

Validation is therefore different to identification in that validation is the checking of that Mode A data shown against a blip, whereas identification is the checking that the blip is the aircraft in question.

MATS Part 1 states that controllers shall validate the Mode A data shown on the radar screen by checking that it corresponds to the assigned code or callsign where code/callsign conversion is used, and this validation shall be done by one of the following methods:

a) Instructing the aircraft to squawk the assigned code and observing that the correct numbers appear on the radar display.
b) Instructing the aircraft to squawk IDENT and simultaneously checking the code numbers associated with the radar return.
c) Matching a radar return already identified by primary radar with the assigned code for the flight.

On most occasions identification and validation can therefore be accomplished simultaneously. Remember however, that although identification and validation may be accomplished simultaneously they are different things. Also, on the occasions that they are accomplished separately, identification must occur before validation.

Chapter 5.8 Verification

In ATC the term 'verification' has a specific meaning although pilots may be unaware of what it is or that it exists.

In simple terms 'verification' is a check that the Mode C level readout is correct. The importance of this for vertical separation is obvious.

MATS Part 1 states:

> Controllers are to verify the accuracy of Mode C data, once the aircraft has been identified and the Mode A validated, by checking that the readout indicates 200ft or less from the level reported by the pilot. If the aircraft is climbing or descending, the pilot is to be instructed to give a precise report as the aircraft passes through a level.
>
> A Mode C readout can be assumed to have been verified if it is associated with a Mode A code that has been previously validated.
>
> An aircraft that has been instructed to climb or descend may be considered to have left a level or to have passed through a level when the Mode C readout indicates a change of 400ft or more from that level and is continuing in the required direction.
>
> Minimum vertical separation may be applied between verified Mode C transponding aircraft provided the intentions of both aircraft are known to the controller whether due to being under his control, by co-ordination or due to standing agreements. If the intentions of a Mode C transponding aircraft are not known or the Mode C data is unverified then the minimum vertical separation is 5000ft for aircraft in receipt of a RCS and 3000ft for aircraft in receipt of a Deconfliction Service and the radar returns are not allowed to merge.

From the above statements of MATS Part 1 the following points can be seen:

Controllers can only verify the Mode C data after the aircraft has first been identified and validated.

When pilots report their passing altitude on departure the controller may need more than one report before he can successfully verify the Mode C data. This is because the tolerance for verification is 200ft from the level reported by the pilot, however, the information on the radar screen is updated every few seconds as the radar antenna sweeps round and so may be slightly out of phase with the actual (reported) level of a departing aircraft with a good climb rate.

The initial verification will always require an RT transmission from the pilot to report his level. After that however, the remainder of the flight may have silent verifications as it passes to subsequent controllers if it has been previously validated. Some pilots may have the habit of giving their passing level when they check in with each controller during the climb. Although this is done with the best of intentions, it can been seen that this practise is unnecessary and is likely to have evolved through the misinterpretation of the requirement to report the SID, passing level and cleared level on departure (see chapter 6.12 for further explanation of this procedure). However this requirement only applies to the first radar controller during departure to enable the first controller to verify the Mode C data, subsequent verifications are then silent as explained. As further evidence that this is where the misinterpretation has evolved from, I have yet to here of a pilot reporting his passing level during the descent (except for when asked to by the controller).

From the previous paragraph you may now be wondering why it is necessary, when checking in with each controller during the cruise, to report your level. However, this is not for reasons of verification, but is a statement of your clearance. It is the same as the requirement during climb and descent to report the cleared level on initial contact, and this procedure is mandatory to enable the controller to check that the pilot has the correct cleared level.

Due to the fact that an aircraft may be considered to have left a level or to have passed through a level when its Mode C readout indicates a change of 400ft or more from that level and is continuing in the required direction, controllers can therefore instruct another aircraft to climb or descend to that level when such 400ft is present. In other words, pilots may think that in order to ensure that 1000ft vertical separation is present at all times, the vacating aircraft must be 1000ft from that vacated level before it can be re-assigned. This would therefore give 2000ft separation at the time the vacated level is re-assigned. However, this is not so. In using the approved procedure, 1400ft vertical separation will exist at the time the vacated level is re-assigned.

Note also, with respect to reporting passing altitude on departure and with reference to chapter 5.3, when giving the passing 'level' whilst at or below the transition altitude, pilots must always report this as an altitude in order for the controller to be able to correlate the report to what is displayed on the radar screen (i.e. altitude is always displayed on the radar screen whenever the aircraft is at or below the transition altitude). Sometimes controllers will use the phrase 'report passing level' when aircraft are still below the transition altitude rather than the phrase 'report passing altitude'. An understanding of the subject matter given in this chapter and chapter 5.3 will aid pilots in resolving such a situation – this being that the use of the word 'level' is meant in the generic sense rather than the misinterpretation that it refers to the similar sounding phrase of 'Flight Level', and what is required is the aircraft's altitude.

The values given in this chapter (i.e. 200ft, 400ft and 5000ft) are used in the UK, but most other countries also use these values. Some countries may use different values although these will be of a similar magnitude.

Chapter 5.9   Unverified

When a controller has traffic relevant to you but that traffic is giving a Mode C readout that is unverified, the controller will usually give you the level information and state that it is unverified, for example, "traffic 12 o'clock, opposite direction, indicating altitude 3000ft, unverified."

The fact that the controller has stated the Mode C readout is unverified has both a practical application (as you now know the exact definition of this from chapter 5.8) as well as a legal application. The legal application is that, as given in chapter 5.8, MATS Part 1 states that if the Mode C data is unverified a minimum vertical separation of 5000ft or 3000ft as appropriate can be applied but the radar returns must not be allowed to merge. Therefore controllers can, and on occasions will, simply because they have no other option (e.g. due to the proximity of other traffic, airspace boundaries etc.) vector you very close laterally to such traffic whilst maintaining the minimum of 5000ft or 3000ft vertical separation from the unverified Mode C readout. On most occasions this practise will not be a problem as such because 5000ft or 3000ft vertical separation exists between the two aircraft and they have not been allowed to coincide laterally. However, it is worth being aware that two unusual situations could exist as follows:

One possible situation is that, if you are very unlucky, the unverified Mode C readout could be wildly inaccurate and the traffic could actually be at, or close to, the same level as you. As you then pass close laterally to that traffic (although the controller will not allow the radar returns to merge) it may look dangerously close and you may think that the controller has not done his job correctly. The controller has, however, operated within the legal boundaries.

Another possible situation is that if, for example, you are receiving a Deconfliction Service and traffic suddenly pops up on the radar screen, the controller may have to suddenly give you avoiding action although in reality there is no risk of collision i.e. the controller has to apply 3000ft vertically, so if the traffic was indicating 2000ft above you unverified then avoiding action is necessary, but if the traffic is really 2000ft above you then on this occasion you may think it is highly unnecessary to be given avoiding action.

In general, therefore, and in the interests of safety and good airmanship, if a controller informs you of unverified traffic it is worth treating the level of that traffic in the worst sense i.e. if the level is similar to yours then treat it as being at your level, and if the level is different to yours the Mode C data could be wrong as it is unverified and therefore think that it could actually be at your level. In both cases it is prudent to have a good vertical scan in order to visually acquire the traffic and think about manoeuvring to avoid the area of that traffic rather than thinking the traffic is at a different level so it is not a problem.

Section 6 — Control of IFR flights

This section explains the methods ATC use to control IFR traffic and why these methods are used.

In chapter 2.5 it was stated that in controlled airspace IFR flights are always separated from each other. This being necessary due to the fact that if aircraft are IFR they could be, at any time, in conditions that preclude flight with visual references and therefore cannot see and avoid each other.

The control of IFR flights therefore begins with an explanation of the term 'separation'. Note that separation of IFR flights occurs in all controlled airspace (Class A – E). Chapters 4.5 and 4.6 give the details of separation as applied to Class F and G airspace.

Chapter 6.1 Separation minima

Recall from chapter 2.1 that 'separation' (or 'standard separation') is when aircraft are kept apart by a prescribed minima. If aircraft are kept apart by this prescribed minima then they are said to be 'separated'. Separation is therefore applied either vertically or horizontally.

Vertical separation

Vertical separation minima are:

1000ft up to and including FL290.
2000ft above FL290 unless RVSM apply, RVSM being 1000ft.

Vertical separation minima can be applied either by using level reports from pilots or by using verified Mode C responses. If the controller does not have radar available and is therefore providing a procedural service, he has to rely on accurate level reports from pilots when providing vertical separation.

Horizontal separation

Horizontal separation is applied both laterally (e.g. aircraft passing side by side) and longitudinally (e.g. one aircraft behind the other). When radar is used the horizontal separation minima are relatively simple and are usually:

10nm if one or both aircraft are more than 80nm from the radar head.
5nm if both aircraft are within 80nm of the radar head.
3nm when authorised in MATS Part 2.

It is more common for approach control and terminal control (i.e. below approximately 20,000ft) to be authorised to provide 3nm horizontal separation so as to enable them to sequence aircraft for approach to the minima of 3nm longitudinal wake turbulence separation and also to use the airspace more efficiently in the terminal environment by applying 3nm lateral separation.

So, in general, whenever 1000ft vertical separation does not exist between aircraft:

- If aircraft pass each other side by side whether travelling in the same direction (i.e. one overtaking the other) or travelling in opposite directions, a lateral separation of 3nm, 5nm or 10nm is used as authorised.
- If aircraft cross each other (e.g. at 90°) 3nm, 5nm or 10nm lateral separation is applied as authorised.
- In the case of aircraft flying head on and climbing/descending through each others levels, there must be 10nm longitudinally between the aircraft whilst ever vertical and lateral separation does not exist i.e. there must be 1000ft (or 2000ft if specified) vertically between the aircraft at the point that the aircraft become 10nm apart longitudinally (if they are not laterally separated). A minima of less than 10nm is not authorised for the case of aircraft approaching each other head on.

If the controller does not have radar available and is therefore providing a procedural service, the horizontal separation minima are greatly increased and their application become a little more complicated.

Procedural horizontal separation is applied by requiring aircraft to fly:

- on different tracks from a navaid in order to provide lateral separation and/or
- at a time or distance interval from a navaid or reporting point in order to provide longitudinal separation, or
- in different geographical locations as determined by visual observations or by navaids.

A procedural service is more commonly given in remote areas where radar is not available or during arrival at airfields that use a procedural approach service. An in depth explanation of the procedural horizontal separation minima would be lengthy and is not required for pilots, but in general the procedural horizontal separation minima are:

- both aircraft reported to be established on radials/tracks which diverge by at least 20° and one aircraft is at least 15nm or 4 minutes (whichever is the greater) from the navaid, or
- 10 minutes longitudinally, or
- 20nm longitudinally by reference to the same on track DME station.

Horizontal separation based on geographical locations is termed 'geographical separation'. Pilots are more likely to encounter geographical separation when flying SVFR, therefore geographical separation is explained in section 7.

Chapter 6.2 Differences between procedural and radar separation

The main point for pilots to note about the difference between procedural and radar separation is that with a procedural service the traffic capacity (i.e. amount of aircraft) the controller has is greatly reduced. This will be around a quarter to a half of the amount of aircraft that can be handled when using radar. Similarly, for the same amount of traffic, the controller's workload is greatly increased when providing a procedural service.

An appreciation of this by pilots will therefore help them to understand that when radar is not available the controller may appear to be giving an inefficient or second rate service and may not allow pilots to do certain things or delay them, which often seems highly unnecessary to the pilot.

There are three reasons why capacity decreases and controller workload increases when radar is not available:

The first reason is that without the radar screen the controller does not have a 2D or 3D picture of where aircraft are and how they are moving, both horizontally and vertically in relation to each other. The controller cannot therefore make an instant judgement of that picture using the eyes, but instead must make up a mental picture by reading all the information on each FPS for every aircraft, which is not an instant process.

The second reason is that, following on from the first reason above, the only way of finding out the positions and levels of aircraft is by asking pilots to report such information. Whereas with radar no such reports are required as the controller can see such information instantly when looking at the radar screen. Consequently the RT loading (i.e. amount of transmissions on the RT) greatly increases compared to the same amount of traffic when using radar.

The above two reasons are due to human restraints, but the third reason is a technical restraint. This being that radar is very accurate and can therefore allow horizontal spacing down to 3nm. The tolerances with navaids or timings (i.e. as used to establish procedural separation) are greater. Therefore, when using procedural separation the minimum distance between aircraft must be increased to account for this.

From chapter 6.1 it can be seen that procedural horizontal separation minima vary depending on what is used to establish the separation (i.e. radials, time or DME distance). In order to give an idea of how much the separation distance is increased when radar is not available one of the more extreme examples is that of oceanic control as used for aircraft flying over the North Atlantic Ocean. Here a longitudinal separation of 10 minutes is used. So with aircraft travelling at a typical groundspeed of 480kts, which is 8nm per minute, this gives an in-trail longitudinal separation of 80nm. Compare this to 10nm in-trail separation when radar is used. In addition to this the lateral (i.e. side by side) separation for aircraft over the North Atlantic is established by requiring aircraft to fly on specific tracks, these tracks being 60nm apart. Again, compare this to a radar lateral separation of 5nm.

The more astute of you may have noticed from chapter 6.1 that although the horizontal separation minima are greatly increased with a procedural service, the vertical separation minima remain the same for both procedural and radar services. Practically however, the points already discussed with regards to capacity decrease and controller workload increase encompass both horizontal and vertical separation minima. This is because in the real world aircraft have to climb and descend through each others levels when passing each other in opposite directions, following each other in-trail, or when in-trail but with the second aircraft flying faster than the one in front. In each of these situations the procedural horizontal separation minima must be applied whilst vertical separation does not exist, whilst with radar the appropriate minima of 3nm, 5nm or 10nm need be applied whilst the aircraft are not vertically separated.

Chapter 6.3   Departure separation

Due to the fact that IFR flights must always be separated in controlled airspace, when IFR flights depart into controlled airspace the tower controller must ensure that when the aircraft are transferred to the next controller (whether procedural or radar) the required separation between the departing aircraft already exists. If this was not so, then as the departure controller receives the aircraft he would be immediately faced with a loss of separation, and therefore would have to take corrective action to establish the required separation. It is therefore a requirement that the tower controller ensures that the required separation exists at the point that the succeeding aircraft lifts off.

Most people are familiar with the idea that aircraft at busy airports (e.g. Heathrow) take-off 60 seconds apart. This is not the full story however. If succeeding departing aircraft are to fly along the same route, then 10nm longitudinal separation will be required for a radar environment, and more for a procedural environment. Therefore, it is not appropriate to depart two such aircraft within 60 seconds of each other.

The departure separation minima as stipulated in MATS Part 1 are given below. Note that if the wake turbulence separation minima are greater than the departure separation minima, then the wake turbulence minima must be used in preference (see chapter 8.6 for further details).

Minimum separation	Provisions
1 minute	Aircraft fly on tracks diverging by 45° or more immediately after take-off. This may be reduced for diverging or parallel runways when approved by the Authority.
2 minutes	Preceding aircraft has filed a speed of 40knots or more faster than the following aircraft.
5 minutes	Preceding aircraft has filed a speed of 20knots or more faster than the following aircraft.
10 minutes	All flights except as above.

In order to both simplify things and give a more efficient service, most busy airports where aircraft depart into a radar environment have the above departure separation minima amended in MATS Part 2. The 1 minute restriction still applies for tracks diverging by 45° or more, but for other aircraft a 'speed group table' is used. In general the speed group table will be:

Speed group	A	B	C	D
Aircraft type	Jet, except BAe 146 and Citations	BAe 146 Citations Saab 2000	Turbo-prop, except Saab 2000 and Shorts 360	Piston and Shorts 360

The required departure separation is then:

Following aircraft	Minimum separation
2 groups or more slower	1 minute
Same speed group or one group slower	2 minutes
Faster group	2 minutes plus 1 minute for each successive group different

Before the tower controller clears an aircraft for take-off he must therefore check the FPS's of the previously departed aircraft to ensure that he applies the required separation between appropriate aircraft. This means the controller may have to keep the FPS's of departed aircraft in front of him for up to 10 minutes in order to check for such separation.

Note that the speed group separation minima are applied to all departures unless the tracks diverge by 45° or more immediately after take-off, in which case 1 minute separation can be used. This ensures, as stated previously, that as the aircraft are transferred to the departure controller the required separation already exists. As an example, aircraft may depart on different SID's, but both the SID's have a common initial part. Therefore, if such a second departing jet aircraft appeared on the radar screen 60 seconds behind a previous departure, radar separation would not exist initially and the controller would have to take action to resolve it.

Note that the above departure separation minima are applicable to IFR aircraft departing into controlled airspace. If an IFR aircraft is departing in uncontrolled airspace, but has filed and received a clearance to enter controlled airspace, then the tower controller will co-ordinate with the departure controller. The tower controller will then only clear the aircraft for take-off when the departure controller has 'released' the aircraft. This 'release' means that the departure controller is assured that the required separation will exist when the aircraft enters controlled airspace

If an aircraft is departing in uncontrolled airspace and has requested a Deconfliction Service before departing, the departure radar controller will again not release such an aircraft until he is assured that the required Deconfliction Service separation minima (5nm or 3000ft, or 3nm or 1000ft) can be maintained once the aircraft has taken off. This is a common occurrence for trainee pilots who are departing for either general IFR handling or departing to practise instrument holds and procedures.

Sometimes the departure separation minima can be by-passed by using appropriate radar control. This allows increased utilisation of the airspace, but to do this the tower controller has to co-ordinate with the departure controller, and the departure controller may then have to co-ordinate with the next controller. Consequently, when controllers have a high workload, there may not be the opportunity for this to happen. To enable this the departure radar controller can use one of two techniques, or both together if he so wishes. These techniques can also be used to establish the Deconfliction Service separation minima without delay.

One option is to allow the tower controller to instruct the second aircraft (before it departs) to stop the climb at a certain level. When the first aircraft has climbed through that level the succeeding aircraft can be cleared for take-off as the clearance assures vertical separation will exist. As the first aircraft leaves successive levels the succeeding aircraft can then be cleared to climb to those levels. So, for example, the clearance for the succeeding aircraft could be "after departure maintain altitude 3000ft". Then as the succeeding aircraft is transferred to the departure radar controller he will instruct a climb to 4000ft, then 5000ft, then FL60 etc.

The other option is to give the aircraft headings to fly immediately after take-off so that lateral radar separation is established earlier than the departure separation minima could be established. This is often used when it is known that the second aircraft will have a much better climb rate than the first aircraft e.g. a jet following a turbo-prop, or an aircraft on a short-haul route following an aircraft on a long-haul route (who are usually close to the maximum take-off weight). Whilst lateral separation exists the second aircraft can be climbed through and above the first aircraft's level. Once vertical separation exists both aircraft can then be put back on the same route with the first departing aircraft (which is now the lower of the two aircraft) being cleared to climb in 1000ft increments as the second departing aircraft leaves such levels. When this is used for a jet following a turbo-prop, due to the speed difference it is often possible to establish the longitudinal separation minima of 10nm (with the jet now in front of the turbo-prop) in a relatively short period of time. In such cases it is therefore no longer necessary to step climb the turbo-prop in 1000ft increments (i.e. for vertical separation) due to the fact that longitudinal separation has now been established.

Chapter 6.4 Visual separation

The term 'visual separation' is often used, and pilots will no doubt know what is meant by it. The reality is, however, that 'visual separation' does not have a defined meaning, nor is it a standard phraseology term! The term has basically evolved as a colloquialism for a procedure that ATC use called 'reduced separation in the vicinity of aerodromes'. The use and details of this procedure are given in MATS Part 1 and are explained below.

The general meaning of the term 'visual separation' is that the pilot(s) will look out of the window to prevent a collision i.e. it is the 'see and avoid' principle. This is not exactly rocket science I know, but the point being made is that it does not have a specific definition, whereas 'separation' (or 'standard separation'), 'traffic information' and 'traffic avoidance advice' do have specific definitions, as explained in section 2. Consequently, although the term 'visual separation' includes the word 'separation', it does not have any specified separation minima as does the term 'separation', as explained in chapter 6.1. 'Visual separation' is therefore, simply, the 'see and avoid' principle.

The term 'visual separation' is not usually used on the RT (by pilots or ATC) for operations outside controlled airspace. This is because outside controlled airspace the pilot is always responsible for his own collision avoidance, therefore, 'visual separation' does not need to be referred to by pilots or ATC as, by definition, it must be in use. Note from the chapters of section 4 that this still applies even when the definition of such a service states that the controller will provide traffic information or issue instructions/manoeuvres to resolve potential collisions.

In this chapter the term 'visual separation' is therefore used with respect to operations inside controlled airspace, as it is in this context that it is usually referring to when spoken on the RT. As such, and as previously mentioned, the term 'visual separation' actually refers to 'reduced separation in the vicinity of aerodromes'. It is used to allow the pilots to use the 'see and avoid' principle (i.e. "visual separation") in situations where otherwise the standard separation minima would have to be applied. Therefore, a more efficient service is given by, for example, allowing an aircraft to depart sooner behind another aircraft than would be possible if the standard separation minima had to be applied.

Note, with reference to the classification of airspace table, that this is not solely applicable to IFR flights. In Class B and C airspace VFR flights may require separation, therefore visual separation could be used for such VFR flights.

Note also, that if traffic information is required to be given, then the term 'visual separation' will not be used on the RT by the controller as, by definition, traffic information implies the 'see and avoid' principle (see chapter 2.4).

The details of the procedure as given in MATS Part 1 are:

> In the vicinity of aerodromes the standard separation minima may be reduced if:

a) adequate separation can be provided by the aerodrome controller when each aircraft is continuously visible to this controller, or
b) each aircraft is continuously visible to the pilots of other aircraft concerned, and the pilots report that they can maintain their own separation, or
c) when one aircraft is following another the pilot of the succeeding aircraft reports that he has the other in sight and can maintain separation.

The following are points to note from the previous statement of the procedure:

It is stipulated to be used 'in the vicinity of aerodromes'. Although no definition (i.e. distance) is given to the meaning of the word 'vicinity', common sense dictates that it can only be used when relatively close to an aerodrome.

Very good weather, visibility and cloud base must be present in order for the aircraft to be 'continuously visible'. For example, a cloud base of 2000ft is not necessarily considered bad weather. However, this can very easily preclude the use of visual separation for departing aircraft, especially jet aircraft that have good climb rates.

Part b) states that the pilots must be continuously visible with the aircraft concerned. Such aircraft could therefore be out of sight of the controller, but this is not a problem as the pilots are using the 'see and avoid' principle. In part a) however, note that it states that the aerodrome controller is to provide adequate separation and the aircraft must consequently be continuously visible to that controller. It does not state, importantly, that any of the subject pilots have to be visible with each other, and nor does it state that the controller has to inform such pilots that he is applying reduced separation between them.

It is useful for pilots to note the above points about part a) as this procedure is often used by aerodrome controllers when the weather is good as it greatly increases the runway utilization when the traffic demand is high, and consequently greatly reduces delays. It can allow, for example, aircraft departing on different SID's, but SID's which have the same initial turn, to depart at 1 minute intervals instead of 3 minute intervals. Recall that the controller does not have to inform the pilots that he his applying reduced separation. The only difference that the pilot may notice, however, is that the aerodrome controller will keep such aircraft on his frequency a little longer than usual, as he must ensure that radar separation exists before transferring the aircraft to the radar controller, as explained in chapter 6.3 i.e. the aircraft have completed the initial turn and are now established on different tracks. Note that this does not require any controller co-ordination which, when busy, would increase controller workload and decrease capacity. Instead of using visual separation, if such aircraft were to be step climbed with vertical separation, then co-ordination would be required, as explained in chapter 6.3.

Visual separation is also used to reduce the time between aircraft departing on tracks diverging by 45° or more immediately after take-off, to less than 60 seconds. Aircraft, on average, take approximately 30 seconds from the start of take-off roll to become airborne. If wake turbulence separation is not required, and the following aircraft will not have a speed catch up on the preceding aircraft, then such aircraft may be allowed to commence take-off roll as soon as the preceding aircraft becomes airborne. Although it may seem a little extreme to be departing aircraft at less than 60 second intervals, the controller is responsible for providing his visual separation, and the aircraft are diverging immediately after take-off. This again greatly increases runway utilization when the traffic demand is high, and is therefore a very useful procedure.

Visual separation/Reduced separation in the vicinity of aerodromes is not to be confused with the term 'visual approach'. This is explained in chapter 6.16.

Chapter 6.5   Avoiding action

CAP 413 states that avoiding action is given when the controller considers that an imminent risk of collision exists if action is not taken immediately. The concept and use of avoiding action are relatively easy to grasp. The controller gives the instruction "[callsign] avoiding action [manoeuvre instructions]" and the pilot initiates such a manoeuvre immediately in order to avoid an imminent collision. There are, however, a few points worth clarifying with respect to avoiding action as detailed below.

'Avoiding action' is not the same as 'traffic avoidance advice'. Traffic avoidance advice is explained in chapters 2.3 and 2.5. A quick read of these chapters now is necessary to recall the major points of traffic avoidance advice before reading the rest of this chapter.

One of the differences between avoiding action and traffic avoidance advice is that traffic avoidance advice is only given if requested by the pilot, whereas avoiding action is given automatically when the controller considers it necessary.

It follows that traffic avoidance advice does not necessarily mean there is an imminent risk of collision. As explained in chapter 2.5, if after being given traffic information the pilot cannot see the conflicting traffic, he can request traffic avoidance advice. Whereas avoiding action implies that there is an imminent risk of collision.

It is not stipulated that avoiding action is only to be given to certain types of flights. Avoiding action may be given to any pilot when the controller considers it necessary. However, in practise, avoiding action is only likely to be given to aircraft on a Deconfliction Service and aircraft inside controlled airspace that require separation. The reason for this is that the remainder of flights i.e. aircraft outside controlled airspace on a Basic Service or a Traffic Service and aircraft inside controlled airspace that do not require separation, are only required to be given traffic information. Such pilots that are responsible for their own separation under the 'see and avoid' principle can therefore fly as close as they wish to such other traffic. In such cases, what may look like an imminent collision on the radar screen is actually not a concern to the pilots as they are seeing and avoiding each other whilst flying relatively close to one another. This is explained in full in chapter 2.4. Chapter 2.4 also explains that the philosophy behind the use of traffic information and the 'see and avoid' principle is both to allow pilots as much freedom as possible whilst at the same time keeping the controller's workload to a minimum.

However, for aircraft on a Deconfliction Service and aircraft inside controlled airspace that require separation, the controller will be providing the appropriate separation against other traffic. Therefore, what looks on the radar screen like an imminent collision must always be treated as such and so avoiding action must be given.

It is a fact, however, that avoiding action can be given to any pilot. So although it is unlikely for certain flights to be given avoiding action, the controller may consider it necessary in an extreme case, for example:

An aircraft outside controlled airspace on a Traffic Service has been given traffic information. The blips become close and are on a collision course. The controller asks the pilot if he his visual and gives an update on the position of the traffic. The pilot does not appear concerned even though he is still not visual, so the controller, fearing the worst, gives avoiding action.

A further point to make is that avoiding action may be given in order to ensure that separation is not lost i.e. the controller realises that if action is not taken immediately then separation may/will be lost. The controller therefore issues avoiding action, and after the completion of the manoeuvre separation had remained at all times.

This does not mean that if you receive avoiding action in the future you should be in the mindset of reacting lazily, thinking that separation will not be lost! This explanation is included to illustrate the fact that controllers may use avoiding action to ensure that separation is maintained.

Chapter 6.6   Essential traffic information

Having previously discussed the defined term 'traffic information' in depth the last thing you would want is another term that sounds similar but is different. Unfortunately that is exactly what we have here, and the term is 'essential traffic information'. This is therefore another example of why pilots should have good RT discipline, and listen to and understand the exact words used by ATC, as in this case the inclusion of the word 'essential' before the more familiar term 'traffic information' means there are some very important differences.

MATS Part 1 states:

> 'Essential traffic' is traffic which is separated for any period by less than the specified standard separation. 'Essential traffic information' is usually passed when radar is not available.

The first point to note is that essential traffic information relates to 'traffic which is separated for any period by less than the specified standard separation' i.e. it is given to aircraft that should be separated, but for whatever reason those aircraft are not being separated. However, traffic information, as discussed in chapter 2.4 relates to aircraft that do not require separating. In such cases the controller gives traffic information to the pilot as an aid to him seeing and avoiding the relevant traffic.

It is stated that 'essential traffic information is usually passed when radar is not available' and as such the most likely occurrence upon which pilots will have essential traffic information given to them is when the radar fails. With reference to the earlier points of this section which detailed separation standards and the differences between radar and procedural separation, try to visualize the situation:

> The radar controller is providing radar separation e.g. 5nm horizontally. At the point at which the radar fails the controller cannot use radar as the basis for providing separation and so the only option is to provide procedural separation. Noting that the procedural horizontal separation minima are much greater than the radar minima (e.g. 20nm instead of 5nm) it will obviously take a certain period of time before these distances, and therefore procedural separation, are established. During this period of time the traffic is therefore separated by less than the specified standard separation and so essential traffic information must be given.

Recall that procedural horizontal separation minima may not simply be a distance (e.g. 20nm) but may require aircraft to establish on different radials from a navaid, or on a radial with a certain DME distance or time difference, or have reported over different navaids and be diverging. Therefore, to establish procedural separation from a radar failure situation can take quite some time.

The more astute of you may have realised that the vertical separation minima are the same for both procedural and radar separation (1000ft or 2000ft as specified) so it would be much easier/quicker in the case of radar failure to establish vertical separation. That way the traffic could still remain 5nm apart horizontally but would be separated procedurally by 1000ft and within a relatively short time period. If this option is possible then it will be the controller's first course of action. However, in a busy environment the radar controller will already have traffic 1000ft above/below other traffic that are separated horizontally. Therefore it may not be possible to immediately separate all traffic vertically. As an interim solution for such situations MATS Part 1 states:

> In the event of radar failure, reduced vertical separation (500ft or 1000ft as appropriate) may be used when standard separation cannot be provided immediately.

As essential traffic is traffic separated by less than the specified standard separation you may think that essential traffic information and avoiding action could be said to be the same as each other. However, avoiding action was defined in chapter 6.5 relating to when an imminent risk of collision exists. Therefore, the instruction "avoiding action" is used as an aggressive instruction where necessary and is not defined in relation to separation, whereas essential traffic information is defined purely in relation to separation.

The philosophy behind essential traffic information is therefore that, like traffic information, it is information on proximate traffic to help the pilot avoid a collision. But unlike traffic information it does not mean the pilot is on a non-separating service and is to use the 'see and avoid' principle. As explained, essential traffic information is given when radar is not available and the controller will be attempting to provide/restore separation. Pilots should not therefore start grossly seeing and avoiding each other in a panic. The controller will immediately commence providing instructions to restore separation. Pilots should therefore comply with such instructions and only undertake a see and avoid manoeuvre if absolutely necessary i.e. if there is an imminent risk of collision. In such situations it is more likely in today's environment that a TCAS TA or RA will be received first.

Should you hear the term 'essential traffic information' on the RT in the future you will now have an understanding of what has happened, what the controller is going to do about it and the fact that you may receive a non-standard level instruction if an interim reduced vertical separation is to be used.

The occurrence of a radar failure is not the only situation that essential traffic information may be given. Aircraft may be receiving a procedural service when the controller discovers (for whatever reason) that two or more aircraft are not separated by the required standard separation. For example, by estimated or actual times at a reporting point, or DME distances along a radial, which now show that the aircraft are not separated. In such cases it is necessary to give essential traffic information and the controller will aim to issue instructions to restore separation.

Chapter 6.7   Flight planned departure time

This chapter, explaining flight planned departure times, applies to both VFR flights and IFR flights. It is included in the IFR section of this book as it is, in general, IFR flights that usually have the problems discussed below.

The time put on a flight plan as the "departure" time is the estimated off blocks time (EOBT) and it means exactly that i.e. it is defined as the time of push-back/engine start, not the take-off time.

The FPS's that tower controllers use have the EOBT printed on them, and this EOBT is taken directly from the flight plan. The EOBT is included on the FPS's for some very important reasons, one of them being to allow controllers to enforce the procedure with respect to flight plans that states:

> In the event of a delay of 30mins from EOBT for a controlled flight and 60mins from EOBT for an un-controlled flight for which a flight plan has been submitted, the flight plan should be amended.

Note that this procedure relates to 'controlled' and 'un-controlled' flights, and does not distinguish between VFR and IFR flights. A 'controlled' flight is defined as 'a flight which is subject to an ATC clearance' and can therefore be either VFR or IFR.

Note also that this tolerance window is not a 'slot' time restriction. The slot time and flight planned departure time are two different things, but both of them have tolerance windows. Pilots are generally familiar with the slot window, however, pilots tend to be generally unaware that the EOBT has a tolerance window. When refused push/start clearance due to the EOBT window pilots are consequently often confused as to why they cannot start if they do not have a slot and often think that the controller is being difficult.

The reason why the flight planned departure time has a tolerance window and why controllers are strict in enforcing it is very important. Every flight plan is processed through a flow management computer. The computer takes the EOBT and adds a taxiing time (which is fixed for each individual airport) to give an estimated airborne time. It then uses this estimated airborne time together with the flight plan details to calculate when the aircraft will pass through each ATC sector along its route. It does this for every flight and therefore identifies if any ATC sectors will have more aircraft at any one time than its specified capacity limit. If a sector will be overloaded then the computer issues slot times that ensure that aircraft will not overload any sectors.

However, very few aircraft get airborne at the exact minute of the EOBT plus the fixed taxi time. Therefore it is unrealistic for the flow computer to use such a single exact minute to calculate whether an aircraft should have a slot placed on it. So, in order to be realistic, the flow computer uses a window based on the EOBT. It is for this reason that controllers are strict on enforcing the EOBT window. If they did not enforce it then ATC overloading could easily occur.

There is also a condition included in the EOBT window which states:

> If a non-regulated flight is not ready for start at EOBT plus 15mins then ATC will not allow the aircraft to push-back or start until the EOBT is modified by the aircraft operator or handling agent.
>
> If an aircraft is ready to start in good time to meet its EOBT parameters and is subsequently delayed by ATC, the responsibility for modifying the EOBT rests with ATC.

What this means in real terms is that a controlled flight can still push and start in the usual window of up to 30mins after EOBT provided the pilot has called for start (i.e. made a request on the RT) no later than 15mins after EOBT.

If start is requested at greater than 15mins after EOBT then start clearance will not be given. This is a fixed rule, it is not dependant on how busy the airfield is. Therefore pilots could call for start at a small quiet airfield 20mins after EOBT thinking that they have 10mins to spare, but consequently have start clearance refused by ATC.

The use of the term 'non-regulated flight' refers to a flight that does not have a slot. If a flight does have a slot then the slot time takes precedence over the flight planned departure time, and the procedures with regards to push and start are as described in chapter 6.8.

These flight planned departure time tolerances, including the window to call for start, are in use in most countries not just the UK.

Chapter 6.8   Slot time

The 'slot' time is the time given by the flow management computer that the aircraft should take-off at i.e. the time the aircraft should become airborne, not the time of push/start. This time is also called the 'Calculated Take-Off Time' (CTOT). As mentioned in chapter 6.7 it is impractical to expect aircraft to get airborne at such a single exact minute, and therefore controllers are allowed to let aircraft take-off within a slot window. The slot window is:

    From 5 minutes before CTOT to 10 minutes after CTOT.

Note that this window relates to the take-off time not the time of push/start. In order to emphasise this to pilots and to ensure that they are ready for their slot time appropriately, in many references to slot times the slot time is defined in practical language for pilots as: 'The time the aircraft should be at the holding point ready for departure'. ATC will be expecting this so pilots should request push/start in sufficient time for it. Note that the important point is to be at the holding point at the slot time. This is so that any delays at the holding point can be accommodated within the extra 10 minutes of the slot window rather than assuming that you will automatically be allowed to take-off if you get to the holding point one minute before the slot window ends.

When airports are busy the time for push/start and taxi can be significant. Such time periods are often advised in the aerodrome briefing pages of aerodrome charts or booklets. The wording of this can be such as: 'Pilots must call for start at least 20 minutes before the slot time' or 'Delays greater than 10mins can be expected at the holding point. Sufficient time must be allowed for start-up, push-back and taxi to account for this'. Again note that the time is referenced to the slot time, not the end of the slot window.

I am sure that the importance of ensuring that aircraft depart within the slot window in order to prevent an ATC overload is obvious and needs no explanation to pilots. What is worth mentioning, however, is that tower controllers are legally required to write on the FPS the time the aircraft becomes airborne to the nearest minute. They are also required to write the slot time on the FPS. Controllers are therefore very strict about not allowing aircraft to depart by even one minute outside of the slot window. Although it may seem very pedantic and unnecessary to pilots, if a controller allowed an aircraft to depart outside of the slot window (even by only a single minute) and an overload occurred, it could be traced using the FPS's to that controller. It may only be a single minute, but legally it is out of tolerance and therefore it is that controller who is at fault.

The slot window of 5 minutes before CTOT to 10 minutes after CTOT is used in most countries. However, some airports may have different tolerances as allowed by local agreements. These are usually for the most busiest of airports and may necessitate a larger slot window due to holding point congestion at the busiest times. Some of the differences may not apply to all aircraft at an airport and may allow, for example, CTOT plus 15 minutes for up to 10 aircraft per hour. Therefore, pilots may not be aware of such increased slot windows and should always prepare for the known policy i.e. request start in sufficient time to be at the holding point at the slot time.

Chapter 6.9   Minimum Departure Interval

Delays in start clearance or delays at the holding point are sometimes incurred due to 'Minimum Departure Intervals' (MDI's). The MDI procedure does not state a specific time to be airborne, nor does it have an associated window, and should not be confused with the slot time as detailed in chapter 6.8. The MDI procedure is, as its name suggests, an interval to be provided between the relevant departing aircraft. MDI's are used when a sector has such an amount of traffic that it can only accept aircraft from the specified airport at the given interval, for example, one aircraft every 3 minutes. MDI's are therefore specific between an airport and each of the (initial) sectors that departing aircraft are fed into when departing from the airport. As MDI's are dependant on the traffic flow through the relevant sector, the MDI may not be in force at all times throughout the day, or its value may change as necessary, for example, from 3 minutes to 4 minutes. MDI's are implemented as deemed necessary by the controller currently controlling the sector, or by the traffic flow/watch manager, or may be stated for enforcement in MATS Part 2 at specific times where a regular traffic flow is known. When MDI's are implemented, or when an MDI (that is currently in use) is increased, this can therefore lead to delays for aircraft intending to use the affected route.

When sequencing aircraft at the holding point(s) for take-off, the departure tower controller must therefore take into account not only the departure separation minima and the wake turbulence separation minima, but also any applicable MDI's. When an airport feeds aircraft into many initial sectors, for example, where many different SID's are used, there may consequently be multiple different MDI's in force.

When MDI's are in force and pilots call for start clearance, tower controllers are able to calculate the earliest time that each aircraft would be able to depart (when taking its place in the departure queue) and therefore give pilots the appropriate time for engine start. As a simplified example, if there are 8 aircraft in front to depart into the same sector with an MDI of 3 minutes, then the aircraft will not be able to depart for another 24 minutes. If the expected time to start and taxi is approximately 10 minutes, then the controller will give a 10-15 minute delay to the start clearance. If the tower controller is aware of the MDI (i.e. when MDI's are already in force) then a delay to the start clearance will be given as necessary as this is more efficient than having aircraft absorb the delay at the holding point with engines running. However, when MDI's are implemented after an affected aircraft has started its engines or begun taxiing, the controller would not have known of this. As MDI's are required for reasons of preventing an overload, the MDI cannot be ignored, so this may require the aircraft to have an inefficient delay at the holding point with the engines running.

Note that when aircraft are subject to MDI's, other aircraft may jump ahead in the start queue or departure queue at the holding point if they do not have a restriction or have a lesser restriction and the traffic environment allows this to be done fairly. In such circumstances, any aircraft subject to an MDI which has other aircraft jump ahead of it is not being treated unfairly as, is shown in the example above, the aircraft is not able to depart for a set period of time as determined by the MDI queue.

When delays are incurred due to MDI's, controllers often state to pilots on the RT "delays due to MDI's in the [name] sector".

Chapter 6.10   IFR departure clearance

Departure clearance for IFR flights is normally given in a set format. This format being:

1. Destination
2. Initial route
3. Level
4. Squawk

For example: "Cleared to Bournemouth, after departure left turn heading 150°, climb to altitude 4000ft, squawk 3174".
or, "Cleared to Malaga, Honiley one romeo departure, squawk 5213".

With reference to chapter 3.3 it can be seen that the format and content of an IFR departure clearance is slightly different to that of a VFR departure clearance. Points to note with regards to such differences are:

- An IFR departure clearance does not include the statement of the flight rules, whereas a VFR departure clearance includes the statement "VFR".
- If a SID has level instructions included within it, the IFR departure clearance only has to state the SID designator and does not need to repeat such level instructions (as shown above for a Honiley one romeo departure).
- An IFR departure clearance often includes the destination, whereas a VFR departure clearance usually does not (see below for explanation).

With reference to the fact that if a SID has a level instruction included within it then the level does not need repeating in the clearance, note that this only applies if you are cleared to fly to that SID level. If a non-standard level is given then this must obviously be included in the clearance and read back by the pilot. For example, if the HON 1R stop altitude is 5000ft, but the clearance is to climb to 4000ft, then the clearance in the example above would be: "Cleared to Malaga, Honiley one romeo departure, climb to altitude 4000ft, squawk 5213".

IFR departure clearances usually include the destination. The exact definition of this is:

> Aircraft shall be cleared for the entire route to the aerodrome of first intended landing when it is planned to remain within controlled or advisory airspace throughout the flight and there is reasonable assurance that co-ordination will be effected ahead of the passage of the aircraft.

Trainee pilots that depart IFR will not usually have the destination included in their departure clearance as they often will not remain within controlled or advisory airspace for the whole of the flight, also the aerodrome of departure will often be outside such airspace. When pilots depart for IFR training and general handling, although it is not a standard phraseology term, the phrase "cleared local training flight" is often used in the departure clearance.

For airline type flights the destination will therefore usually be included in the departure clearance. However, if such flights have a portion of their route in Class G airspace then the destination will not be included in the departure clearance. This is still the case even if the portion of the flight that is in Class G airspace in very small, for example, a flight that departs from an aerodrome within Class G airspace but will enter controlled airspace in 10nm and then remain within controlled airspace for the rest of the flight.

Whilst it is obvious to state that pilots must have a clearance to enter controlled airspace before they do so, this can be easily forgotten in the real world especially for (professional) pilots who usually operate from airports within controlled airspace but on this occasion are departing from a seldom visited or unfamiliar airport that is in Class G airspace. On such occasions it is therefore good airmanship to make a mental note and include in the departure briefing that the airspace is Class G (with the associated requirement to look out for traffic as per the 'see and avoid' principle) and that a specific clearance to join controlled airspace must be received.

At some airports within Class G airspace the procedure for passing departure clearance may further lead to the confusion of pilots or to the mindset that a clearance to join controlled airspace has been given when actually it has not. This may occur when two clearances are passed separately – one being the 'airways joining clearance' and the other being the 'local departure instructions'. If there is a delay between issuing the two clearances to the pilot this can enable or add to the confusion. The tower controller may receive these clearances separately as the airways joining clearance is issued by the appropriate area controller and the local departure instructions are issued by the approach controller for that airport (the approach controller being responsible for providing a service in the airspace surrounding the airport) Again, it is necessary for pilots to be aware of the environment they are operating in and to listen to the exact words used by ATC, in this case ensuring that a clearance of "cleared to join controlled airspace" has been received. An example of such could be:

Airways clearance: "Cleared to join controlled airspace at BASIL, climb FL190, squawk 5362".

Departure clearance: "After departure fly heading 150°, climb to altitude 4000ft, squawk 6341".

The term 'Request level change en-route' may be included in an IFR departure clearance. The exact meaning of the term is very important and must be fully understood by pilots. The definition and explanation is written in chapter 10.2.

The glossary lists some of the standard symbols that you may wish to use in order to quickly write down departure clearances given to you by ATC.

Chapter 6.11   Revisions to departure clearance

It is a common occurrence for controllers to give a departure clearance but later (before take-off) change part or all of the clearance. The usual reason for the change is due to other traffic in the area which now requires the departing aircraft to change its initial direction and/or altitude in order to guarantee separation. This can also include the technique of effectively reducing the departure separation minima as explained in chapter 6.3. What this does in virtually every case is to allow the aircraft to depart sooner than would otherwise be possible. However, revisions to departure clearances are often misinterpreted by pilots even though pilots read back such revised clearances correctly. The issue here is that the phraseology of such transmissions suggests things or puts the pilot into a certain mindset that is incorrect. This chapter is intended to resolve such issues for pilots.

Revised departure clearances are mainly misinterpreted with respect to level instructions. It is specified in MATS Part 1 that a revised clearance automatically cancels the earlier restriction. Note, however, that this refers to the horizontal and vertical profiles separately. This therefore means that two major differences occur which must be fully understood by pilots.

The first difference is that if the revised departure clearance refers only to the vertical profile, then it is only the vertical profile that is changed. The horizontal profile therefore remains as previously cleared. So, for example, if the clearance was given as a HON 1R departure and the controller subsequently says "[callsign] after departure maintain altitude 3000ft", the horizontal profile of the HON 1R departure is still valid, but the vertical profile has changed to a stop altitude of 3000ft. It does not therefore mean that the entire original clearance is cancelled and should be interpreted as climb straight ahead to altitude 3000ft.

The second difference is that, in the UK, as a revised clearance automatically cancels the earlier restrictions, if the original departure clearance had step climb restrictions (as do many SID's) but the revised departure clearance specifies a level, the step climb restrictions are consequently cancelled. So, for example, if a SID had an initial stop altitude of 3000ft, then a climb to 4000ft, then a climb to FL50, and the revised clearance is "[callsign] after departure maintain altitude 4000ft", the step to 3000ft is cancelled and the aircraft can consequently climb to 4000ft straight away. Note that as the clearance is to maintain altitude 4000ft, in such an example it does not mean that the aircraft can climb to 4000ft and then climb as per the SID step to FL50. If maintain altitude 4000ft is given then 4000ft shall be maintained until further instructed. Similarly, for the same SID and step climb, if the revised clearance is "[callsign] after departure maintain FL60", all the step climb restrictions are cancelled and the aircraft can climb to FL60 straight away.

The policy described above with respect to step climbs is valid in the UK. However, outside the UK, country specific or ICAO procedures may involve a different policy. Such procedures may be the opposite to those used in the UK i.e. a revised clearance may not automatically cancel previous restrictions, and so such restrictions are still valid unless specifically cancelled using the appropriate standard phraseology. In this case, using the first example above, the initial step to 3000ft must be obeyed before climbing to maintain 4000ft. In the second example this would mean that all the SID steps must be obeyed, and then, when at the end of the SID (at FL50) a climb to FL60 is to be commenced.

The use of two conflicting policies on such a serious issue as level clearances is not an ideal situation. However, the only practical solution at present is for pilots to be aware that such conflicting procedures are in use and to reference the relevant documents to ensure that the procedure for the state being flown in is known. A frequent check of such documents is also required to ensure that pilots are aware of any changes to such procedures that may occur in the future.

If ever in doubt with respect to the clearance given never be afraid to ask the controller to clarify the clearance. If you are still unclear after the controller replies then continue to ask until all doubt is removed. It may be the case that your query does not seem to be resolved even after multiple enquiries. In this case it is likely that the greatest chance of obtaining a definitive answer is by stating what you understand the clearance to be, with the inclusion of the word 'confirm' so that the controller has to reply as to whether you are correct or not. For example: "Confirm maintain altitude 3000ft until 8DME then climb FL50?".

The term 'unrestricted' is sometimes used, although it is not necessarily a standard phraseology term, to indicate to the pilot that any previous step climb restrictions are cancelled. For example, "[callsign] after departure climb FL60 unrestricted". Again, if in doubt then always ask the controller to clarify. The use of the term 'unrestricted' is not commonly used in the UK due to the policy as previously explained that a revised clearance automatically cancels the earlier restriction.

Many controllers, when issuing a revised clearance with a level that is lower than the previous clearance, will often include the phrase "until instructed" as a practical approach to making clear to the pilot that such a level is to be maintained until ATC instruct otherwise and consequently any step climbs above that level are cancelled. For example, "[callsign] after departure maintain altitude 4000ft until instructed".

Chapter 6.12   Initial transmission after departure

CAP 413 and MATS Part 1 state:

> Pilots of all aircraft flying instrument departures shall include the following on first contact with approach/departure control:
>
> 1. Callsign.
> 2. SID designator where appropriate.
> 3. Current or passing level.
> 4. Initial climb level. For SID's including stepped climb profiles, state the initial level to which the aircraft is climbing.

Note that the above states 'all aircraft flying instrument departures'. Therefore, the initial transmission on the departure frequency should always be in this given format for all IFR departures not just those with a SID. The use of this format provides a concise transmission. For example, "London, [callsign], Brookmans Park 6G departure, passing altitude 2300ft, climbing FL60".

The inclusion of the current or passing level enables the controller to verify the Mode C readout as explained in chapter 5.8 without having to make a transmission to ask the pilot to do so, therefore decreasing RT loading. During procedural control the current or passing level must still be included. Although this has no use with regards to verification, during procedural control the controller can still use the report to check the aircraft's level and this may allow him to provide vertical separation, again without having to make a transmission to ask the pilot to report his level.

The inclusion of the initial climb level is a safety measure that confirms to the controller that the pilot has understood the correct initial cleared level, again without the need for the controller to make a transmission to request it.

As the use of this procedure is mandatory, should pilots omit part or all of it from the initial transmission, the controller will ask the pilot to report the relevant (missing) details.

The procedure as detailed in this chapter is a UK procedure and is not necessarily required in other countries. However, it is advised that pilots always use this procedure wherever they are in the world as it gives a very concise transmission and includes all the information the controller needs initially without the controller having to make a transmission to request it. Also, with reference to step climbs outside the UK as discussed in chapter 6.11, the (voluntary) inclusion of the initial level may alert the controller to the fact that you may be climbing to a level that is different to the one the controller is expecting. An exception to using this procedure would be if the aerodrome briefing pages state otherwise, for example, 'pilots contact departure frequency immediately after take-off with callsign and cleared level only'.

Chapter 6.13 Expected approach time

The term 'Expected approach time' (EAT) has a defined meaning. Its abbreviation EAT should not be confused with ETA (Estimated time of arrival).

MATS Part 1 states:

> An Expected approach time (EAT) is the time that approach control estimate that an aircraft will be able to leave the holding facility, following a delay, to commence its approach for landing.
>
> EAT's are based on the landing rate and are calculated according to the traffic situation. They are to be expressed as actual times, not as time intervals, and revised as necessary.
>
> EAT's shall not normally be issued when the delay is expected to be less than 20 minutes. The phrase 'no delay expected' is only to be used if it genuinely reflects the situation.

Expected approach times are issued as a protection should (aircraft or ATC) radio failure occur. ICAO radio failure procedures state that if an EAT has been given aircraft should commence the approach from the holding facility at the last acknowledged EAT. The first (i.e. lowest) aircraft in the hold is given the earliest EAT. The next aircraft in the hold (i.e. the one that is second vertically) is given the next available EAT and so on. EAT's are spaced at time intervals according to the landing rate at that time. For a particular airport the landing rate can differ due to factors such as weather, number of runways in operation, etc. Should a radio failure occur, the use of EAT's therefore ensures that separation will not be lost as the EAT means that the radio failure aircraft will not leave the hold to commence an approach (at its EAT) until all preceding aircraft (i.e. those ahead in the queue and below the radio failure aircraft) have left the hold to commence an approach.

It is worth reminding that in such a situation you are to remain in the hold at your last assigned level until you reach your EAT. So, for example, if the minimum hold altitude is 5000ft and you are instructed to join the hold at 10000ft, you shall remain in the hold at 10000ft until the EAT, only then (at the EAT) may you start to descend. If this means that you are too high to commence the approach procedure at the EAT, the ICAO radio failure procedure states that (at the EAT) descend in the hold as necessary before commencing the approach procedure.

The main point of this, therefore, is that you are not to descend in the hold (early) so as to be at the minimum hold/procedure altitude at the EAT. If you did this you would be descending through other aircraft in the hold that are remaining at their last assigned hold level until their EAT.

ICAO radio failure procedures state that aircraft should carry out the approach procedure and land if possible within 30 minutes of the EAT. However, EAT's are generally issued with intervals in the region of 5 to 10 minutes. So, should a pilot in such a situation have to go-around from the procedure and decide to use the remainder of the 30 minutes to conduct subsequent approaches, this could lead to the situation where the aircraft conflicts with other aircraft commencing their approach at their EAT. To prevent this from happening MATS Part 1 states:

> The level occupied by the radio failure aircraft in the holding stack, and subsequent levels which the aircraft will have to pass through, may be re-allocated to succeeding aircraft 15 minutes after the latest time they should have been vacated.
>
> The lowest level in the stack and the level at which, according to published procedures, radio failure aircraft are expected to leave the vicinity are to be kept clear for 30 minutes after the time descent should have begun plus an appropriate period to allow the aircraft to leave the vicinity.

If an aircraft has radio failure the controller will therefore issue clearances, including revised EAT's, to other aircraft in order to establish the procedure given above.

The fact that EAT's are normally given for delays of 20 minutes or more means that you could be instructed to hold and, without being given any warning, use up to an extra 20 minutes of fuel. If fuel is a concern then simply ask the controller for the length of the expected delay.

Delay not determined

The phrase 'delay not determined' has a defined meaning. MATS Part 1 states:

> If, for reasons other than weather (e.g. a blocked runway), the extent of the delay is not known, aircraft are to be advised 'delay not determined'. As soon as it is possible for aircraft to re-commence approach, EAT's are to be issued.

As explained earlier in this chapter EAT's are issued as a protection should radio failure occur. If a situation exists which prevents aircraft from commencing the approach and landing, and it is not known when such movements will be able to re-commence (such as a blocked runway), it is obviously not appropriate for ATC to issue EAT's. If EAT's were issued and radio failure subsequently occurred, such aircraft would commence approach with the intention of landing into an unsuitable environment. The meaning and the use of the phrase 'delay not determined' must therefore be understood.

ICAO radio failure procedures state that if 'delay not determined' is given and radio failure occurs, aircraft should not attempt to land at that airfield but proceed to their nominated diversion airfield or other suitable alternate.

If 'delay not determined' is given, this obviously has implications with respect to fuel as you are now holding indefinitely. In such situations it is not recommended that you wait until minimum diversion fuel before diverting to another airfield, because often other aircraft will be doing the same thing and divert at the same time going to the same airfield. This can therefore require extensive vectoring and speed control and possibly more holding at the diversion airfield, all of which increases the fuel burn.

Holding for weather improvement

MATS Part 1 states:

> If aircraft elect to hold for the weather to improve before attempting an approach and landing the controller shall inform the first aircraft entering the holding pattern 'no traffic delay expected'. Subsequent aircraft entering the holding pattern are to be passed 'delay not determined [number] aircraft holding for weather improvement'.

The required landing minima are not always the same for every aircraft or aircraft operator, and the weather with respect to such minima can change over a relatively short period of time. So, when pilots elect to hold for weather improvement, there is not an obstruction of indeterminate length that is preventing aircraft from commencing an approach and landing. The first such aircraft into the hold is therefore given 'no traffic delay expected' rather than 'delay not determined'. Subsequent aircraft will enter the hold above the first aircraft, but, as it is not known at what time the lowest aircraft will commence an approach, EAT's cannot be given. If EAT's were given and radio failure subsequently occurred, this could result in such aircraft descending through other aircraft in the hold. Subsequent aircraft are therefore given 'delay not determined'.

In such a situation when you have been given 'delay not determined' it is still the case that if you experience radio failure you should not attempt to commence the approach but should proceed to your nominated diversion airfield or other suitable alternate.

If a pilot wishes to make an approach but is above other aircraft that are holding for weather improvement, if radar is available the controller will vector the aircraft away from the hold and then, when horizontal separation exists, descend the aircraft and vector it onto final approach.

If the controller does not have radar this can be a little more complicated. In such a situation, if the airfield has more than one holding facility, each with its own approach procedure, and both holds are deemed separated, the controller can instruct the aircraft to route from one hold to the other maintaining its level (so as to remain vertically separated), then when it is established in the second hold (now horizontally separated from the other hold) it can descend and commence the approach procedure. If, however, there is only one holding facility at the airfield, aircraft must remain in the hold until there are no aircraft below as in this situation there is no horizontal separation between any part of the holding or approach procedure. Aircraft must therefore remain vertically separated at all times.

It may also be the case that (with or without radar) if an aircraft, that is not at the lowest holding level, is holding for weather improvement and aircraft above it wish to make an approach, such aircraft may be routed away from the hold, descended, then routed back into the hold underneath the aircraft that is holding for weather improvement. As all such aircraft that are beneath the one holding for weather improvement are wishing to make an approach they may now be issued with EAT's.

Chapter 6.14   Instrument approach procedures

This chapter explains a number of items with regards to instrument approach procedures. Again, some points may seem a little pedantic, but the intention is that pilots are made aware of the actual facts, therefore reducing the possibilities for incorrect actions or misinterpretation.

Level to descend to

Pilots will be familiar with the phrase 'cleared for the procedure' with respect to flying instrument approach procedures. This instruction obviously means that you are cleared to fly such a procedure and therefore, by definition, you are cleared to descend to the levels as specified on the approach plates for such procedure. However, misinterpretation sometimes exists with respect to which level must be maintained until the start of the procedure.

In most cases, when "cleared for the procedure", it is left to the discretion of the pilots to choose the level to descend to whilst routeing to the start of the procedure. Pilots must therefore ensure they themselves choose an appropriately safe level to descend to whilst routeing to the start of the cleared instrument approach procedure. Such an appropriately safe level is:

- The minimum hold level, if in the hold.
- The minimum route level, if on an airway or STAR.
- The MSA or grid MORA, if proceeding direct (i.e. not on an airway or STAR).

Note that if under radar control and cleared to proceed direct and the controller gives a level to descend to (i.e. the radar vectoring minima, which will often be lower than any MSA's, grid MORA's or procedure altitudes that are available for reference by pilots) you may descend to the level specified by the controller providing you are assured that you are radar identified and will remain radar monitored by the radar controller.

The charts must therefore be checked carefully to ensure that the correct level is used until the start of the procedure. The main trap is that once cleared for the procedure you must not automatically descend to the first level specified on the procedure. The following example is used to illustrate:

> A procedure starting at beacon DEF, showing an altitude over DEF of 3500ft and descending outbound to an altitude of 2500ft. Once cleared for the procedure do not automatically descend to 3500ft because that is the first level specified on the procedure. In the majority of cases the minimum hold level will be the same as the level at the start of the procedure. But if, in this example, the minimum hold level is an altitude of 4000ft, whilst in the hold you must maintain 4000ft until overhead DEF, at which point you can descend to 2500ft whilst routeing outbound on the procedure. If you were routeing to DEF on an airway or STAR, and such charts give a minimum level of FL50 until DEF, then you must maintain FL50 until overhead DEF, at which point you can descend to 2500ft whilst routeing outbound on the procedure. And if you were proceeding direct to DEF, but not on any specified route, and the MSA or grid MORA was an altitude of 4200ft, then you must maintain 4200ft until overhead DEF.

Pre-conditions

It is also important when being cleared for the procedure to listen carefully to any pre-conditions/instructions included in the clearance for the procedure. An example of this is that controllers will sometimes use the phrase 'cleared for the procedure, maintain [level]' or 'cleared for the procedure, report beacon outbound maintaining [level]'. Pilots may misinterpret this as meaning maintain the level until the start of the procedure and then descend in accordance with the procedure. This (misinterpretation) is incorrect. The actual meaning is to maintain the level indefinitely. It is therefore similar to a revised departure clearance, as explained in chapter 6.11, in the sense that you are cleared to follow the horizontal profile (i.e. the procedure route) but the vertical profile is amended (e.g. maintain FL50 until instructed). The reason for the vertical restriction will almost certainly be due to other traffic. The controller will be expecting such traffic to have cleared in the near future however, so that he can clear you to rejoin a sensible vertical profile.

Instrument approach procedure phraseology

It is common for most pilots to make certain RT calls when flying holds or instrument approach procedures. These RT calls to which I am referring are ones which many pilots seem to make instinctively as if they were mandatory reports, however, there is no mention anywhere that such reports are mandatory. It is therefore simply a common habit that most pilots have of making these reports. The reports in question are:

"[callsign] taking up the hold"
"[callsign] beacon inbound/outbound"

So, in the interests of correctness, should you be told otherwise, the above reports are not mandatory and therefore only have to be made if specifically instructed to do so by the controller. The routine use of these calls is not necessarily a bad thing, and some may argue that it is actually a good idea in the interests of airmanship etc. But they are not mandatory as some people may have you believe. However, a time when it is best not to make such reports is when the RT is very busy. In this case all unnecessary RT calls should be omitted to prevent frequency/controller overload.

Should you be wondering why such reports are not mandatory, if the controller has radar then he can see the aircraft's positions easily on the radar screen, so such calls are not necessary. When the controller is providing a procedural service he writes on the FPS's to indicate certain clearances and/or physically moves the FPS's into certain blocks in the strip bay to indicate the clearance or aircraft position. Due to this practise, if an aircraft has been cleared into the hold or cleared for a procedure the controller knows the clearance of that and other aircraft relative to it. So it may not be necessary, for example, to report taking up the hold as the controller has cleared you for the hold and therefore knows it is safe for you to do so. It may be the case that the controller is waiting for a certain event, for example, the previous aircraft to land, before he can clear you for the procedure. So, in this case, it does not matter whether you have already entered the hold or are on the way to the hold, your clearance to the hold is safe and your next event (i.e. your clearance for the procedure) cannot occur until the previous aircraft has landed.

When asked to report beacon inbound/outbound it is standard phraseology to use the word "beacon". However, in the interests of safety, it is preferred if the actual name of the beacon is used, for example, "[callsign] DEF outbound". This practice informs the controller of exactly what you are doing, and is a good double check at airfields that have more than one beacon associated with them. Similarly, it is preferred when asked to report taking up the hold to include the beacon name, for example, "[callsign] taking up the hold at STH". The good thing about this practice is that you are not making an extra RT transmission, but are simply replacing the generic term "beacon" with the beacon's actual name in a transmission that you are already having to make.

When cleared for an instrument approach procedure pilots should read back the clearance with the exact name of the procedure. This is important both from the practical points of view that you the pilot know the exact procedure you are cleared for, and also that the controller knows you have received the correct clearance. So, for example, rather than saying "cleared for the procedure runway 02 [callsign]", use the exact phrase "cleared ILS DME procedure runway 02 [callsign]".

The exact procedure names are written in the top corner of the approach plates and so can be easily read verbatim from the plate when needed. Some procedures will also have an alphabetical or numerical identifier included in the name. It is very important that such identifiers are also included in the name. The usual reason for these identifiers is that there is more than one procedure using the same navaids for that runway. It could be that one procedure is a DME arc procedure starting at 20nm north of the airfield, and the other is a teardrop procedure starting overhead the beacon on the airfield. It is important to confirm, therefore, which procedure is to be flown. An example is 'VOR ILS DME Yankee procedure runway 10' and 'VOR ILS DME Zulu procedure runway 10'.

When giving the exact procedure name it should be spoken exactly as written on the top of the approach plate. In contrast to the earlier paragraph explaining that the beacon name should be used for reports of beacon inbound/outbound and taking up the hold, the beacon name should not be used when reading back the approach procedure clearance unless the procedure name includes it. This may seem a little confusing, but for approach procedures simply read the title as given on the approach plate, as that is the official name for the procedure, for example, "cleared NDB DME procedure runway 06 [callsign]".

Missed approach

When cleared for an instrument approach procedure you are also, by definition, cleared for the whole of the missed approach procedure which, in most cases, will include entering the same hold from which the approach began. It has to be the case that you are also cleared for the missed approach procedure as well as the approach procedure as a landing can never be guaranteed 100% until it has been completed. As such, missed approach procedures are always procedurally separated from any inbound routes, approach procedures, holds and departure routes at that and nearby airfields. This means that in the high workload situation of a go-around, not only is a safe clearance already present without requiring a transmission/instruction from ATC, but also that radio failure situations have a safe missed approach clearance.

With reference to the hold at the end of a missed approach procedure, by looking at the plates for any airfield you will see that when the same hold is used for the missed approach and approach procedure, the missed approach hold level is always (1000ft) below the minimum hold level specified for the approach procedure. This therefore ensures that separation is automatically provided.

Procedural service

Chapter 6.2 explained how traffic capacity greatly decreases when a procedural service is given compared to a radar service. This is still true with respect to a procedural approach service. If the controller has radar, then although aircraft may still be required to enter the hold, once they leave the hold the controller can vector aircraft relatively close together e.g. 5nm in-trail, and vector them onto final approach with minimum wake turbulence separation e.g. 3nm in-trail. With a procedural service, due to the proximity to each other, the hold, outbound legs and final approach track are not usually deemed separated. In this case it means that often a second aircraft cannot be cleared for the approach until the tower controller has confirmed to the approach controller that the first aircraft has landed. Due to the fact that a full instrument approach procedure can take in the region of ten minutes to fly, a procedural approach service is much less efficient compared to a radar service that has the potential to land one aircraft every sixty seconds. However, as explained in chapter 6.2, in such a situation the workload for the procedural controller can still be high.

As explained earlier, the missed approach procedure must be protected in case of radio failure. This can be one reason why a second aircraft may not be cleared for the approach procedure until the first aircraft has landed as it could otherwise result in more than one aircraft routeing to the same missed approach hold at the same (missed approach) level.

At some airfields it may be possible to clear more than one aircraft for an approach procedure at any one time. This is usually possible if the airfield has two holds that are deemed separated, for example, one to the north of the airfield at beacon NOR and one to the south of the airfield at beacon STH. The controller will clear the first aircraft for the procedure from NOR and ask the pilot to report established on the final approach track. When the pilot reports on the final approach track the controller can then clear a second aircraft for the procedure but this time from STH. This is possible as the initial approach track from the beacon and the final approach track are deemed separated (due to their directions and distance between them) and the fact that longitudinal in-trail separation is deemed to exist with one aircraft on the final approach and the other aircraft just leaving the beacon. If the first aircraft has to go-around the missed approach will route to NOR and be deemed separated from the approach procedure route from STH and the final approach track. Should the second aircraft also go-around the missed approach procedure will route to STH so that both aircraft remain separated during the missed approach.

Summary

Below is a summary of the main points in this chapter.

- When routeing to the start of the cleared procedure, ensure that an appropriately safe level to descend to is chosen. Such a level being:

    - The minimum hold level
    - The minimum route level
    - The MSA or MORA

- When cleared for the procedure, listen carefully to any pre-conditions/instructions included in the clearance.

- Use the actual beacon name spoken in the phonetic alphabet.

- Use the exact instrument approach procedure name.

Chapter 6.15　　　Radar vectors to final approach

MATS Part 1 states that when vectoring aircraft onto the ILS:

> To reduce the possibility of unstable and rushed approaches, the controller should provide a conditional clearance to the pilot to descend on the ILS glidepath once established on the localiser. Alternatively, where it is necessary to ensure that an aircraft joining the ILS does not commence descent until specifically cleared, the controller shall solely instruct the pilot to report established on the localiser, and if deemed necessary, may reiterate the previously assigned level.

It is therefore important that pilots listen to the exact clearance given as they will be in the mindset of expecting to hear in one transmission a conditional clearance to establish on the localiser and when established descend on the glidepath. However, the controller may have solely given an instruction to establish on the localiser (without a clearance to descend on the glidepath). Such circumstances will almost certainly be due to other traffic, so it is important that a descent is not commenced until a clearance to do so is given by the controller. In such circumstances the controller will be expecting the traffic to clear the area so as to be able to issue a clearance to descend on the glidepath in sufficient time. Note that if a sole instruction to establish on the localiser is given the controller is not required to reiterate the assigned level, so pilots should not be in the mindset of thinking they will always be given this reminder as a backup.

To complete the explanation of the previous paragraph and to ensure that no confusion remains, if a clearance is given to establish on the localiser (without a clearance to descend on the glidepath) and a level is specified or reiterated, the pilot must maintain the specified level until a new clearance is received i.e. its meaning is not to maintain that level initially and then descend on the glidepath when the glidepath is intercepted.

MATS Part 1 also states:

> Controllers shall not instruct pilots to establish on the localiser at ranges outside the localiser Designated Operational Coverage (DOC). Controllers shall not instruct pilots to descend on the ILS when the glidepath intersect would be outside the glidepath DOC.

This therefore explains why, in cases where pilots establish on the localiser whilst being beyond the protected range of the glidepath and request descent on the glidepath, the controller will not give such a clearance (possibly giving step down altitudes as an alternative until within the protected range of the glidepath).

It has been explained that a clearance to establish on the localiser does not mean that you may descend on the glidepath, a separate clearance to descend on the ILS (or glidepath) is also required. In the UK the two phrases of "establish on the localiser" and "descend on the glidepath" will be used although the may be given together as a conditional clearance. In other countries the one phrase "cleared ILS" may be used e.g. "[callsign] turn right heading 050° cleared ILS". The instruction "cleared ILS" is relatively free from misinterpretation and means that you are cleared to intercept the localiser and descend on the glidepath.

Unfortunately, some airfields use the phrase "final vectors ILS" as the instruction to clear pilots for the ILS. This instruction has some ambiguity as it only states that final vectors are being given and does not state any form of clearance onto the ILS. However, the phrase is in use and hopefully you are now forearmed should you encounter it. In some cases the use of such non-standard phraseology is detailed in the aerodrome charts, so this is another good example of the need to read the aerodrome briefing pages of the aerodrome charts. Should you be in doubt at anytime, including after receiving the instruction "final vectors ILS", the phrase "confirm cleared ILS" can be used to resolve the situation.

MATS Part 1 states that controllers shall always instruct the pilot to report established on the localiser (i.e. irrespective of whether a conditional clearance to descend on the glidepath has been given or not). Therefore, in the UK such an instruction and report will always be required. In other countries this may not be a requirement so pilots may not receive such an instruction in those countries.

Chapter 8.6 details the wake turbulence separation required for aircraft on approach. Recall from chapter 3.8 that for VFR flights the controller is only legally obliged to inform the pilot of the recommended wake turbulence separation, it is then the pilot's responsibility to ensure that such separation is applied. When IFR flights are being radar vectored to final approach it must obviously be the controller's responsibility to ensure that the appropriate wake turbulence separation is applied. As such the controller will therefore provide the required wake turbulence separation without informing the pilot that he is doing it or what the actual distance of the separation is.

At busy airfields maintaining the flow of traffic is essential in order for the airfield to run efficiently and prevent a backlog of traffic (both holding for approach and at the holding points waiting to depart). Controllers will therefore space aircraft on final approach exactly on the wake turbulence separation minima with great accuracy (to within ¼ of a mile). This is done through combinations of appropriate vectoring (i.e. early or late turns onto the final approach or taking aircraft through the localiser for spacing) and speed control. To the trained controller this technique of achieving great accuracy comes with relative ease, and to the general public it often comes with relative bemusement! However, when such instructions are given it does require prompt compliance from pilots otherwise the controllers efforts will be in vain.

When controllers sequence aircraft onto final approach they do this in accordance with procedures known as 'Pack' and 'Gap'. These terms are not standard phraseology terms and are not for use by pilots. The exact details of such procedures are detailed in MATS Part 2 as they are often different, although possibly similar, to each airfield. The terms used are a statement of how the spacing on final approach is to be managed in order to provide the most efficient overall traffic flow for both arrivals and departures. The relevant tower and approach controllers will therefore agree between them the current procedure to use.

The nature of the 'Pack' and 'Gap' procedures are that if 'Pack' is in use then the approach controller can space all arriving aircraft on final approach to the wake turbulence separation minima – the aircraft are therefore "packed" without any "gaps". If 'Gaps' are in use then the approach controller must provide between each arriving aircraft a 'gap' sufficient to enable a departure. The actual size of the 'gap' will be specified in MATS Part 2 and may differ between airfields, or between different runways or runway directions at the same airfield, for a variety of reasons. One such reason is when departing aircraft have to backtrack the runway. The length that must be backtracked (once the landing aircraft has passed by) will dictate how much (extra) distance is required between arriving aircraft to provide a sufficient 'gap'. At a "standard" airfield with no backtrack requirements, a 'gap' of 6nm is often suitable to allow a departure between arriving jet aircraft. Note, however, that this should not be assumed to be the convention - MATS Part 2 will give the actual procedures to be used at each airfield.

Different variations of the 'Pack' and 'Gap' procedures will be used as appropriate to the traffic conditions. For example, if there are more departing aircraft than arriving aircraft then 'Double gaps', or '10nm gaps' may be used. If there are more arriving aircraft than departing aircraft then 'Pack 3, gap 1' may be used, or if there are no departures for a while, then 'Pack' may be used. It can be seen that the use of the 'Pack' and 'Gap' procedures can produce a large variance in the spacing between aircraft on final approach, this can lead to incorrect perceptions by pilots with regards to the traffic environment. This is detailed further in chapter 8.8.

Note that if the wake turbulence separation minima is greater than the specified 'gap' distance, then the wake turbulence separation must be provided. For example, if gaps of 6nm are used and the required wake turbulence separation between two arriving aircraft is 8nm, then 8nm spacing must be provided between the two arriving aircraft.

Chapter 6.16   Visual approach

The term 'visual approach' is another term with a defined meaning. Its meaning is often the cause of much confusion, firstly with respect to what it actually is, secondly with respect to whether the flight is now VFR or still IFR, and thirdly with respect to what separation is applied. However, I shall endeavour to make all this very simple!

The term 'visual approach' actually relates to IFR flights. Although when a VFR flight makes an approach the pilot must obviously be operating visually and therefore in real terms is making a "visual" approach, when spoken on the RT (and within the ATC community) the term 'visual approach' is only used with respect to IFR flights as given by its definition below. The ICAO definition of 'visual approach' is:

> An approach by an IFR flight when part or all of an instrument approach procedure is not completed and the approach is executed with visual reference to terrain.

It is often difficult to find the definition of 'visual approach' in aviation literature so the reproduction above should be of use. CAP 413 does not define the term exactly but says:

> On occasions IFR aircraft do not complete the instrument approach procedure but request permission to make a visual approach.

So the first part of the puzzle is knowing the actual definition of 'visual approach' and the fact that it only relates to IFR flights.

The second question is: once the pilot of an IFR flight has accepted a visual approach does it become a VFR flight? The answer to this is no, it remains an IFR flight.

This leads onto the third question of: if the flight is IFR but operating visually, what separation is applied, if any, and how is it applied? The answer to this is given very neatly in MATS Part 1 which states:

> Standard separation shall be applied between IFR flights making a visual approach and other arriving and departing IFR and/or SVFR flights. Separation from other traffic is to be provided unless the pilot cancels his IFR flight plan.

So the only remaining question is: how is separation applied if the pilot is now operating visually? ATC will vector aircraft behind the one making a visual approach so as to provide the required separation. If, for example, the aircraft making a visual approach is on the downwind leg and the number two aircraft is being vectored for a straight in approach, the number two aircraft may require some early speed control or vectors through the final approach to establish from the other side in order for such separation to be applied. Although controllers know roughly at which point aircraft will turn in visually from the downwind leg when making a visual approach, it is not possible to pre-empt it to the exact second. Therefore the number two aircraft may be subject to conservative speed control just in case the number one aircraft extends downwind a little longer than anticipated before turning in visually. Radar controllers often ask pilots making a visual approach to report turning base as this ensures that the controller is made aware as the turn actually commences, whereas the radar screen will take a few seconds to portray that the turn has commenced.

If an aircraft is making a visual approach but is number two to another aircraft (that may be on final or also making a visual approach) then in this case the controller may instruct the number two aircraft to report when ready to turn base for the visual approach. When the controller receives the report he can then assess if the required separation will be maintained if the aircraft did turn in visually at that point. This may therefore require the controller to instruct the number two aircraft to continue downwind for a few extra seconds before turning in.

Recall from chapter 6.4 that when standard separation is required, the separation may be reduced if appropriate under the terms of 'reduced separation in the vicinity of aerodromes'. As IFR flights making a visual approach are required to have standard separation applied to them, when appropriate they therefore may also be subject to 'reduced separation in the vicinity of aerodromes'. Chapter 6.4 details the use of this procedure. A quick re-read of chapter 6.4 will show that aircraft making a visual approach may be allowed to use visual separation against other relevant traffic, and similar for traffic following the one making a visual approach. In the examples in the previous paragraphs, if visual separation can be applied between relevant aircraft the controller may therefore not have to provide vectors, speed control or request a report before turning in.

Recall also that reduced separation in the vicinity of aerodromes can be applied if each relevant aircraft is continuously visible to the controller without those aircraft being visual with each other. So the controller can, for example, allow an aircraft on a right hand downwind leg to make a visual approach with the controller visually separating it from an aircraft on a left hand downwind leg or a long final if the pilots cannot see each other.

Chapter 8.6 details the wake turbulence separation that is required for aircraft on approach, including those making a visual approach. A read of chapter 8.6 will show that when an aircraft makes a visual approach and reduced separation in the vicinity of aerodromes is used, it and/or the following aircraft as appropriate will be informed "Caution wake turbulence. The recommended distance is [number] miles". Recall from chapter 3.8 that this same phrase is used for VFR flights and it means that the pilot is now responsible for ensuring that the relevant distance is applied.

Additionally, MATS Part 1 states that controllers should not clear pilots for a visual approach when the RVR is less than 800m. Although it may seem obvious that such a visibility is not suitable for a visual approach it may be the case that with, for example, low lying fog, the aerodrome is easily visible from the air but the visibility decreases considerably when closer to the ground. Pilots should therefore be aware that controllers may be required by law to refuse clearance for a visual approach for this reason, or any other (local) reason as given in MATS Part 2.

Summary

- The definition of 'visual approach' relates to IFR flights.
- When making a visual approach the IFR flight remains IFR (it does not become VFR).
- Standard separation is still applied to aircraft making a visual approach due to the fact that they are still IFR.
- Reduced separation in the vicinity of aerodromes (i.e. visual separation) may be applied to aircraft making a visual approach. In such cases pilots may be informed of (and therefore become responsible for) the recommended wake turbulence separation.

Section 7   Control of Special VFR flights

This section explains the methods ATC use to control Special VFR (SVFR) traffic and why those methods are used. Pilots (especially low hour pilots) are often confused as to what SVFR actually is and what rules and procedures apply to SVFR flights. This confusion is generally because definitions of SVFR flight are often difficult to find in aviation literature and are lengthy and difficult to understand. So, to start the topic of SVFR flight, consider the following as a practical explanation of SVFR:

- Pilots cannot fly VFR in Class A airspace at anytime or in any other control zone at night or when the weather is below VFR limits. However, should a pilot wish to fly using visual references (i.e. he does not wish to fly IFR) in Class A airspace at anytime or in any other control zone at night or when the weather is below VFR limits, he can do this by requesting a SVFR clearance.

- SVFR flight is a flight where the pilot flies using visual references (as he does in VFR flight).

- Due to the fact that pilots flying SVFR are flying visually, but in situations where otherwise flight by visual references would not be allowed, ATC use precautionary procedures to protect the traffic with respect to preventing collisions (as explained later in this section).

- The weather limits that apply to SVFR flights are that the pilot must remain clear of cloud and with the surface in sight. No visibility limits are specified.

- SVFR flight can only occur in control zones i.e. Class A – E airspace and therefore not in Class F or G airspace.

Another way of clearing up the confusion about SVFR is to think of when it is required. From the above it can be seen that SVFR can only occur in control zones, so first of all you must obviously be in a control zone. Then there are only three occasions when a SVFR clearance must be given. One is due to weather conditions, one is at anytime that it is night, and the other is at anytime when the airspace is Class A.

When SVFR operations take place ATC use precautionary procedures to protect the traffic with respect to preventing collisions. MATS Part 1 states that unless otherwise specified in MATS Part 2, standard separation shall be applied between SVFR flights as well as between IFR flights and SVFR flights. Chapter 6.1 detailed separation in depth so you will be familiar with what it means both in legal definition terms and practically. The precautionary procedures that ATC use for SVFR flights are therefore based on separation.

If a flight is made SVFR due to either the weather being reduced below VFR limits or the flight taking place at night (therefore visual acuity is reduced) then it makes sense that ATC use precautionary procedures (i.e. separation) to protect traffic with respect to preventing collisions. If a flight is made SVFR due to it taking place in a Class A control zone then the nature of Class A airspace is such that it requires all flights in it to be separated. Note that in the case of Class A control zones a SVFR clearance is therefore given irrespective of weather or time of day. This could mean that such a flight with visual references requires a SVFR clearance in excellent weather during daylight, whereas in other control zones a SVFR clearance is reserved for flight at night time or during poor weather (below VFR limits).

The question now is: how do ATC actually control and separate SVFR flights? Remember that during SVFR flight the pilot is flying using visual references. It cannot be assumed by ATC therefore that such a pilot is qualified to fly using instrument navigational aids, so such navaids cannot be used by ATC to provide separation to SVFR flights. With reference to chapter 6.1 it can be seen that the only method available for procedural horizontal separation (for a pilot flying visually) is geographical separation as determined by visual observations. Such visual observations will involve VRP's, as discussed in chapter 3.6 and may also involve the following of a specified feature e.g. a river, in order to comply with a 'specified route'.

SVFR flights can take the following three forms:

- Taking off and departing from a control zone SVFR.
- Entering and landing in a control zone SVFR.
- Transiting through a control zone SVFR (i.e. without taking off or landing within it).

SVFR clearances are given in a similar format to that of VFR clearances (as discussed in section 3) due to the fact that a SVFR flight is operating with visual references. So, typical SVFR clearances are:

"Cleared to leave the control zone via Echo, not above altitude 2000ft, Special VFR".
"Cleared to enter the control zone via Golf, not above altitude 2000ft, Special VFR".
"Cleared route H4, not above altitude 1500ft, Special VFR, hold at Bunting power station".

SVFR clearances will (usually) involve a VRP. As stated earlier VRP's are used in the provision of separation, but the reason why it is preferable to give a VRP in a SVFR clearance whereas a VFR clearance will often not have a specific point e.g. "cleared to leave the control zone to the east" is that when operating in the poor met conditions of a SVFR flight, pilots require an easily identifiable feature that stands out from its surroundings in order to confirm that they are at the zone boundary. Otherwise they could easily misidentify the zone boundary or miss it completely. If the controller has radar it could be argued that the controller can inform the pilot when he has reached the zone boundary, however, it is still very much a necessity that the pilot identifies and confirms to himself where the zone boundary is. For SVFR flights following a specified route, VRP's are usually used to positively confirm the start and end of such routes and also as points for traffic to hold at if necessary as may be required in the provision of separation e.g. "hold at Bunting power station".

To provide separation between SVFR flights ATC will generally use one of two methods. One method is to essentially divide the control zone into areas. Only one SVFR flight is then allowed into each of these areas at any one time, this therefore ensures separation. The other method is to require pilots to fly on a specified route. The route is divided into segments, again, only one SVFR flight is allowed in each segment at any one time, this therefore ensures separation.

Chapter 7.1 SVFR clearance by areas

To illustrate the method of SVFR clearance by areas, use the example of an airport with an east/west runway and a control zone with VRP's 'November' and 'Sierra' on its north and south zone boundaries respectively. The control zone will essentially be divided into two areas. One area being the part of the control zone that is north of the runway and the other area being the part of the control zone that is south of the runway. These areas are not given names or referred to in clearances, but the procedures used by ATC for SVFR clearances are based on these areas.

To ensure that separation is provided, only one SVFR flight can be allowed in each area at any one time. So in this example ATC can allow two SVFR departures, or two SVFR arrivals, or a SVFR departure and a SVFR arrival at the same time as long as only one is in the northern area (routing via November) and only one is in the southern area (routing via Sierra) and this will be deemed separated in MATS Part 2. Until either the departing SVFR flight has reported at the (zone boundary) VRP or the inbound SVFR flight has landed, that relevant area is considered as blocked and another SVFR flight cannot be allowed into that area as separation cannot be assured.

Note that the use of such procedures for SVFR flights means that the traffic capacity is very much reduced compared to that for VFR flights. However, such procedures are necessary in order to assure separation of SVFR flights.

If the controller has radar available you may think that rather than using the above inefficient procedure where only one SVFR flight is allowed in a certain area, the controller can now use standard horizontal radar separation minima (i.e. 3nm or 5nm) to allow more than one SVFR flight in each area and therefore retain a larger traffic capacity. However, this is not so and for a very good reason, as explained below.

Recall that the weather limits that apply to SVFR flights are clear of cloud and in sight of the surface. Pilots could therefore (although it is not necessarily recommended) be flying in very poor visibility and/or at low level, just underneath the cloud base to obey the 500ft rule. Such weather can also be patchy with even lower visibility and/or lower cloud in places. Pilots flying SVFR attempting to route inbound or outbound in a straight line (via a VRP) may therefore need to make turns through $90°$ or $180°$ and fly in an apparent wrong direction for a while in order to fly around an area of worse weather and/or areas of rising terrain or obstacles which cannot be over flown due to the cloud base.

The problem this would create for ATC is that if a horizontal radar separation was applied (e.g. 3nm or 5nm) between SVFR flights, such aircraft could make sudden turns and fly in a different direction for a while (due to weather) which would encroach the separation minima and therefore the aircraft would no longer be separated. With reference to the above, it is also inappropriate to attempt to radar vector SVFR flights as the weather could/will prevent the pilots from complying with such vectors. The use of radar vectoring to resolve conflicts and maintain separation between SVFR flights cannot therefore be guaranteed.

So even if the controller has radar available the procedure will still be used whereby only one SVFR flight is allowed in each area as this is the only method that can guarantee separation between SVFR flights.

As a practical note it is worth highlighting that the zone boundary is essentially a barrier that cannot be passed without ATC clearance. It is likely that the weather outside the zone boundary is the same (i.e. as poor) as that inside it. However, as ATC have no legal responsibility to provide separation or indeed any type of service at all to aircraft outside the zone boundary (i.e. in Class F of G airspace), ATC can and must instruct aircraft to remain outside of the zone until an arriving or departing SVFR flight has vacated that area of the control zone, and then only one aircraft at a time can be allowed into the zone.

So, although ATC will give you some extra protection (i.e. separation) as a SVFR flight when inside the control zone, whilst attempting to enter the zone the controller may legally be required to essentially make things worse for you by making you remain outside the zone in poor weather.

Chapter 7.2   SVFR circuits

It may be a surprise (for those of you who are not familiar with the practise) to learn that pilots can be cleared for SVFR circuits. You may wonder why anyone would want to fly circuits in weather which is obviously poor - being less than the VFR minima. However, the rules allow it should you choose to do so.

Recall from chapter 3.7 that ATC shall not issue any further VFR clearances to aircraft other than helicopters when the visibility at the aerodrome is less than 5000m and/or the cloud ceiling is less than 1500ft. So if the visibility is not completely dire but is less than 5000m (for example 4000m), then the pilot may still wish to carry out circuits as the visibility will still allow him to remain visual with the airfield whilst in the circuit, but ATC cannot give a VFR clearance. So a clearance for SVFR circuits is given. Or it may be that the cloud is below 1500ft but still allows circuits to be flown at 1000ft or at lower levels if the pilot wishes to fly bad weather circuits. Again, this would require a clearance for SVFR circuits.

Recall also that pilots cannot fly VFR in a control zone at night. So should a pilot wish to fly circuits at night in a control zone then the clearance must be for SVFR circuits irrespective of weather conditions.

It still remains that SVFR flights must be separated (unless otherwise specified). Therefore it is usual to allow a maximum of only two SVFR circuit aircraft at any one time with one flying left hand circuits and the other flying right hand circuits. This again provides one SVFR flight per area. For example, for runway 09, one aircraft circuiting to the north and the other circuiting to the south, this being deemed separated in MATS Part 2. On each circuit the aircraft that is second to land will be instructed to hold at the end of the downwind leg and report visual with the preceding aircraft. Again it will be stated in MATS Part 2 that holding at the end of the downwind leg is deemed separated from the opposite circuit and from the final approach. Once with pilot is visual with the preceding aircraft, or both aircraft are continuously visible to the controller, then 'reduced separation in the vicinity of aerodromes' (as explained in chapter 6.4) can be used to allow the pilot to turn base and join the final approach.

Note that (unless the airport has additional procedures) whilst SVFR circuits are being conducted, that area of the control zone (e.g. to the north or south of the runway) will be considered to be blocked. As such the controller cannot allow a SVFR departure or arrival through that area whilst there is an aircraft conducting SVFR circuits in that area.

Chapter 7.3   SVFR clearance by specified route

Pilots may be unfamiliar with SVFR clearances that involve a specified route. A good example of specified SVFR routes is in the London control zone which is Class A airspace and requires helicopters to fly along specific routes called "H1", "H2" etc. (the AIP gives full details). One of these routes follows the river Thames and has VRP's established on it (e.g. the Thames barrier) and requires pilots to fly along the right hand bank of the river.

Separation must be applied between SVFR flights that are required to follow a specified route. To do this traffic is usually held at VRP's along the route, with the procedure being that only one SVFR flight is allowed in the segment of the route between two VRP's, and only one SVFR flight is allowed to hold over a VRP at any one time. This therefore ensures separation by dividing the specified route into segments, with only one SVFR flight allowed in each segment, and is a slightly different concept to the previous method which divided the control zone into areas. In addition, in the example of the London control zone which requires pilots to fly along the right hand bank of the river, this therefore allows two SVFR flights per route segment provided they are opposite direction flights. This is because with each pilot flying along his respective right hand river bank, the two opposite direction flights are assumed to remain in such a position laterally to be deemed separated at all times.

Chapter 7.4 Separating IFR flights from SVFR flights

It was explained earlier in this section how SVFR flights are usually separated from each other by using geographical separation. Recall also that separation must be applied between IFR flights and SVFR flights. As SVFR flights generally operate at low level, IFR flights in the control zone, whether being radar vectored or under procedural control, will usually be provided with vertical separation (i.e. 1000ft) against SVFR flights. This is possible until IFR flights are on final approach or initial climb-out and therefore are also at low level. In such cases SVFR flights can be instructed to hold at specified points e.g. at the end of the downwind leg, in order to provide geographical separation (in the same way as discussed in chapter 7.2).

For SVFR clearance by specified route, the routes will have VRP's established on them that enable such SVFR flights to be held clear of, and therefore separated from, the final approach track, aerodrome and initial climb-out.

When appropriate, reduced separation in the vicinity of aerodromes will be used to provide a more efficient service in allowing SVFR flights to cross or operate close to the final approach track, aerodrome or initial climb-out.

Chapter 7.5 Weather limits applicable to SVFR flights

Recall that the weather limits applicable to SVFR flights are clear of cloud and with the surface in sight. Chapter 3.7 explained the actions taken by ATC when the weather reduces below certain limits as applicable to VFR flights. It also explained that the change over from VFR to SVFR operations due to met occurs when the reported met conditions at the aerodrome reduce to less than the specified minima, and controllers are strict with the exact figures as they are legally binding. So should a pilot request SVFR when the met conditions are at or above the specified minima then the controller will refuse. Similarly MATS Part 1 also states:

> Controllers shall not issue a SVFR clearance to any aircraft, other than helicopters, for departure from an aerodrome within a control zone when the official met report indicates that the visibility is 1800m or less or the cloud ceiling is less than 600ft. When the reported visibility consists of two values, the lower of the two values shall be used when determining if a SVFR clearance can be issued.

As was done in chapter 3.7 it is also worth dissecting and explaining the above statement from MATS Part 1 so that it is fully understood. In the explanation below some similarities can be seen in the terminology used to that in chapter 3.7.

The first part states that it does not apply to helicopters. It states 'for departure' and therefore it does not apply to aircraft already airborne.

The relevance of the use of the above procedure is that when the met conditions reduce to the limits stated, it is obviously appropriate for ATC to prevent pilots from attempting to get airborne to fly with visual references (i.e. SVFR) as the conditions are approaching those that cannot sensibly allow flight by visual references for a fixed wing aircraft. So any further departures must be under IFR rules. However, for aircraft already airborne, controllers cannot make the pilots accept an IFR clearance as the pilot and/or the aircraft may not be licensed for IFR. It is expected in such circumstances that pilots will use good airmanship and common sense and either be attempting to land without delay, remaining clear of the area of reduced met conditions if that area is localised, or request an IFR clearance. However, as stated, it is not possible for controllers to force such pilots to accept an IFR clearance, and so the rules can only be to prevent further SVFR departures.

The reason for the use of a cloud ceiling of less than 600ft is that pilots must always obey the 500ft rule i.e. they should not fly at a height of less then 500ft above ground or water except for the purposes of taking-off and landing. So if the cloud ceiling is less than 600ft it is appropriate for ATC to prevent pilots from attempting to get airborne to fly with visual references (i.e. SVFR) as the conditions do not allow for compliance with the 500ft rule if flying visually.

The term 'official met report' is used and so this again relates to the weather at the aerodrome itself as reported by the official met observer.

Controllers will be strict with the change over at '1800m or less' and 'less than 600ft'. If the weather is above these figures then operations will continue as they were. However, the met conditions given are visibility 'or' cloud ceiling so it only requires one of those conditions to occur not both. Also, the term 'cloud ceiling' is used rather than 'cloud base'.

MATS Part 1 also states:

> At aerodromes situated in Class A airspace, ATC shall inform SVFR flights when the reported met visibility is less than 10km. Pilots must be asked their intentions and, if necessary, IFR clearance obtained from approach control.

Note from the above that the requirement is to inform pilots and ask their intentions. It does not state that SVFR flights cannot continue. So when asked, if pilots choose to do so they can remain SVFR.

Section 8 — Miscellaneous information

This section details information from a variety of topics. Some parts are more of an explanation of certain procedures, whereas other parts are more of an explanation of human factors – such as the equipment controllers have at their working positions and how this can affect the amount of traffic that can be controlled at any one time.

Chapter 8.1 Filing of flight plans

Details of how to file a flight plan, when one is required to be filed, and the flight plan form itself are covered during pilot training. Although necessary, it is not the most excitable of subjects, and this chapter is not intended as a repeat of such lectures. The aim of this chapter is to give a more practical picture which you can hopefully remember more easily with regard to the types of flight plans and when/where to file them.

There are two types of flight plans – a full flight plan and an abbreviated flight plan. An exhaustive list of when a flight plan is required to be filed by law is given in the ANO. It should be remembered that if your flight does not require a flight plan to be filed then, by law, you are required to inform your aerodrome of departure of the brief details of your flight. This procedure is called 'booking out'.

So, in brief, for any flight you must either file a flight plan (full or abbreviated) or book out.

Filing a full flight plan basically involves filling in the flight plan form giving full details of the flight.

An abbreviated flight plan is used to obtain a clearance for a portion of the flight. Note that the word 'clearance' is used, therefore it relates to controlled airspace. The classification of airspace table (given in the glossary) gives details of when an ATC clearance is required. To file an abbreviated flight plan you can either telephone ATC (before departure) or call them on the radio whilst in the aircraft giving the relevant (brief) details. For example:

> "[callsign], Cessna 172, 5 miles east of [place], altitude 3000ft, request to route west through the control zone en-route [place]".

From this you can see that the mystery surrounding abbreviated flight plans is not really a mystery at all. It is simply calling ATC on the radio and asking to enter their controlled airspace. The format of the transmission that you use to do this is the same as what you have already been using for initial contact with ATC.

The usual way to book out is to write your relevant details in the 'booking out' book which is kept on the counter at the airfield club house or tower, or to telephone and ask them to write it in the book for you. If you forget to do this, when you get to your aircraft you can simply call on the radio and ask them to book you out as you request start. For example, "[callsign] request start and request to book out".

Note that when filing a flight plan whilst airborne it must be done in sufficient time for a clearance to be issued before the aircraft reaches the boundary of controlled airspace. Aircraft must always remain clear of controlled airspace until a clearance to enter has been received. It is recommended that if a pilot wishes to cross or join an airway, that such a request is given at least ten minutes before reaching such a boundary. This is to allow sufficient time for the controller to plan and arrange the traffic flow in order to have separation established between you and other traffic when you enter that controlled airspace. It is important to remember that aircraft already in controlled airspace have priority over those outside controlled airspace wishing to enter. So, should the airspace be very busy, it may mean that you have to remain outside controlled airspace for an indefinite period as the constant stream of aircraft in the airway makes it impossible to establish an extra separation gap for you to fit into.

Chapter 8.2 Control of the manoeuvring area and apron

The 'manoeuvring area' and 'apron' have a defined meaning. Just as ATC have different responsibilities for aircraft in the air depending on whether the aircraft are IFR or VFR and the class of airspace they are in, ATC also have responsibilities with regards to ground movements. These ground movement responsibilities also differ with respect to persons, vehicles and aircraft, and whether they are on the manoeuvring area or the apron. Note that the title of this chapter states 'control' and therefore it only applies to aerodromes where an aerodrome control service is provided.

To further your understanding, the callsigns used when an aerodrome control service is provided are 'Tower' and 'Ground'. In general terms they provide you with exactly the same service whilst on the ground i.e. one is not a lesser control service, they just have different names. The two are used because 'Tower' control is designed to provide a control service for the aerodrome airspace, the runways and ground movements. However, when a busy traffic environment or extensive airfield layout exists it is necessary for 'Tower' control to control the aerodrome airspace and runway(s), but the ground movements to be controlled by a separate person – that being 'Ground' control.

The details in this chapter may not necessarily be applicable to PPL type pilots who fly from small grass airfields only. However, those learning to fly at or wishing to visit larger airports will find it relevant, as will those of you intending to find a career in airline type flying.

To begin, here are the exact definitions of the manoeuvring area and apron as given in MATS Part 1:

> The manoeuvring area is that part of the aerodrome provided for the take-off and landing of aircraft and for the movement of aircraft on the surface, excluding the apron and any part of the aerodrome provided for the maintenance of aircraft.

> The apron is that part of an aerodrome provided for the stationing of aircraft for the embarkation of passengers, the loading and unloading of cargo, refuelling and for parking.

With respect to ground movements, MATS Part 1 states:

> An air traffic control service is provided for the purpose of assisting in preventing collisions between:
> - Aircraft moving on the apron and the manoeuvring area.
> - Aircraft and obstructions on the manoeuvring area.

> The movements of aircraft, persons or vehicles on the manoeuvring area and the movement of aircraft on the apron are at all times subject to permission from aerodrome control.

To help you visualise where the manoeuvring area starts it is worth remembering that there is an ICAO standard marking which delineates the apron from the manoeuvring area. This standard marking is a double white line. The nature of the double white line is visually the same as the double yellow lines seen on roads that signify that you are not allowed to park, the difference being that the double white lines are, of course, white.

The next time you visit an aerodrome that has a control service I am sure you will now notice the double white lines and will now also understand what they are there for. At large airports with a terminal or pier the double white lines run parallel to the terminal or pier, usually coincident with the tails of the airliners parked there. On one side of the double white lines is the stands where the airliners are parked nose-in to the terminal or pier (this being the apron) and on the other side is the taxiway (this being the manoeuvring area). The stands adjacent to each other are delineated by a single white line. This means that the stands are boxes marked by a single white line on either side and a double white line across the end.

At airports with a general aviation or light aircraft park, such an area is still delineated (as the apron) by a double white line, but that apron is not usually separated into further parts by single white lines. This is because it is an apron (a general aviation apron) and not separate stands like those found at the terminal.

In locations where there is a cul-de-sac, the double white lines may run across the end of the cul-de-sac so that the whole of the cul-de-sac is an apron. This sometimes occurs where two piers form a cul-de-sac and the double white lines run across the end of the two piers (this is more common outside of the UK).

So what does all this mean to you as a pilot? It can be seen from the previous statements that you must call ATC before moving your aircraft on the apron. This is so that ATC can assist in preventing collisions between aircraft moving on the apron. However, ATC have no such responsibility to prevent collisions between vehicles or persons or each other on the apron, and neither do ATC have a responsibility to prevent collisions between aircraft and vehicles or persons on the apron. This is why, when you see airliners parked on stand at a terminal (i.e. on the apron) the catering trucks, refuelling trucks, tugs, baggage handlers, engineers etc. can all move or walk around the aircraft freely without permission from ATC - because they are on the apron side of the double white lines. It also allows you and anyone else to walk out to your light aircraft on the general aviation apron without asking permission from ATC.

However, no such vehicle or person is allowed to cross the double white lines onto the manoeuvring area (usually the taxiway) without permission from ATC. This is why you will often here ATC giving permission over the RT for ops vehicles, tels vehicles, tugs and the fire service to move on the taxiways (i.e. manoeuvring area). The only exception to this is that when an aircraft is cleared to push-back, its tug and ground crew are permitted to move directly back onto the stand (apron) without a separate clearance once the push-back is complete. Note that persons on foot require permission from ATC to enter the manoeuvring area. Usually the only such persons that move on foot on the manoeuvring area are ops personnel and maintenance workers e.g. for runway or taxiway re-surfacing or lighting. But these persons must carry a hand held radio with them in order to request the permission and maintain a listening watch.

Some airports may have roadways which cross taxiways (but never runways) to allow ground vehicles such as catering trucks and refuelling trucks to go about their business. Such ground vehicles do not require permission from ATC to cross taxiways via these designated road networks. However, any such driver must hold an airside driving licence and must hold clear of the taxiway until any aircraft in the vicinity have passed clear.

Chapter 8.3   Taxiing

The subject of taxiing may seem simple, but there are some details worth explaining which could otherwise present problems to pilots. This applies not just to low hour pilots, but also to experienced pilots who are unfamiliar with a particular airfield or seldom used route or procedure. Some of the details have more of a safety nature, whereas others are more to do with providing an efficient operation. All such details discussed in this chapter are given in the aerodrome briefing pages of the aerodrome charts or booklets in order to make pilots aware of such procedures. The reality is that if pilots do not read such briefing pages (which pilots may have a tendency to do, especially for large airports with many such briefing pages) this could lead to inappropriate actions, confusion, inefficiency or safety related occurrences as described below.

The RT frequency to be used and the details of the initial call may be stated as a standard procedure. This may require one frequency for clearance delivery, another for engine start, and another for push-back. The details of the information required on initial contact may include such as the ATIS code, QNH, flight planned cruising level, stand number, cleared taxi route, or may simply require callsign only. The correct use of the procedure reduces frequency congestion not only by (in some cases) decreasing the amount of information given in transmissions, but by also removing the need for controllers to make additional transmissions to gain the required information from pilots.

Some airports have standard taxi routes that are referred to by controllers on the RT by route designators, for example, "[callsign] taxi route east, hold short runway 25L" or "[callsign] taxi route north, stand G14". The use of such phraseology reduces RT loading, however, pilots must read the details of such standard taxi routes beforehand in order for the procedure to be effective. An example of a standard taxi route is: 'Route east: Taxiways F to F4, G to G2, M to hold short runway 25L'.

The description of the standard taxi routes may also include a statement as to whether the clearances automatically clears or does not clear pilots to cross runways on the route. This therefore has safety implications and some thought may also be given to the issues raised in chapters 1.7 and 1.8 with regards to crossing runways and red stop bars.

Specific procedures to use after landing may exist. At some aerodromes these procedures state that after landing, and without further instruction, pilots are to vacate onto the parallel taxiway and must not stop on the runway turn-off exit. However, at other aerodromes the procedures state that after landing, if no further clearance is given, pilots are to vacate onto the runway turn-off exit but must hold short of the parallel taxiway. Adherence to the correct procedure is important for safety reasons. Inappropriate holding on a runway exit could necessitate a go-around if local ATC procedures require the runway to be considered as occupied until such exits are clear of all aircraft, or could constitute a collision hazard with a subsequent landing or departing aircraft due to the proximity of the runway to the aircraft holding on the runway exit. Similarly, inappropriate vacation on to the parallel taxiway could constitute a collision hazard if other aircraft are using the taxiway and expecting vacating aircraft to give way to them. Such problems are also exacerbated at night when it can be surprisingly very difficult to see aircraft even with their lights switched on, especially when encompassed by the many other lights present at an airport.

Procedures may also state, as relevant to that given in the previous paragraph, whether aircraft already on the taxiway must give way to vacating aircraft or vice versa. Some taxiways may also be used as one-way routes and procedures may state that, without further instruction, pilots are to use the relevant one-way taxiway for their taxiing direction.

Runway operational procedures may state that certain exits are not to be used or that if a 180º turn to backtrack the runway is required this must be done at the runway end only. On occasions where pilots have not read such details this can lead to the slightly inefficient and annoying situation (for the pilots) whereby during the landing roll a moderate to high amount of braking is used, then just as the aircraft is at a sufficiently low speed and attempts to either vacate or make a 180º turn the controller sees that the pilot is not adhering to the given procedure and consequently gives the instruction to roll to the end to either vacate or make the 180º turn. A read of such procedures beforehand would have made the pilots aware that they should plan for an appropriate amount of braking to roll to the end of the runway.

Procedures may state that after landing, when vacated, pilots are to change to the ground frequency without instruction from the tower controller. The correct ground frequency to use should be checked as different ground frequencies may be specified for different areas of the airport or for different runways. Adherence to the correct procedure is therefore necessary to prevent (possibly lengthy) un-cleared taxiing and the associated implications for collision prevention, with the pilot in the (incorrect) mindset that the tower controller on the selected frequency is monitoring his taxi progress.

All the examples given in this chapter highlight the need for pilots to read the aerodrome briefing pages. For pilots such as PPL's that may not use aerodrome charts or booklets with such briefing pages, the relevant details are given in the AIP (which your flying club will have a copy of) and so this should be read thoroughly before flying to such aerodromes. If you are based at an aerodrome with such procedures your flying club may even have copies of the appropriate pages pinned to the notice board in the club house.

Chapter 8.4   Runway-in-use

The term 'runway-in-use' has a defined meaning. Although its meaning is obvious in general terms, it does on occasions lead to the confusion and dissatisfaction of experienced professional pilots, but this is only because they do not fully understand its definition and what it means with regards to ATC operations. To begin, MATS Part 1 states:

> The term 'runway-in-use' is used to indicate the particular runway and direction selected by aerodrome control as the most suitable.
>
> Normally the runway-in-use should be that most closely aligned to the surface wind direction but other factors shall be considered such as the length of runways and approach aids available.
>
> The pilot may request to use other than the runway-in-use. Permission may be deferred until the traffic situation permits the use of another runway and the expected delay shall be passed to the pilot.

The first two paragraphs of the above statement will be the same as most pilots current understanding of the term 'runway-in-use'. In addition to this, many large airports with long runways have local procedures that dictate that a particular runway direction will be used even if a light tailwind exists. Information with respect to this will be included in the aerodrome briefing pages and will state the maximum tailwind component allowed for the use of that runway-in-use (usually 5kts or 10kts is specified).

It is the third paragraph of the above statement that often becomes the cause of dissatisfaction for pilots. To aid in the understanding it is necessary to think of what the runway-in-use means in the real world. It is a statement made, either by the controller himself or via the ATIS, to all aircraft that a particular runway and its direction is the one in operation. Therefore, all pilots can plan for the use of that runway and direction whether arriving or departing. Not only that, but importantly, ATC can do the same thing i.e. area control will feed aircraft to approach control using the procedures and routes that are to be used for that runway-in-use, approach control will use holds and vector aircraft according to that runway-in-use, and similar for departures. So, essentially, all pilots and controllers are working and conforming to the same standard as dictated by the statement that the "runway-in-use is [number]".

If a pilot wishes to use another runway, or more specifically, the opposite direction of the runway-in-use, this can only be allowed in the interests of fairness if it will not affect any other traffic. Otherwise it would mean that pilots conforming to the given standard as dictated by ATC are then being penalised. For example, if a pilot wishes to depart from the opposite direction runway it is unreasonable to give arriving aircraft delaying vectors or holds in order to allow that departure, nor is it reasonable to force such arriving aircraft to land on the opposite direction runway to allow such a departure.

The usual cause of such situations is where an aircraft requires a specific direction for take-off due to performance reasons. For those readers new to aviation but intending to gain a career in aviation, you will become familiar in the future with the conundrum that for a relatively short runway with a relatively high climb gradient requirement, an aircraft at a particular weight can be too heavy to depart even with a 5kt headwind, but (due to a lower climb gradient requirement and possibly more runway length available) is legally able to depart from the opposite direction runway with a 5kt tailwind. However, in such a situation, as explained it is unreasonable to expect all other traffic to be delayed in order to allow such a flight to depart immediately from the opposite direction to the runway-in-use.

To summarise, in the real world the implications of the specified runway-in-use do not simply finish at the end of the piece of tarmac that is the runway, it has implications for the whole traffic flow to and from the airways system. If a pilot wishes to use other than the runway-in-use for arrival or departure he must accept whatever delay is necessary as other aircraft cannot be delayed if they are using the specified runway-in-use.

Chapter 8.5   Flight priorities

Controllers have to give priority to certain flights. It is obvious that search and rescue flights, medical flights, flights declaring a MAYDAY etc. must be given the highest priority, but MATS Part 1 gives a full list of the priority sequence and to which flights they apply to. The list includes many types of flights which you may not realise have a priority position at all, such as radio and flight calibration flights. It is not vital that an exhaustive list is included and discussed in this book as it is fair to say that if your flight is delayed or held for any of the types of priority flights then you will understand that the delay is necessary due to the nature of that flight. The only one of these situations that pilots sometimes become unhappy about is when light aircraft are held seemingly unfairly for a long time to allow movements of heavier traffic. This chapter therefore explains the situation so that pilots do not misunderstand the situation should they encounter it in the future.

The priority list basically states that flights that have filed a flight plan and conform to normal routeing procedures have priority over flights that have not. At a large busy airport this will generally mean that larger airline, cargo or commuter flights will have priority over smaller light aircraft, general aviation or training flights. Although this may appear to be about size it is actually because those larger aircraft have filed an IFR flight plan to fly within the airways 'normal routeing' system, whereas light aircraft tend either not to file a flight plan at all (which is absolutely fine as there is nothing wrong with not filing a flight plan) or have filed an abbreviated flight plan by basically asking on the RT to enter or depart controlled airspace (as explained in chapter 8.1) which is not necessarily 'conforming to normal routeing procedures' as is an IFR airways flight. Some may think that this is unfair against light aircraft, but that is the explanation of the situation.

It is also important to think of the situation in real terms. At a busy airport with a constant stream of heavier/faster aircraft both inbound to the airport and at the holding point awaiting departure, it is impossible to instantly provide a gap with the necessary speed difference and vortex wake spacing that is required to fit a light aircraft into the departure or arrival sequence. The arranging of such a gap takes time to implement and essentially means that either the approach controller has to start backing up the arriving traffic and/or the departure controller has to delay a flight planned IFR departure by departing a light aircraft in its departure gap. If there is more than one or many such light aircraft then it would require extensive delays and holding for the arriving traffic and/or an extensive holding queue at the holding point for departing traffic.

It is important to realise that with a busy arriving traffic flow, the aircraft are already airborne following each other and cannot therefore be told to stop, nor is it reasonable to unduly delay/hold such flight planned traffic. With a busy departure traffic flow of aircraft taxiing out to the holding point it is also unreasonable to unduly delay such flight planned traffic.

It is a fact that flight planned flights have priority over non-flight planned flights, and one of the reasons for this is that flights that have filed a full flight plan have been checked by the flow management computer which, as explained in chapter 6.7, will allow ATC sectors (a sector meaning not just area sectors but also approach sectors and tower and ground control positions at the airport) to have traffic movements up to, but not over, their specified capacity limit. Therefore it will mean on many occasions that the amount of aircraft inbound to the airport and also on stand at the airport that will in the near future require start, taxi and take-off, will put the controllers at that airport to their capacity limit. So any extra non-flight planned traffic that ask for an approach to or departure from the airport may require a long delay before the controller(s) can accommodate them.

There are occasions when VFR flights wishing to cross through the overhead, approach or initial climb-out of an airport may also be held for a period of time until other arriving and/or departing aircraft are clear. Again this often fits into the non-flight planned light aircraft versus larger flight planned IFR aircraft scenario.

Chapter 8.6 Wake turbulence separation

Wake turbulence separation between aircraft is provided by using either time or distance. For departing aircraft time is used i.e. when an aircraft departs a following aircraft cannot depart until the required number of seconds has passed. For arriving aircraft under radar control distance is used i.e. the required number of nautical miles must exist between the two aircraft. For arriving aircraft receiving a procedural service time is used although in most, if not all, of these cases the procedural IFR separation minima will be greater and so the IFR minima must be used (chapter 6.1 gives details of the procedural IFR separation minima).

The times or distances required between aircraft for wake turbulence separation are specified by the regulatory authorities. Consequently these times and distances are part of the law for controllers, or in other words controllers cannot decide their own wake turbulence separations. Controllers will work to those minima exactly i.e. if 4nm is required then the controller will achieve 4nm not 3¾nm or 4¼nm, if 2mins is required then the controller will achieve 120secs not 1min 40secs or 2mins 20secs. This may seem pedantic and you may think that adding a little extra for safety is a good idea. However, airport operators have contracts with air traffic providers to provide a safe and efficient service, part of which will be an agreed movement rate. Such movement rates will depend on certain physical constraints (e.g. airfield layout) as well as legal constraints (e.g. wake turbulence minima). The wake turbulence minima are a safe minima as specified by the regulatory authorities and therefore at busier airports it would result in less traffic flow and undue delays if controllers were to add a little extra to those minima, even if by only a small amount. Obviously during less busier times it is not as critical in terms of maintaining the traffic flow to achieve the minima exactly, and so if the wake turbulence separation achieved was slightly greater than the minima this would not result in undue delays.

It should be noted that the wake turbulence separation requirements may differ between countries. Many countries use the ICAO wake turbulence categories and minima although at present Europe alone has 15 differences to the ICAO recommendations. These differences may occur in either the timings, distances or the wake turbulence categories. In the UK the wake turbulence categories and minima are specified by the UK CAA.

Wake turbulence categories are based on the aircraft's maximum certified take-off weight. The UK and ICAO categories are:

UK			ICAO	
Heavy	$\geq$ 162,000kg		Heavy	$\geq$ 136,000kg
Medium	> 40,000kg	< 162,000kg	Medium	> 7000kg < 136,000kg
Upper Medium	> 104,000kg	< 162,000kg	Light	$\leq$ 7000kg
Lower Medium	> 40,000kg	$\leq$ 104,000kg		
Small	> 17,000kg	$\leq$ 40,000kg		
Light	$\leq$ 17,000kg			

Note that some aircraft may be placed in a different category to that dictated by their weight due to results of tests on their wake turbulence characteristics. Details of the wake turbulence separation minima for the A380 are combined in this chapter under the heading of 'A380 operations'. Note also that there is progress with some of the major regulatory authorities with regards to a reclassification programme of the wake turbulence categories and minima for all aircraft. This has been enabled through new technologies that allow a more accurate determination of wake turbulence characteristics and such a reclassification could therefore occur in the near future.

For all operations on parallel runways separated by less than 760m, such runways are considered to be a single runway for wake turbulence reasons for both landing and departing aircraft. Also, wake turbulence separation must be applied, when specified, to crossing or diverging runways, or parallel runways more than 760m apart when it is deemed that the projected flight paths of aircraft using those runways will cross.

Departure wake turbulence separation

The procedures used for departure wake turbulence separation are based on the following:

- The required separation is provided using time. These times shall be applied to the second and not rounded to the nearest minute i.e. 1 minute shall be 60 seconds.
- It is a scientific fact that vortices start to be generated by aircraft when the nosewheel lifts off the runway and continue until the nosewheel touches down. Therefore to be strictly accurate the wake turbulence separation time for departing aircraft should begin when the preceding aircraft's nosewheel lifts off rather than when the preceding aircraft begins its take-off roll (as is common practice amongst pilots), and end when the following aircraft is at the point at which the preceding aircraft's nosewheel lifted off.
- The separation must be applied between successive aircraft, both VFR and IFR.

Both the UK and ICAO departure wake turbulence separation minima are:

- 2 minutes when the preceding aircraft is of a heavier wake turbulence category and both aircraft start their take-off roll from the same position.
- 3 minutes when the preceding aircraft is of a heavier wake turbulence category and the following aircraft starts its take-off roll from an intermediate position.

Note, in the above the word 'heavier' is used and not 'Heavy' i.e. it does not solely relate to the Heavy wake turbulence category.

Also note that in the UK it is specified by the authority (as written in MATS Part 1) that for departure only (therefore not for arrival) both the Medium and Small wake turbulence categories are to be classed as the same category for departure wake turbulence separation purposes.

For both the UK and ICAO minima there is no departure wake turbulence separation required between aircraft of the same wake turbulence category.

It is not a requirement (in most countries) to provide 2 minutes departure wake turbulence separation between a 737, A320 or similar following a 757. It is a common misconception amongst pilots that such 2 minutes should always be given (i.e. in every country). Such aircraft are in the same wake turbulence category, and so in the interests of expedition, whilst remaining legally safe, controllers will not attempt to provide any such departure wake turbulence separation. There are a minority of countries that class the 757 as a Heavy for departure wake turbulence separation purposes, and so in such countries 2 minutes wake turbulence separation is provided between a departing Medium or Light aircraft when the preceding departing aircraft is a 757. This can leave pilots in the awkward position of not knowing what wake turbulence separation minima to expect when operating in different countries. The only answer to this is to reference such details from either the AIP of each relevant country or from the en-route navigation manuals kept in the flight deck. In the en-route navigation manuals the information is usually given in the 'Air Traffic Control' section, with each country having its own sub-section detailing procedures specific to that country. Whilst this situation is not ideal it is the only practical solution until such time as the wake turbulence separation procedures are standardised between all countries.

Should pilots wish to have 2 minutes separation when departing behind a 757 then it is reasonable for them to ask the controller for this, and some operators may have SOP's that require this. Although pilots may not always know which aircraft they will depart behind (particularly if holding bays and intersections are being used at busy airports) such requests should be made in good time, especially if the likelihood of such an occurrence appears to be high. If this request is left too late then at the very least it may mean another aircraft could have departed in that time if the controller had been informed earlier, and in the worst case it could necessitate an arriving aircraft having to go-around.

Should pilots have any strong views on this subject or be involved in any form of delay or occurrence due to it, please remember that it is not a requirement (in most countries) for controllers to provide such 2 minutes. Controllers are only able to continue providing an efficient (and safe) traffic flow if pilots inform the controller that they require such 2 minutes in good time.

Intermediate departures

In the previous pages the term 'intermediate departure' is used. This is another term with a specific meaning. It is similar to what pilots call an 'intersection take-off', however, the two are not exactly the same. Pilots will be familiar with the term 'intersection take-off' - this being a departure from any runway entry point other than the runway end. To explain an 'intermediate departure' some theory and practicality is required.

As stated previously, aircraft begin to generate vortices when the nosewheel lifts off the runway. It is generally the case that aircraft of lighter wake turbulence categories have a shorter take-off roll than those of heavier wake turbulence categories. If an aircraft of a lighter category departs behind an aircraft of a heavier category, and both aircraft start the take-off roll from the same position, the two flight paths will not therefore coincide. However, if the lighter aircraft had started the take-off roll from further along the runway compared to the heavier aircraft, the two flight paths will now coincide or be very close to coinciding. It is therefore specified that in this case the departure wake turbulence separation must be increased to provide the same amount of safety, and so 3 minutes is used instead of 2 minutes.

An 'intermediate departure' therefore occurs when an aircraft of a lighter wake turbulence category begins its take-off roll from a position further along the runway than the preceding departing aircraft of a heavier wake turbulence category. This is therefore different to an 'intersection take-off', and the following two situations will illustrate this further:

Firstly, imagine a runway orientated left to right with multiple entry points, the left-most being 'A', the next 'B' and so on. All departures from 'B' onwards are therefore intersection take-offs. If a heavier wake turbulence category aircraft departs from 'C' and the following departure is a lighter wake turbulence category aircraft from 'B', both departures are from intersections, however the lighter aircraft is not an intermediate departure (as it did not begin its take-off roll from further along the runway compared to the preceding aircraft). In this case 2 minutes wake turbulence separation is required.

Secondly, if two runway entry points (i.e. intersections) are sufficiently close to each other it may be specified that they are considered to be the same intersection for departure wake turbulence separation purposes. If this was applicable to entry points 'C' and 'D' then a heavier departure from 'C' followed by a lighter departure from 'D' would not be classed as an intermediate departure, and so 2 minutes wake turbulence separation is required rather than 3 minutes.

With reference to the case of two runway entry points being classed as the same intersection for departure wake turbulence separation purposes, again it is the regulatory authority that will determine this during the licensing of the aerodrome rather than it being left to the individual controller to determine. Such procedures are therefore written in MATS Part 2 and controllers must learn all the permutations of which intersections are, and are not, classed as intermediate departure points.

Remember that intermediate departures are only concerned with the relative positions that successive aircraft begin the take-off roll, rather than being relative to the runway end. The details above explain why pilots may on occasions receive 2 minutes departure wake turbulence separation when they were expecting 3 minutes, and vice versa.

Touch and go

An aircraft performing a touch and go will use a large portion of the runway during the manoeuvre. An aircraft performing a touch and go behind a heavier wake turbulence category departure is therefore always treated as an intermediate departure irrespective of where the previous aircraft departed from. 3 minutes wake turbulence separation is therefore applied between such touch and go aircraft and the preceding heavier departure.

Opposite direction operations

On the occasion that after an aircraft has landed, another aircraft then departs in the opposite direction, no wake turbulence separation is required. This is due to the fact that the departing aircraft will rotate and become airborne before the point at which the opposite direction landing aircraft ceased producing vortices. Recall from earlier in the chapter that vortices continue until the nosewheel touches down, this being near the landing threshold and therefore after the point at which the opposite direction departing aircraft becomes airborne. The departing aircraft will then climb-out above the flight path of that arriving aircraft, therefore continuing to avoid the wake turbulence trail.

However, 2 minutes wake turbulence separation must be applied between a Medium, Small or Light aircraft and a Heavy aircraft, and between a Medium or Small aircraft and a Light aircraft whenever the heavier aircraft makes a low or missed approach and the lighter aircraft either departs or lands on the same runway in the opposite direction or lands on a parallel opposite direction runway separated by less than 760 metres.

Displaced landing threshold

When a runway has a landing threshold that is displaced by a sufficient amount the following will be specified, again due to the fact that the flight paths of the aircraft will, or will be close to coinciding:

When operating on a runway with a displaced landing threshold 2 minutes wake turbulence separation must be applied when a departing Medium, Small or Light aircraft follows a Heavy arrival or a departing Light aircraft follows a Medium or Small arrival, or, an arriving Medium, Small or Light aircraft follows a Heavy departure or an arriving Light aircraft follows a departing Medium or Small aircraft.

Arrival wake turbulence separation

The wake turbulence separation minima for arriving aircraft are given in the table below as specified by the UK CAA and ICAO. When radar is used for the application of wake turbulence separation the distance in 'nm' is used, when a procedural service is given the time in 'mins' is used:

Leading aircraft	Following aircraft	UK CAA	ICAO
Heavy	Heavy	4nm, 2mins	4nm, 2mins
	Upper Medium	5nm, 3mins	-
	Lower Medium	5nm, 3mins	-
	Medium	-	5nm, 2mins
	Small	6nm, 3mins	-
	Light	7nm, 4mins	6nm, 3mins
Upper Medium	Upper Medium	3nm, 2mins	
	Lower Medium	4nm, 2mins	-
	Small	4nm, 2mins	-
	Light	6nm, 3mins	-
Lower Medium	Small	3nm, 2mins	-
	Light	5nm, 3mins	-
Medium	Light	-	5nm, 3mins
Small	Small	3nm, 2mins	-
	Light	4nm, 2mins	-

A minority of countries class the 757 as wake turbulence category Heavy for arrivals. This means that Medium and Light aircraft following a 757 on approach will have the appropriate increase in separation behind a 757. However, with a 757 following a Heavy aircraft on approach the separation between the 757 and preceding Heavy aircraft is effectively reduced as the 757 is also considered by ATC to be a Heavy rather than a Medium. As this policy may be deemed by some operators to be a reduction in safety, such countries usually also state in their procedures that pilots of 757 aircraft should report to ATC in good time if they require spacing as a Medium for the eventuality of following a Heavy aircraft. Note also that a minority of countries class the 757 as a Heavy for departures, but a Medium for arrivals, and others class it as a Medium for departures, but a Heavy for arrivals.

As stated earlier, although not ideal, the only practical method for pilots to know such differences is to reference either the AIP or the en-route navigation manuals.

It may also be the case that at certain aerodromes the regulatory authority allows different wake turbulence minima to that it specifies as the nominal standard. Such information is often included in the airfield briefing pages of the aerodrome charts, and so this is another example of the need to read such briefing pages.

As stated earlier in the chapter, reclassification of the vortex wake separation minima may occur in the near future.

A380 operations

The wake turbulence separation minima as detailed in this chapter are amended as follows for the A380 aircraft, as specified by both the UK CAA and ICAO. Note that, at the time of publication, the UK CAA uses revised minima to that of ICAO for arriving aircraft, however, this is subject to review in the near term and therefore may change in the near future:

Departure: For a Light, Small, or Medium aircraft departing behind an A380, 3 minutes must be applied. This is increased to 4 minutes for such an intermediate departure.
For a Heavy aircraft (including A380) departing behind an A380, 2 minutes must be applied. This is increased to 3 minutes for such an intermediate departure.

Opposite direction operations: When an A380 makes a low or missed approach and a Light, Small, or Medium aircraft then departs or lands in the opposite direction, 3 minutes must be applied.

Displaced landing threshold: For runways with a displaced landing threshold if a Light, Small, or Medium aircraft departs behind a landing A380, or a Light, Small, or Medium aircraft lands behind a departing A380, 3 minutes must be applied.

Arrival: The following are applied behind an arriving A380:

Following aircraft	UK CAA revision	ICAO
A380	4nm, 2mins	4nm, 2mins
Heavy	6nm, 2mins	6nm, 2mins
Upper & Lower Medium	7nm, 3mins	-
Medium	-	8nm, 3mins
Small	7nm, 3mins	-
Light	8nm, 4mins	10nm, 4mins

<u>Wake turbulence separation for VFR and Visual approaches</u>

The arrival wake turbulence separation given on the previous page must be provided by controllers to arriving IFR flights. In doing so the controller will not give any information to pilots with regards to how far behind other aircraft they are or what wake turbulence separation is required as this would be wasted RT time due to the fact that for IFR aircraft the controller is solely responsible for providing the wake turbulence separation. However, this is not so in the following cases:

- VFR flights.
- IFR flights that accept a visual approach under the terms of 'reduced separation in the vicinity of aerodromes' when visual with the preceding aircraft.

In such cases the responsibility for providing the wake turbulence separation lies solely with the pilot. To confirm to the pilot that he is now solely responsible for the provision of his own wake turbulence separation the following phrase is used:

"Caution wake turbulence. The recommended distance is [number] miles"

Note that to the unsuspecting pilot this is another hidden instruction whereby the pilot may not realise that he is now solely responsible for the provision of the separation and that the controller will not therefore issue any further instructions to maintain the separation. The phrase given above is used in the UK and must consist of the two parts i.e. the caution of wake turbulence and the recommended distance. The phraseology used in other countries may be slightly different and may not require the recommended distance to be passed. However, the minimum the phrase usually consists of is "caution wake turbulence", and so pilots should be aware that when this phrase is used the pilot is now solely responsible for the provision of his own wake turbulence separation. As the recommended distance may not be passed in some locations it is therefore good airmanship for pilots to know the (ICAO or country specific) wake turbulence separations for their aircraft type.

Whether in the UK or abroad, once the phrase has been given (the pilot thereby becoming responsible for the separation) the controller will not give updates on the distance between your aircraft and the one in front, even if the controller has radar available. So, for example, if you turn in early from the downwind leg and are consequently 2nm behind the preceding aircraft but the recommended distance is 4nm, the controller will not inform you of this. Some may feel that this is not in the best interests of safety especially as wake turbulence separation is a serious matter, however, the rules are there to allow the pilot to assess the situation. Also, on a practical note, in such situations it is likely that the pilot will be under the control of the tower controller who, by nature of his job, does not have radar available and so cannot provide such information.

Chapter 8.7   250kts below FL100

Some misconceptions exist with regards to the speed limit of 250kts below FL100. This chapter explains the facts as dictated by air law as well as some practical details which may be the reason for the misconceptions.

<u>Air law</u>

Starting with the restrictions as given by UK air law, aircraft flying below FL100 are to comply with a speed limit of 250kts IAS except:

- For any aircraft in Class A or B airspace and IFR aircraft flying in Class C airspace there is no airspeed restriction by law (i.e. speed restrictions will only exist if the controller gives you a speed restriction over the RT).
- For VFR aircraft in Class C airspace and both IFR and VFR aircraft in Class D airspace a speed limit of 250kts IAS below FL100 applies unless otherwise instructed by ATC.
- For both IFR and VFR aircraft in Class E, F or G airspace a speed limit of 250kts IAS below FL100 always applies (i.e. the speed restriction cannot be removed by ATC).

So, for an IFR flight in the UK below FL100 the speed limits are simply: No speed limit in Class A, B or C airspace and a maximum of 250kts IAS in Class D airspace unless otherwise instructed by the controller. In Class E, F and G airspace a maximum of 250kts IAS always applies.

The difficult part for the pilot is knowing what class of airspace you are flying in. To the G/A or VFR pilot it may seem odd that an IFR pilot (in particular airline or biz-jet pilots) may not know what class of airspace he is flying in. VFR charts used regularly by G/A pilots show clearly the airspace class boundaries and altitudes. However, the IFR SID/STAR charts used by IFR pilots do not show airspace class boundaries. The IFR en-route charts do show airspace class boundaries and altitudes, but such information is often difficult to depict and is impractical to use during initial departure or arrival stages of flight. It is also often the case that major airports have one class of airspace surrounding them from the surface up to a particular level, above that level the airspace is of a different class e.g. Class D up to 3000ft and Class A above 3000ft.

The reason why the speed restriction of 250kts below FL100 does or does not apply in certain circumstances is due to the service provided by ATC and the subsequent need to uphold the 'see and avoid' principle. This can be seen with reference to the classification of airspace table (given in the glossary) and is explained as follows:

In Class A and B airspace all aircraft must contact ATC, comply with ATC instructions, and ATC must separate all aircraft. Therefore the controller is controlling all aircraft in that airspace and will issue instructions in sufficient time (irrespective of the speed the aircraft are flying) in order to maintain separation.

Similarly, IFR flights in Class C airspace are always separated from all other traffic. However, for VFR flights in Class C airspace and for IFR and VFR flights in Class D airspace there are occasions where traffic information may be passed i.e. collisions are prevented by pilots using the 'see and avoid' principle. In such circumstances it must therefore be the case that the speed limit applies initially, but, as in such airspace (i.e. Class C and D) the controller is aware of the behaviour of all aircraft (as all aircraft must be in contact with ATC and comply with ATC instructions) it is permissible for the controller to remove the speed restriction if he is satisfied that an increase in speed in that traffic situation will not cause a collision hazard.

In Class E, F and G airspace there are occasions where some aircraft may not be in contact with ATC and may not need to comply with ATC instructions. In such airspace the controller cannot therefore guarantee the behaviour of all aircraft, and therefore the speed restriction of 250kts below FL100 must always apply.

SID and STAR charts

The air law requirements are purely governed by the class of airspace, as explained above. The second part of the puzzle is that the air law rule may be amended by information given on the SID and STAR charts. This is where some confusion and misconceptions may arise.

For most of the aerodromes in the UK each SID chart has a note stating: 'A speed restriction of 250kts IAS below FL100 applies unless otherwise cleared by ATC'. So, stating the obvious, it is stating that the pilot does not need to know what class of airspace he his flying in during the departure as he must comply with a maximum of 250kts IAS until FL100 unless otherwise instructed by ATC.

For most of the aerodromes in the UK where the STAR remains in Class A airspace, each STAR chart has a note stating: 'A speed restriction of 250kts IAS applies at the SLP or 3mins before reaching the holding facility' – 'SLP' being the speed limit point shown on the STAR chart. The difference between such SID and STAR charts is therefore that FL100 is not relevant during the arrival. For such STAR's the 250kts speed restriction is based on the aircraft's position (not flight level) - that position being the SLP or 3mins before the holding facility.

FMS

The third part of the puzzle is that the Flight Management Systems (FMS) used in some aircraft have 250kts below FL100 automatically preset in their programming (i.e. a default setting). Therefore, when reviewing the information in the FMS it can appear that 250kts below FL100 is a valid air law restriction, when in fact it could just be the FMS default setting.

Country

Finally, note that the air law speed restrictions may differ between countries. Some countries may not have a speed restriction below FL100 or may have a speed restriction based on another level. Unfortunately the only way to find such differences is by referencing the ANO for each country.

With reference to the explanation earlier regarding SID and STAR charts, some countries have speed restrictions such as '250kts IAS below FL245' printed on STAR charts and '250kts IAS below FL150' printed on SID charts.

Summary

The following points are a summary of how to determine the speed restriction below FL100 or other such applicable level:

- Note the air law speed restriction for the relevant country and class of airspace.
- Check if the SID/STAR charts amend the air law speed restriction, and use such details for that specific procedure only i.e. the restrictions for the SID may be different to that of the STAR.
- Check the aircraft's FMS reflects exactly the reality of the air law restriction as amended by the SID/STAR charts.

It is worth mentioning that if pilots would like to fly faster than an air law or SID/STAR speed restriction then simply ask the controller. Either of the phrases "request high speed" or "is there any speed restriction" are quick and easy to use for this purpose.

Many pilots will probably wonder why, if speed restrictions are given by law and published on the majority of SID/STAR charts, do controllers nearly always say "no ATC speed restriction" when asked. This is simply because the relevance of speed restrictions to controllers is to help in keeping aircraft at a more appropriate speed for sequencing and vectoring during arrival and departure. Whereas the relevance of the speed restrictions for pilots, as explained earlier, is to aid in upholding the 'see and avoid' principle. So, in most cases, controllers are satisfied that the traffic conditions are suitable for aircraft to have "free speed". Recall, however, in Class E, F and G airspace a maximum of 250kts IAS below FL100 must always be adhered to even if ATC use the phrase "no ATC speed restriction".

Chapter 8.8   Speed control during arrival

When ATC issue speed control instructions during arrival it is often the case that pilots do not fly the instructed speed, or they fly the speed initially but later decide to change the speed without asking permission from the controller. The reason for this non-compliance is usually due to the pilot's perception of the situation, this perception arising from one or a combination of the following factors:

- The pilot using the TCAS display and deciding he is either too close to the aircraft in front or there is a large distance to the aircraft in front.
- The pilot deciding that the controller has forgotten to remove the speed control.
- The pilot's viewpoint on the controller's competency.
- Whether the instructed speed requires the use of flap earlier than would normally be used.
- The proximity of the instructed speed to the SOP speed that is normally used (i.e. the manoeuvring or minimum flap speed).

When speed control is used by ATC during arrival it is for reasons of both sequencing and to maintain separation. If you, as a pilot, wish to change speed for whatever reason then simply ask the controller. Having the perceptions as described above and changing speed at your free will is not only incorrect but is also an example of bad airmanship as you do not have the controller's accurate picture of the overall traffic situation (although you may think you do) and neither do you know what the controller's plan for such traffic is. This speed non-compliance is a common habit amongst pilots, however, you would not change heading or altitude without asking the controller first, so neither should a speed instruction be ignored – a speed instruction is just that, it is an 'instruction'.

Controllers much prefer pilots to ask if they wish to change speed rather than the common habit of not flying the instructed speed or changing speed at their free will as this all too often results in a disruption to the traffic flow and sometimes a go-around is necessary.

It is worth highlighting that in situations where the pilot perceives a large spacing to the aircraft in front, the controller may be planning for one or more aircraft to depart in that gap. So although it may be slightly inefficient for you to slow down and possibly use flap earlier than normal, the controller is managing the overall traffic flow and the speed control is necessary to maintain the movement rate of that traffic situation. Similarly, when the pilot perceives he is getting too close to the aircraft in front, the controller will be sequencing to minimum wake turbulence separation in order to maintain the traffic flow. This separation can be as close as 2.5nm where approved and, as described in chapter 8.9, the controller will be achieving such spacing with great accuracy.

If you reduce speed without asking the controller, there could be traffic behind you so any spacing that has been or is in the process of being implemented will now be eroded.

If the instructed speed is close to your SOP speed, the instructed speed should still be flown as this is the correct and safest procedure and is the only way the controller can ensure the required spacing will be achieved. So, should a speed instruction of 180kts be given and your SOP flap 1 minimum manoeuvring speed is 190kts or 187kts, the next flap setting should be used and 180kts flown rather than thinking that the 190kts or 187kts will do. If the aircraft's systems are such that it also requires the undercarriage to be lowered at an earlier stage than normal in order to fly the instructed speed, then this should be done even though it may make the approach less efficient than you would ideally wish for.

It is another practical point that when a lower speed is selected the aircraft must be monitored to ensure that it decelerates in a reasonable amount of time and actually achieves the new selected speed. In normal circumstances the deceleration is not a problem, but in situations such as high descent rates or strong tailwinds, although a lower speed may be selected, the aircraft may have difficulty in decelerating and achieving the new speed. This then gives the situation where the pilot may think he has done correctly be selecting the new speed, but he does not actually fly the instructed speed. In this situation some intervention (e.g. speedbrake) is therefore required by the pilot to fly as per the instruction issued by the controller.

Chapter 8.9 Telephone calls and RT loading

It is of great benefit to the system in general when pilots have an appreciation of how busy the controller they are talking to is, and consequently, how much spare capacity the controller does or does not have. The main point referred to here is the fact that controllers can be at or near to the limit of their capacity even though the frequency may not appear to be very busy. Obviously it cannot be expected that pilots are fully aware of all the fine details of a controller's job if they have not been a controller themselves. However, this chapter is intended to paint a picture and clarify some of the more common misunderstandings with regards to how busy controllers are.

In chapter 6.2 it was explained that in a procedural environment the movement capacity (i.e. amount of aircraft) that controllers have is greatly reduced compared to a radar environment. A similar explanation can be given for other situations, in this case telephone calls and RT loading.

Firstly, the subject of telephone calls. Controllers will sometimes be heard to use the expression "sorry, I was on the phone". You may wonder who the controller is phoning and what are they talking about? Controllers have to co-ordinate a variety of things with other controllers and this is done via a direct line telephone system. The telephone system is connected to the controller's headset so the controller can hear RT transmissions at the same time rather than having to remove the headset and pick up a hand held telephone. There is not a definitive list of what must be co-ordinated due to the fact that no two controlling positions are exactly alike - they vary due to airport or airspace layout, equipment being used, agreed procedures, etc. Below is a list of some of the more common items that may require a telephone call (i.e. co-ordination) between controllers:

- Tower controller requesting departure instructions/clearance from the approach controller.
- Tower controller requesting from the approach controller where in the arrival flow he would like a gap to allow an aircraft to depart.
- Approach controller informing the tower controller of the order of inbound aircraft.
- A request to an adjacent controller to transfer aircraft earlier than the standard agreement (i.e. different to that specified in MATS Part 2) so that the receiving controller can offer a more efficient service.
- A request to an adjacent controller to use one or more of that controller's levels in order to offer a more efficient service.
- A request to an adjacent controller for him to accept an aircraft into his sector on a specific heading or route (i.e. different to the flight planned route or agreed route).
- Passing relevant details of a flight (e.g. aircraft type, intended route, squawk) to an adjacent controller when that controller does not have any details of the flight (i.e. usually for operations outside controlled airspace or when a flight plan has not been filed).

The main point of the subject of telephone calls is that (as can be seen from the list above) on many occasions aircraft do not effortlessly transfer from one frequency to another. Due to the nature of the ATC system there is often much information that must be passed verbally from one controller to the next. Whilst this co-ordination is occurring the controller is therefore unable to speak on the RT. He is also unable to listen accurately to the RT and may need to ask the pilot to repeat any transmissions made whilst the controller was on the telephone. So although the frequency may have frequent periods of quietness it does not mean that the controller is not busy. Nearly all of the dead RT space may be filled for the controller with co-ordinating telephone calls.

The second point of discussion is that of RT loading. Pilots will no doubt be aware that some controllers talk non-stop on the RT. So why is it that some frequencies appear quieter (due to the need to make endless telephone calls) but other frequencies have an apparent gunfire of transmissions from the controller? As mentioned previously, every controlling position is different. They are different not just in the type of position (i.e. tower is different to area, and procedural is different to radar), but in the airspace layout, equipment available, procedures used, etc. So what is effectively the same position at one airport or centre can have a very different way of operating at another airport or centre.

One example of this is that at many busy area control positions there are actually two controllers sat working at that position. One of these controllers is the one talking on the RT and is designated as the 'Controlling position' for that sector. The controlling position makes all the RT calls and controls the traffic just as any other controller does. However, due to the busy nature of the sector he does not have sufficient spare time to make the essential co-ordination via the telephone, so he marks any required co-ordination on the FPS's. The other controller at that position is designated as the 'Co-ordinating position' and he will make any co-ordination that is required as determined by the annotations made on the FPS's by the controlling position. So although a controller on a particular frequency may sound extremely impressive as he makes a non-stop stream of transmissions, he is probably only doing 50% of the job that you think he is doing as the controller sat next to him is doing the remainder of the essential work. Note that although the analogy is used that each controller is probably only doing 50% of the job that you think he is, the reality is that both the controllers (i.e. the 'controller' and the 'co-ordinator') are doing 100% of their respective jobs because that sector is designed to be operated by two such people working to capacity.

Another example that often gives pilots a different perception of the service being given is with approach control. At most busy major airports the approach control function will be split into numerous positions so that controllers can sequence aircraft from the holding stacks towards the final approach, and the final 'Director' will feed aircraft onto the ILS at the required spacing. This is all done with great finesse using speed and heading control to give extremely accurate spacing on the final approach that leaves many of the general public (and some pilots) in amazement at how good the controllers are to achieve such feats of accuracy. Whilst I would not dream of dispelling such thoughts, it is a fact that such accuracy is made possible by the system in place – this being that the job is simplified in some respects to allow the accuracy to be achieved. This means that the initial approach controller(s) can concentrate on sequencing a one-way stream of aircraft from the holding stacks to the final approach, and the final director can concentrate solely on the final approach (including the turn onto the final approach) to provide accurate spacing.

Compare this to an approach controller who's coverage is a 30nm radius (60nm diameter) around the airfield and includes operations outside controlled airspace. In this scenario the controller cannot concentrate his attention on a single stream of traffic. He must, for example, vector aircraft from all corners of the radar screen towards the final approach, whilst in one corner of the radar screen give a Deconfliction Service to one or more aircraft near to a gliding area, whilst in another part of the radar screen give traffic information to aircraft wishing to transit the zone near to the approach or climb-out, etc. The controller is therefore constantly dividing his attention and switching between different areas of the radar screen to different aircraft wanting different types of service. It is also likely that telephone calls will often have to be made to pass departure instructions/clearances to the tower controller and co-ordinate all inbound and outbound airways traffic with one or more area sectors.

The details given above therefore explain how controllers can be very busy, and doing the best job possible, even though pilots may think otherwise from the perception given by the RT loading and other factors.

Chapter 8.10   Controller's equipment

This chapter gives a description of the equipment controllers have at their controlling positions. This should help pilots not only in the understanding of how controllers do their job, but also in the future, should a certain piece of information be needed, pilots will now be aware that the controller can help with relative ease.

Telephone panel

Each controlling position has a telephone panel. As mentioned in chapter 8.9 controllers need various direct telephone lines to other controllers. The telephone panel is therefore a set of buttons with each button having the name written on it of the controlling position that it is connected to e.g. 'Bournemouth Approach' or 'Capital' sector. To make a call, simply press the button. When one of the direct lines is calling a controlling position the appropriate button (e.g. 'Bournemouth Approach') will flash and a buzzer or ringer will sound. To answer that direct telephone line and therefore talk to that controller, simply press the appropriate button (e.g. 'Bournemouth Approach') and the telephone line is immediately opened and connected to the controller's headphones and microphone. On occasions, when a controller is transmitting on the RT you may hear a buzzer sounding in the background. This will almost certainly be the telephone buzzer, especially if it is an annoying sound!

Obviously each controller cannot have a direct line button for every other controller in the country, as this would require hundreds of buttons. The direct lines available are therefore, in general, to the adjacent controlling positions, as it is usually only these that it is necessary to co-ordinate with. The telephone panel will usually have a maximum size in the region of 16 buttons i.e. a panel of 4x4. With respect to adjacent controlling positions, these will be, in general:

For Tower controllers:
- All other positions in that tower e.g. 'Ground', 'Delivery' and 'Tower'.
- All approach and departure positions for that airfield.

For Approach controllers:
- All other approach positions for that airfield and adjacent airfields.
- 'Tower' positions for that airfield and adjacent airfields.
- Adjacent area sectors.

For Area controllers:
- Adjacent area sectors.
- Adjacent approach positions.

Tower controllers (and possibly approach controllers) will also have direct lines to other necessary airport personnel outside of ATC, for example (see next page):

- Airport operations – to request runway inspections, bird control, airport lighting serviceability checks, etc.
- 'Ramp' – for information on stand allocation.
- Airport fire service – for emergency and non-emergency use.
- Telecommunications engineers – for information on the serviceability of navaids, ILS, radio frequencies, etc.

The telephone panel also has an external line connection with a number keypad (0-9) to allow calls to any telephone worldwide. This is used when necessary, usually in non-standard or emergency situations. At each ATC unit there is an ATC telephone book listing available external numbers for all ATC units and controlling positions in the country, and possibly some abroad. The use of this, and the external dialling keypad, allows controllers to contact any other unit should it be necessary.

Should this information on telephones be of use to pilots in the future please remember that the controller's primary task is to control traffic, any extraneous duties and requests from pilots can only be accommodated if the controller has sufficient spare capacity and judges it safe to do so. Obviously in emergency situations the controller's priorities will change and controllers will try to provide as much assistance as possible.

RT frequencies

In an aircraft the radio box will have either knobs or a number keypad that allows the pilot to select the required frequency. At controlling positions no such radio box is provided as that position is, in general, assigned to a single frequency e.g. 'Tower' on 118.4 MHz. Each controlling position is therefore hardwired to its specific frequency, the frequency being set by the telecommunications engineers in the telecommunications equipment room. However, it is necessary for each controlling position to be able to transmit and receive on other frequencies for such times as when positions are combined during quieter periods or when equipment failure occurs at another position. So, at each controlling position there is a set of buttons or switches each being labelled with a specific frequency. The controller simply selects which of these he requires to transmit and receive on. The frequencies available to the controller will usually be those of adjacent positions and are therefore similar to the list of direct telephone lines given earlier.

When a controller selects more than one frequency to transmit and receive on he can therefore transmit on all of those frequencies at the same time and will also hear anyone transmitting on any of those frequencies. This often leads to the situation where pilots can hear the controller transmitting on the RT to an aircraft but cannot hear a reply from that aircraft. This is due to the controller transmitting on all the frequencies he is controlling, but the replying aircraft is transmitting on only one of those frequencies (that frequency being different to the one you are listening to).

The combining of frequencies is called 'band-boxing' and occurs during quieter periods where one controller can safely control more than one frequency from his position. This usually means that 'Tower', 'Ground' and 'Delivery' frequencies are band-boxed onto one position, multiple approach frequencies are band-boxed onto one position, and multiple area sector frequencies are band-boxed onto one position.

At airports, ground vehicles usually transmit on UHF frequencies rather than the VHF frequencies used by aircraft. 'Tower' and 'Ground' controllers must therefore always have the UHF frequency selected as well as the VHF frequency for that position. This means that even without band-boxing it is normal for pilots to hear tower controllers transmitting to vehicles on the RT, but not to hear a reply from those vehicles.

Controlling positions also have 121.5 MHz available. It is not usual for controllers, even in emergency situations, to use 121.5 MHz as there is a dedicated controller assigned to 121.5 MHz for the whole of each Flight Information Region.

Aerodrome lighting

All of the aerodrome lights are controlled by switches on the aerodrome lighting panel in the control tower. Such lighting consists of runway, taxiway, approach and lead-on/lead-off lights, PAPI's and stop bars for the whole of the aerodrome. It is necessary for controllers to be in control of such lights in order for them to execute their job safely and effectively. Therefore the control tower positions are arranged so that each controller is within arms reach of the lighting controls that are relevant to him. For example, the ground controller may not have the approach lights available at his position, but the air controller that controls the runway must have them available. At certain airports that are very busy and have extensive taxiway lighting, procedures may be in place whereby trained lighting assistants are in control of the lighting panel. The assistants monitor the relevant ground control frequencies and select the lighting as appropriate to the controller's RT transmissions in order to help guide pilots taxiing.

It is standard practice to have the approach lights and PAPI's only selected for the runway to which approaches are being made. For example, if the landing runway is 27R then the approach lights and PAPI's will be selected on for 27R, but selected off for 09L, 09R and 27L. It is also standard practice in some locations that during the day the approach lights and PAPI's are selected on to aid in flying the final approach, but all other lighting (e.g. runway and taxiway lights) are selected off. This is an approved procedure due to the fact that the edge of the runways and taxiways can be visually identified during the day. At airports having extensive layouts or where confusion may exist, the relevant lights may still be selected on and off during the day to help guide pilots and prevent incidents.

Pilots may be unaware that the brightness of all the aerodrome lights can be changed by the controller. This is to ensure correct illumination at all hours of the day and prevent the lights from being too bright or too dim depending on the daylight outside. To illustrate this, think of switching on a torch or car headlights. During bright daylight such lights do not appear to shed any light and it is possible to look directly at the bulb itself. As the daylight fades the torch or headlight appears to become brighter, and at night time it is impossible to look directly at the bulb as it is blindingly bright. As daylight changes, controllers adjust the intensity of the aerodrome lights so that they maintain the same apparent brightness. The brightness controls are located on the lighting panel and allow separate control of each type of lighting e.g. runway, taxiway, PAPI, etc. Where necessary this may be further separated e.g. individual runways or large sections of taxiways.

In the future, should it appear that certain lights are not illuminated, or are too bright or too dim, you are now aware that a quick transmission to the controller will probably solve the problem. The most common occurrences are approach lights and PAPI's not being selected to the correct approach after operations on the runway in the opposite direction, and PAPI's being too dim during the day. Again, please remember that any such requests should be kept concise and restricted to those of importance rather than long conversations about trivial items, especially if the frequency is busy.

Weather displays

Each tower and approach control position has available a display showing the current airfield ATIS. This usually consists of a small TV screen with the ATIS written on it. This allows the tower and approach controllers to pass any updated weather information to pilots when they have not received the latest ATIS broadcast. In non-standard situations it is therefore possible for the pilot to ask the controller to read to him the ATIS details as this is quicker and less demanding on the pilot compared to having to select another frequency and listen to it on a second box. However, under normal circumstances, to avoid frequency congestion, pilots should listen to the ATIS broadcast on the dedicated ATIS frequency.

A display of the current surface wind is available (i.e. the actual wind at the present time) as this may be different to the wind reported on the ATIS. This is described in more detail in chapter 9.1.

If the airport has an automated instrument RVR system (IRVR) then the current IRVR values are displayed at the tower and approach control positions. This allows controllers to pass the latest RVR values to pilots during low visibility operations.

Section 9 Weather

When controllers pass weather information to pilots there are some rules and definitions that apply to such information. Some of this is covered during pilot training. This section is intended to give an understanding of such weather information from ATC's perspective as well as a practical explanation of how and why certain procedures and phraseology are used.

All of the information given in this section applies equally to METAR's, ATIS and that spoken by controllers on the RT.

Chapter 9.1   Wind

The subject of reporting the surface wind may seem very simple, but there are a few details that are worth explaining in order to give a complete understanding. This involves details of where the wind reading is taken from, how the wind speed is measured and how the wind direction is measured.

Anemometers

The surface wind is measured by an anemometer at the runway threshold. For any given single runway there is therefore two anemometers i.e. for runway 09/27 there is one anemometer at the 09 threshold and one at the 27 threshold. If an aerodrome has two runways there will be four anemometers, etc. Some large aerodromes may also have an anemometer at the mid-point, although this is not a requirement. Consequently the wind readout displayed to the controller is not taken from the windsock, although the windsocks and anemometers are usually in close proximity to each other.

The controller can select which anemometer to use for his wind readout display. Controllers are required to pass the surface wind to pilots as measured abeam the relevant threshold for both departures and arrivals. Being able to select either anemometer not only allows the correct/required information to be given, but also allows the wind to be checked at both ends of the runway in conditions where there is a significant difference between both ends.

It is a requirement that anemometers measure the wind at a height of 30ft above the runway elevation (windsocks must also be situated at 30ft above the runway elevation). This wind is called the 'surface wind'. Note that this is the only position that controllers have wind readouts from i.e. abeam each threshold (and possibly mid-point) at a height of 30ft. Controllers have no information on the current winds present on the final approach path. The only wind information available to controllers for the final approach path is from the same upper wind forecasts that pilots use, or from recent reports from pilots on final approach.

It can often be the case that the wind on final approach is very different to the surface wind reported by the controller. This can often lead to confusion or disbelief by the pilot, but it must be remembered that the surface wind given by the controller is measured at 30ft above the threshold elevation. On occasions it is the case that the surface wind is reported as calm or even a 5kt headwind, but the pilot is experiencing a 30-40kt tailwind during the final approach. The tailwind can be persistent and may give a 10kt tailwind even at 200-300ft. If the pilot is uncomfortable with such conditions he is of course always within his rights to go-around in the interests of safety. However, in such circumstances, unless there is a technical problem with the anemometer, as the aircraft enters the flare at approximately 30ft the wind will have changed to that as reported by the controller, as that is where the surface wind reading is taken from.

For those readers who are not familiar with glass cockpit instrumentation such displays show the current wind experienced by the aircraft as calculated by the aircraft's inertial reference system. Therefore, pilots of such aircraft are able to see when the wind at their position (e.g. on final approach) is significantly different to the surface wind reported by the controller.

Averaged wind

When the wind speed and direction are given it is actually the average wind speed and direction calculated over a set period of time. When the surface wind is given it is a legal requirement to give the wind as averaged over the last two minutes when spoken by the controller on the RT and when given on the ATIS. However, for METAR's it is a legal requirement to give the wind as averaged over the last ten minutes.

The averaging of the wind speed and direction are calculated by the measuring equipment and the controller can select on his wind readout display whether to display the 'two minute' or 'ten minute' wind. Most displays also have available an 'instant' wind display i.e. with no averaged time period. As stated, when the surface wind is given on the RT (either by the controller or on the ATIS) it is the two minute average that is used.

Magnetic and true directions

When the surface wind direction is given it is given in degrees magnetic when spoken by the controller on the RT and when given on the ATIS. For METAR's it is given in degrees true. The rationale behind this is that runway directions are specified in degrees magnetic, therefore a magnetic surface wind is required when given on the RT so that pilots can easily correlate the wind direction to the runway direction. METAR's are more generally used for planning purposes (as are forecasts). Plotting charts and maps are drawn in degrees true, therefore METAR winds are given in degrees true to facilitate an easy correlation.

Wind variations

In the UK variations in wind direction are only required to be given if the variation is by 60° or more. Such variations are to be given as averaged over the last ten minutes. This applies even when giving the two minute surface wind. Therefore, when a controller gives the surface wind e.g. "surface wind 240° 12kts varying 180° to 300°" he is giving the two minute averaged wind with variations from the last ten minutes. The controller's wind readout display shows the directional variations in a simple easy to use format and does not (as it is not a requirement) show variations of less than 60°.

Maximum and minimum wind speeds

When maximum and minimum wind speeds are given in the UK (also referred to as gusts and lulls) it is only a requirement to give such speeds if they differ from the main (i.e. averaged) wind speed by 10kts or more. Such differences are to be given as averaged over the last ten minutes. This applies even when giving the two minute surface wind. Therefore, when a controller gives the surface wind e.g. "surface wind 240° 12 gusting 24kts" he is giving the two minute averaged wind with the maximum gust from the last ten minutes. The controller's wind readout display shows the maximum and minimum speeds as averaged over the last ten minutes.

Chapter 9.2 Visibility

There are a few details on the subject of reporting the visibility that are worth explaining in order to give a complete understanding. In particular the type of visibility is important as this has relevance to where the visibility is measured from, in which direction it is measured and how it is measured. There are two types of visibility - these being 'MET VIS' and 'RVR'.

MET VIS

When the MET VIS is given on the RT by a controller or on the ATIS it is preceded by the word 'visibility'. In other words, whenever the term 'visibility' is used (e.g. "visibility 6km") it therefore refers to the MET VIS. It is also the MET VIS that is given in the surface visibility section of a METAR.

MET VIS is measured by a person. This can either be a dedicated 'met man' or a controller with a met observers certificate. To determine the MET VIS the area around the airfield is surveyed during the licensing of the airfield. A list is then provided of visibility features and their distance from the met observation point. There will usually be at least ten features listed in order to give an accurate variation in visibilities. These features can be anything that is easily depictable. The following are a few examples:

- [name] power station   15km
- [name] block of flats   8km
- Electricity pylon bearing 300°   2500m
- Holding point 'B'   400m

To report the MET VIS the observer must view all directions. The visibility is then reported in accordance with the definition of 'prevailing visibility' - where prevailing visibility is the visibility that is present within at least half of the aerodrome surface.

The use of prevailing visibility could therefore lead to situations where the MET VIS is reported as good, but in a particular sector (of less than half the aerodrome) the visibility is actually poor. To prevent such situations occurring there is also an attached condition that prevailing visibility is forecast and reported unless the minimum visibility is less than 50% of that prevailing or less than 1500m whichever is worst. In such cases the minimum visibility and direction are also given in addition to the prevailing visibility.

Note that the term 'prevailing visibility' is not used by controllers on the RT. The word 'visibility' is used as a shorter phraseology term and it is actually the 'prevailing visibility' that is being given.

The MET VIS is determined (using the rules given above) according to which of the visibility features are and are not visible. For example, if a factory at 6km is visible but a block of flats at 8km is not visible, the visibility is reported as 6km.

It is important for pilots to realise that the position on the airfield from where the MET VIS is measured can have a major effect on the reported visibility. This is due to the fact that visibility can be markedly localised, so the visibility reported from a particular point on the airfield can be different to that at other points around the airfield or in the vicinity of the airfield. If the visibility is, in general terms, good then any variations around that reported visibility distance will have little or no effect on flight operations. However, in poor visibility conditions such variations can have consequences for pilots. Below are some practical examples to highlight such matters:

- A reported visibility in the region of 2500m. The observation point being near to one threshold, but the pilot is at the other end of the runway. At the pilot's position the visibility may appear to be much less or much greater than that reported.
- Mist and fog are often much denser around large expanses of fields or near to water compared to that around large expanses of concrete. So the visibility observed from the control tower on a large apron maybe, for example, 1000m. But as the pilot taxis onto the runway, which has grass either side and a large expanse of fields on one side, the visibility at that position may only be 500m.
- With a visibility around 5km this can mean the commencement/cessation of VFR/SVFR operations. However, the pilot maybe experiencing a markedly different visibility and so he may feel that the present operations (i.e. VFR or SVFR) are inappropriate.
- The reported visibility is obviously correct, but recall that this is as per the definition of prevailing visibility and is as viewed from the met observation point. Pilots should therefore always be prepared for the fact that they may encounter a visibility of only 50% of that reported and this could occur when it is least expected or wanted.
- The MET VIS is measured from a position on the ground. When airborne the visibility can change markedly even at only a few hundred feet above the ground, so this could give a difference between the visibility experienced by the pilot and the reported MET VIS.

The important point to remember about the reported MET VIS is that it is the prevailing visibility observed from (some) point on the airfield. Add to this the fact that visibility can be localised, this therefore gives the explanation that the visibility experienced, whether on the ground or in flight, can be different to the reported MET VIS.

You may have noticed that I have not yet mentioned exactly where the visibility observation point is on an airfield and you may think, after the points raised in this chapter, that it would be a good idea for pilots to know where the observation point is. Unfortunately I cannot tell you this because it is not the same at every airport. Neither is the observation point stated on any type of airfield briefing or aviation literature available to pilots. So, basically, pilots will not be aware of the exact location of the observation point, just that it is somewhere on the airfield. It is often the case that the met observation point is in the control tower, but this is by no means a convention and so should never be assumed to be true. It is sometimes the case that the met observation point is in a small hut on the far side of the airfield. Also, some aerodrome charts show a symbol or 'MET' or 'AIS + MET' location. Note, however, that this does not refer to the met observation point. Pilots should refer to the legend of such charts to obtain the correct definition of any such symbol or abbreviation, but in most cases any such 'MET' location usually refers to the place where pilots can obtain weather information, rather than the location of where the met observation is conducted by the official met observer i.e. it is the reception desk where pilots can get a paper copy of METAR's, TAF's, etc. This may often be at the same location as the 'AIS' (Aeronautical Information Service) which usually refers to where NOTAM's etc can be obtained.

RVR

When the RVR (Runway Visual Range) is given on the RT by a controller or on the ATIS it is preceded by the abbreviation 'RVR' e.g. "RVR 700m". The RVR, as the name suggests, is a visibility measurement along the runway direction and is measured at the runway threshold unless otherwise stated. RVR is therefore different to MET VIS (or "visibility") as the RVR is always measured at that specific point and in the relevant direction.

RVR is measured in two ways – either by human observer method or by automated instruments called 'transmissometers'. The automated instrument system is known as 'IRVR'. Note, however, when spoken on the RT or on the ATIS the term "RVR" is used for both human observer method and IRVR determined values.

The human observer method involves a person stood to the side of the runway threshold (or mid-point or stop-end where stated) who counts the number of runway edge lights visible. This number is applied to a conversion table to obtain the RVR. The IRVR method utilises the transmissometers which are permanently fixed at the side of each of the runway thresholds and the runway mid-point. The transmissometers automatically calculate the RVR and this is displayed on a readout at the relevant ATC controlling positions.

The brighter the runway edge lights are means that more of the edge lights further along the runway become visible and consequently the greater the RVR is. However, if the runway lights are simply turned to full intensity those lights closest to the pilot may be blindingly bright, especially at night. Therefore it is a requirement to have the runway lights set within a certain range of intensity depending on the outside conditions. The IRVR system automatically allows for the runway light intensity when calculating the RVR.

The MET VIS is still reported whenever the RVR is being reported. With reference to the previous paragraphs detailing the position on the airfield of the MET VIS observation and the localisation of the visibility, it can be seen that the MET VIS and RVR values can be markedly different. Due to the bright intensity of the runway edge lights the RVR can often be greater than the MET VIS. However, it is possible for the RVR to be less than the MET VIS due to localisation of denser mist/fog around the runway.

Most RVR equipment do not give values above 1500m. When the RVR is above 1500m the controller's display shows ' +1500m '.

It is the convention at most airfields to commence reporting RVR values when the MET VIS or RVR is less than 1500m. This can therefore give a poor MET VIS but a good RVR, and vice versa. For example, "visibility 1000m, RVR greater than 1500m", or "visibility 2000m, RVR 1100, 1200, 1100".

Visibility obscurant

There are some rules that apply to the reporting of the type of visibility obscurant. Although these are covered in pilot training, the major points are given below to ensure a complete understanding is given in this chapter regarding visibility. Note that a height value is included in many of the definitions. The letters given in brackets, after the title, relate to the METAR code.

Mist (BR):	For mist to be reported the visibility must be between 1000m and 5000m inclusive. The obscurant is water droplets.
Fog (FG):	For fog to be reported the visibility must be less than 1000m. The obscurant is water droplets.
Haze (HZ):	For haze to be reported the visibility must be 5000m or less. The obscurant is extremely small dry particles.
Widespread Dust (DU):	For widespread dust to be reported the visibility must be 5000m or less. The obscurant is dry particles that are larger than those for haze.
Sand (SA):	For sand to be reported the visibility must be 5000m or less. The obscurant is dry particles that are larger than those for dust.
Duststorm (DS):	For duststorms to be reported the visibility at 2m or more above the ground must be less than 1000m.
Sandstorm (SS):	For sandstorms to be reported the visibility at 2m or more above the ground must be less than 1000m.
Shallow (MI):	This is only used in combination with fog (FG) and indicates that the visibility below a height of 2m above the ground is less than 1000m, but the visibility at 2m or more above the ground is 1000m or more.
Drifting (DR):	The obscurant is raised by the wind to a height of less than 2m above the ground.
Blowing (BL):	The obscurant is raised by the wind to a height of 2m or more above the ground.
Vicinity (VC):	The phenomena occurs within 8km of the aerodrome perimeter but does not occur inside the aerodrome perimeter. (Note that this definition of 'vicinity' is purely for use with respect to weather, no definition of vicinity is given for use in other context, for example 'reduced separation in the vicinity of aerodromes').

Chapter 9.3   Cloud

There are some definitions and rules that govern how cloud is reported that are worth explaining in practical terms.

Cloud level

The first point to remember with regards to cloud reports is that the reported cloud level is the vertical distance of the cloud above the aerodrome i.e. height above the aerodrome. Although this may seem obvious it can be easy to forget when flying with QNH set on the altimeter. Practically this means that with QNH set, the aerodrome elevation must be added to the reported cloud level in order to find the reading on the altimeter at which the cloud will be present.

Although it may not seem vital to do this when flying in the UK, as most aerodromes in the UK are below 500ft amsl, it is a good habit to get into for future reference should you fly in areas of higher terrain or for those of you that will undertake instrument flying.

When making instrument approaches it is the decision altitude (DA) or minimum descent altitude (MDA) that is used by pilots rather than the decision height (DH) or minimum descent height (MDH) i.e. QNH is set on the altimeter. If, for example, an aerodrome is reporting cloud overcast at 400ft and the MDA for the VOR approach is 550ft, at first glance you may think it is not worth attempting an approach as the cloud is 150ft below the MDA. However, if the aerodrome elevation is 250ft it must be remembered that the cloud is reported as a height above the aerodrome. This means that that the altitude of the cloud is 650ft and so is actually 100ft above the MDA, which makes the approach now a viable option.

Format of cloud reports

When cloud is reported it is done so in a certain format, this being:

1. The lowest layer whatever the amount.
2. The next higher layer of scattered of more.
3. The next higher layer of broken or more.

In addition, cloud more than 5000ft above aerodrome elevation is not reported, the exception being that towering cumulus and cumulonimbus cloud is always reported irrespective of height or amount.

When cloud is not discernible, for example due to fog, the term 'sky obscured' is used.

This explains why cloud reports may seem unusual, for example, when "broken 1000ft, broken 1600ft" is reported. You may think in this case that broken 1000ft would suffice, as it is only the lowest significant layer that is important.

Pilot perceptions

Due to the fact that cloud more than 5000ft above aerodrome elevation is not reported, it is possible that the aerodrome could have an overcast layer at 5100ft but the report does not specify any cloud. Although this is unlikely to have any major affects for pilots due to the height above the aerodrome, it can lure you into the false perception that the aerodrome will have glorious blue sky, when in fact a solid cloud layer is present. It is therefore good airmanship to always remember the possibility of this worst case.

The amount of cloud reported can also lead to another false perception. When few, scattered or broken is reported it does not necessarily mean that the cloud is evenly distributed. So, for example, if there is a solid layer of cloud to the west of the aerodrome, but to the east there is none, or just an odd whisper, then the total amount of cloud present may be 4 oktas which means the report will state scattered. A pilot approaching from the east may therefore be presently surprised when he experiences blue sky and no cloud. However, a pilot approaching from the west and expecting (intermittent) ground contact may be caught out as he actually experiences a solid cloud layer.

Although this type of cloud split is not common, it can happen if a front is approaching or if an aerodrome has high terrain on one side and cloud is stagnating around that higher barrier. As no directions are given in cloud reports, just the total amount of cloud present in the sky, in such cases there is therefore no warning that a report of scattered or broken may actually be much more solid (i.e. tending towards overcast) in certain portions of the sky.

Cloud base, cloud ceiling and CAVOK

The term 'cloud base' is defined as: 'The height above the aerodrome of the base of any cloud'. This can therefore be as little as one okta of cloud.

The term 'cloud ceiling' is defined as: 'The height above the aerodrome of the lowest part of any cloud that is sufficient to obscure more than one half of the sky'. This therefore refers to 5 oktas or more, or reports of broken or overcast layers.

The term 'CAVOK' is defined as:

- Visibility 10km or more, and
- No significant weather at or in the vicinity of the aerodrome, and
- No cloud below 5000ft above the aerodrome or MSA (whichever is greater), and
- No cumulonimbus or towering cumulus cloud at any level.

Note that all the above conditions must apply before the term CAVOK can be used. Also, similar to that mentioned earlier with respect to cloud, when CAVOK is given it does not necessarily mean that the aerodrome has glorious blue sky. The weather can be a visibility of 11km and cloud overcast at 5100ft and the report of CAVOK is still valid. The use of the term 'vicinity' with respect to weather reports is defined as within a radius of 8km of the aerodrome but not occurring inside of the aerodrome boundary fence. Note that this definition of 'vicinity' is purely for use with respect to weather, no definition of vicinity is given for use in other context, for example 'reduced separation in the vicinity of aerodromes'.

Chapter 9.4   ATIS and validity of weather reports

Although the following may not seem of vital importance it is included so that you know what the rules actually are should you be told otherwise. This being that MATS Part 1 states:

> Pilots of departing aircraft need not acknowledge report of an ATIS message. Pilots of arriving aircraft are required to acknowledge receipt of the ATIS message on initial contact with approach control. If a non-current code letter is used, or if receipt of ATIS is not acknowledged, approach control must pass the relevant information.

This explains that on occasions when controllers appear to be obsessed with getting pilots to clarify the ATIS code it is because they have to by law. Should a pilot give a non-current ATIS code the usual practise is for the controller to pass any changes or state "no significant changes". The ATIS display available at the controller's position (as described in chapter 8.10) gives a highlighted background around any details that have changed compared to the previous ATIS code. This therefore allows the controller to easily pass any updated details without having to solely rely on his memory.

Some aerodromes have ATIS that include a specific request. This will apply to departing aircraft as well as arriving aircraft unless otherwise stated. For example, "pilots report aircraft type and receipt of information [code] on first contact".

On some occasions the term 'unverified' is included in an ATIS broadcast. The use of this term is as follows:

> Some aerodromes have electronic equipment that observe and measure all the relevant weather details required to produce a weather observation report. This equipment is slaved to the ATIS broadcast equipment and therefore allows an automated ATIS to be completed and broadcast without any human input.
>
> During aerodrome opening hours this equipment is set to 'verified' mode, which means that the weather information (which is displayed on a computer screen) is not automatically broadcast but must be confirmed to be correct by the met observer. When confirmed, the met observer then uses the verified prompt, which enables the equipment to compile and broadcast the new ATIS. If any of the automated details are different to the actual weather the met observer can change those details using the computer screen and keyboard. Examples can be such as rain being light rather than moderate, cloud being scattered rather than few, or visibility being 5km rather than 9km.
>
> When the aerodrome is closed, or if it is open but no official met observer is present, it is permissible to leave the equipment transmitting automated ATIS broadcasts so that pilots can still obtain a reasonable idea of the weather at the aerodrome. However, as such reports have not been confirmed by an official met observer they cannot, by law, be classed as correct. Therefore the term 'unverified' is included to indicate this.

The term 'unverified' is used in automated ATIS broadcasts. However, some aerodromes do not have an automated system, so at such aerodromes if there is no official met observer present the controller will use the phrase "unofficial observation" to indicate that the weather information given has not been confirmed by an official met observer.

Chapter 9.5 Runway surface condition

When controllers report the presence of surface water on runways the terms used are subject to specific definitions rather than being general terms as interpreted by the controller. These terms are defined in MATS Part 1 and are therefore bound by law. Controllers are therefore very strict on using these terms correctly. It consequently makes sense, and is good airmanship, for pilots to be aware of these definitions so that you know exactly what surface water is present when the controller reports such terms. The terms and definitions as stated in MATS Part 1 are given below:

Term	Surface condition
Dry	The surface is not affected by water, slush, snow or ice.
Damp	The surface shows a change of colour due to moisture. NOTE: If there is sufficient moisture to produce a surface film or the surface appears reflective, the runway will be reported as wet.
Wet	The surface is soaked but no significant patches of standing water are visible. NOTE: Standing water is considered to exist when water on the runway surface is deeper than 3mm. Patches of standing water covering more than 25% of the assessed area will be reported as water patches.
Water patches	Significant patches of standing water are visible. NOTE: Water patches will be reported when more than 25% of the assessed area is covered by water more than 3mm deep.
Flooded	Extensive patches of standing water are visible. NOTE: Flooded will be reported when more than 50% of the assessed area is covered by water more than 3mm deep.

Individual pilots or aircraft operators may have their own definitions of the terms used to report surface water. However, it is important to realise that controllers only use the definitions given above for those terms, so if you or your company have different definitions then be aware. Again it is stressed that the wording of the definitions is used exactly and, as can be seen from the table, the wording is clear and unambiguous so as to be easily understood.

A practical point to note is that it is the aerodrome authority that is responsible for assessing and reporting the runway surface condition. In reality this means that it is not the official met observer or the controller that looks out of the window and decides if the runway is damp or wet etc, but it is a person from the airport ops department that must go out onto the runway (in an ops vehicle) and report the runway surface condition to the controller (usually via the RT).

On occasions it may appear that the runway surface condition is different to the official report. Examples being at the onset of rain where the runway is no longer dry, and after the rain has stopped where the runway is drying out and is no longer wet. In the interests of safety MATS Part 1 states:

> Under no circumstances are controllers to pass information which suggests that the runway surface condition is better than the official report. However, if an observation from the control tower indicates a worse surface condition this information is to be passed.

This can sometimes lead to the situation where the runway is reported as wet but it is obviously damp or even dry. This can occur easily in the hot summer months when the runway dries quickly in the sun after a rain shower. This can be a source of frustration for pilots when they are performance limited on wet runways. Recall, however, that it is the airport ops personnel that are responsible for assessing and reporting the runway surface condition and that controllers are not allowed to pass information that suggests the surface condition is better than the official report, even if it is obviously so. During transitioning periods of the surface condition, and when the airport ops personnel are busy undertaking the many other duties that they are responsible for, it may therefore take a while before the ops person can physically get out to the runway to determine if it is damp rather than wet, or wet rather than water patches, etc.

Section 10   Emergencies

During emergency situations, and situations of a less critical (minor incident) nature, controllers will obviously provide as much help as possible to pilots. Controllers will try and help with requests of any nature (i.e. not just those solely confined to ATC or to the controller's normal area of responsibility) from pilots of emergency traffic, for example, a request to telephone the airline's maintenance office for technical advice. Where possible, and if necessary, the controller may effectively move all other traffic out of the way in order to give the emergency traffic as much freedom as possible, for example, instructing aircraft to enter the holding pattern so that the approach area and final approach track are free of traffic.

In emergency situations controllers may be required by law to perform certain tasks or be responsible for specific aspects. This section is intended to make pilots aware of what controllers must do and why those things must be done during emergencies. It may be the case during an emergency or incident that the pilot feels the controller is not being as helpful as he could or is performing an unnecessary task. However, if this is so, I am 100% certain that it will be due to the procedures specified by law rather than the controller being purposely difficult. The need for such procedures by law should mean that they are actually of benefit to the emergency traffic even though the pilot may not think so.

Although it may not be of vital importance, it is a fact that the standard phraseology for a MAYDAY situation is to state 'MAYDAY' three times i.e. "MAYDAY, MAYDAY, MAYDAY", whereas for a PAN situation the word 'PAN' is said six times as "PAN PAN, PAN PAN, PAN PAN". What is worthy of note is that some states do not recognise the word PAN. Importantly, as this is solely an aviation term rather than being an obvious word in the English language (with respect to controllers who's first language is not English), controllers in those states may have no understanding of the word 'PAN' and so the use of it by pilots may lead to long, confused transmissions which have no positive affect on flight safety. In states where the word 'PAN' is not recognised pilots should declare a MAYDAY in situations where otherwise a 'PAN' call would have been made and should not fear that the initiation of a MAYDAY is too high a state of emergency – if urgent assistance is required in such states then a MAYDAY call is the only recognised phrase to alert to an other than normal situation.

Again, not of vital importance but often asked, is the question of when and how often are the terms 'MAYDAY' and 'PAN' to be included in transmissions. The official answer as given in CAP 413 is that the initial emergency message should be prefixed with the appropriate phrase 'MAYDAY, MAYDAY, MAYDAY' or 'PAN PAN, PAN PAN, PAN PAN', and for following transmissions pilots and controllers may use 'MAYDAY' or 'PAN' as a callsign prefix at their discretion where it is judged that this would have a beneficial effect. This therefore clearly states that after the initial emergency message it is at the decision of the individual (pilot or controller) as to whether 'MAYDAY' or 'PAN' is included as a prefix to the callsign. To clarify this further, should there still be any doubt, it therefore means that if the controller continues to use 'MAYDAY' or 'PAN' as a prefix, it does not automatically mean that the pilot must also use it as a prefix. However, the controller may request that the pilot does so if he judges it to be beneficial in that situation. Also, should a change of frequency be required, it is therefore not a requirement to repeat the emergency message or include 'MAYDAY' or 'PAN' as a prefix on initial contact with the next frequency (unless specifically asked to do so by the controller).

Chapter 10.1 Categories of emergencies

In order to simplify what has occurred and the appropriate actions to take when an emergency exists, phrases are used to determine the 'category of emergency'. These are effectively standard phraseology definitions for the emergency and therefore provide the parties involved with a quick, simple and unambiguous explanation of the general nature of the emergency.

These phrases or terms are used by ATC, the aerodrome fire and emergency services, the airport operations department and the airport public telephone switchboard (this is who would answer any telephone calls from the public ringing for information on an incident). Please note that these terms are not for use by pilots, and as such are not specified in any pilot standard phraseology literature such as CAP 413. An in depth description of the categories of emergency and their definitions is not necessary for pilots, but what is important for pilots to realise is that by law controllers must initiate the appropriate category of emergency as dictated by the nature of the incident. Also, the procedures as specified by law for that category of emergency mean that ATC and the aerodrome fire service must take certain actions.

Examples of categories of emergency are 'full emergency' and 'aircraft ground incident'. However, please remember that it is the controller who, by law, determines the category of the emergency. So, should you have knowledge of the definitions of the categories of emergencies, it is not appropriate for pilots to request that a specific category of emergency be initiated.

A category of emergency that I will describe in more detail is that of a 'local standby due weather' or 'weather standby'. The usual definition of this is that the weather conditions are such as to render a take-off or landing difficult or difficult to observe by the aerodrome controller, for example, strong crosswind, poor visibility, LVP's in force, contaminated runway, etc. Although a weather standby is listed in the categories of emergencies it is fair to say that it is not an emergency situation as such. This category is therefore initiated as a precaution as determined by the weather conditions. Again, it is not left to the judgement of the controller to decide if the weather is bad enough to warrant a weather standby – the weather minima are specified in MATS Part 2 and consequently a weather standby must, by law, be initiated whenever these minima are reached. The minima may be, for example, a crosswind component of 20kts or more, or a cloud base below 300ft, or a MET VIS or RVR of 1500m or less.

When a weather standby is initiated the usual procedure is for the firemen to sit in the fire trucks, park outside the fire station and have the engines running i.e. the fire service is in a state of 'readiness'. As a pilot you will no doubt notice this practice in the future and now be aware that it does not necessarily mean that an emergency as such has occurred.

Due to the fact that the firemen must be in the fire trucks for the whole time that a weather standby is active, this can mean the firemen have to remain in the fire trucks for hours at a time and possibly for the whole time they are at work that day. So, when there is a break in the traffic (i.e. no movements for 10 minutes or more) controllers will often stand down the fire service to allow them to have a quick break (whether this be for an essential toilet break or just a nice cup of tea). What this means to pilots is that if you are that last movement, after you have taken-off or landed you may hear the controller say on the RT "fire service stand down" or "fire service, weather standby cancelled". As a pilot you will now be aware of what this means rather than thinking why was the fire service alerted to begin with as, as far as you are concerned, there was no problem. Similarly, if you are the first movement you may hear the controller initiating the weather standby with the fire service on the RT.

During emergencies or minor incidents pilots may feel that the actions taken by ATC or the aerodrome fire service are inappropriate. Often this is because too much of a fuss is created. After reading this chapter pilots will now be aware that ATC and the aerodrome fire service have no choice in the matter. If an aircraft has an abnormal condition it will fit into one of the category of emergency definitions which means that, by law, specified actions must be taken. If those actions are not taken and the pilot requests little or no assistance because the problem is "nothing to worry about", but the situation unexpectedly worsens, the implications for ATC and the fire service would be very serious.

Similarly, when pilots report an abnormal condition it may seem that ATC ask a lot of questions regarding the exact nature of the problem. Although controllers understand that during abnormal situations pilots have relatively little spare time and capacity to answer questions, they need to know a certain amount of information in order to initiate the correct category of emergency. Such clarification could be sought to determine, for example, if a "flap failure" means a zero flap landing or a landing with intermediate flap, or if a "hydraulic problem" is relatively minor or leaves only one hydraulic system remaining or will have a major affect on the flying controls, flaps or brakes.

It is a fair point to make, and is also in the interests of safety, that due to the legalities of initiating the correct category of emergency and the fact that controllers do not have an in depth knowledge of aircraft systems, it is likely that on most occasions controllers will err on the safe side when determining which category of emergency to initiate.

Chapter 10.2   Radio failure

Radio failure procedures are detailed in the AIP and this should be used as the authoritative source. The radio failure procedures that controllers use are specified in MATS Part 1 and 2 and are the same as those specified in the AIP. The point to note is that should radio failure occur, controllers know the radio failure procedures and will expect pilots to follow them (i.e. as given in the AIP). This is of importance to note by pilots because controllers will be controlling other traffic in a manner that is based on the assumption that the radio failure aircraft will continue to follow the correct procedures. So, should a pilot not follow the correct procedures, safety may be compromised.

The procedures to follow for radio failure during initial, intermediate and final approach (i.e. after the Initial, Intermediate, and Final Approach Fixes) are usually specified on the last page of the aerodrome charts carried in the cockpit for each individual airport. These can therefore be referenced relatively quickly and easily in flight. However, the general procedures to use for radio failure on departure, en-route, or during initial descent are not as easily accessible in flight as they are often embedded somewhere in the text manuals in the flight documents bag carried in the cockpit and are lengthy to read. Such procedures often have subtle but important differences depending on the point at which radio failure occurs (see later in this chapter for further details). There may also be differences for use in specific countries compared to the ICAO standard procedures. There may also be a section in the text manuals for specific procedures at individual airports for radio failure whilst on a SID or STAR, these procedures unfortunately are not usually included in the aerodrome charts carried in the cockpit and so are confined to the aforementioned lengthy text manuals.

It may therefore be advantageous to make concise notes of these subtle but important details to take with you in your flight bag so that you have them in an easy to read and easily accessible format should you need them or simply wish to refresh your memory. Or, alternatively, make notes of the relevant page and paragraph numbers and a highlight of the difference or subject matter so you can quickly locate the necessary paragraphs to read from the lengthy text manuals should you need them.

It is important to remember that the AIP and the text manuals in the aircraft are the authoritative source and therefore should be used as the definitive version and should be checked regularly to update yourself (and your notes) of any changes.

This chapter is not intended as a repetition of the procedures detailed in the AIP but is intended to highlight some of the points that can often be forgotten or may need a practical explanation in order to be fully understood. Remember that ATC will be controlling other traffic by issuing clearances that assume the radio failure aircraft will continue to follow the correct procedures.

Class of airspace

The classification of airspace table (given in the glossary) shows that for all flights in Class A, B, C and D airspace ATC clearance is required before entry. In Class E airspace IFR flights require clearance before entry but VFR flights do not. No clearance is required for Class F and G airspace.

If you are operating outside of controlled airspace (i.e. operating in Class F or G airspace) and experience radio failure you should not therefore enter such airspace that requires ATC clearance before entry. Although that may seem an obvious point to make, the mindset can be different if for example your home base is inside controlled airspace (Class A – E) and you experience radio failure whilst flying outside of its airspace. In such a situation do not automatically re-enter the airspace under the assumption that it is what ATC will expect you to do because it is your home base. You should therefore divert to an airfield within airspace that does not require a clearance before entry.

Departures and en-route

It was mentioned earlier in this chapter that radio failure procedures differ depending on the point at which radio failure occurs. Below are some of the (subtle) items, but not a definitive list, that are worth highlighting in the interests of fully understanding and using the correct procedure. Again note there may be differences between countries:

- Specified time to maintain speed and level may differ depending whether under radar vectors, proceeding direct, or on the flight planned route.
- The point at which such timing is to commence.
- The level to climb to.
- Whether to follow the clearance of the current flight plan or the filed flight plan.
- Whether a 'request level change en-route' or 'temporary restriction to climb' clearance has been given.

Request level change en-route

The phrase 'request level change en-route' has a specific meaning as detailed below. It is good airmanship to keep a copy of its meaning in your flight bag so that it is easily accessible should you need it.

> If an aircraft which has been given a clearance which includes 'request level change en-route' experiences a radio failure within controlled airspace it can be assumed that the pilot will:
>
> a) Proceed in accordance with the clearance given, climbing to the assigned level within controlled airspace.
> b) Turn left or right 60° and leave controlled airspace.
> c) Remain clear of controlled airspace for at least 5 minutes.
> d) Rejoin controlled airspace at the flight planned level.

Temporary restriction to climb

Unlike 'request level change en-route' this is not a standard phraseology term and does not have its own specific procedure. As such, the words "temporary restriction to climb" will not be heard on the RT, but what this refers to is when the climb is temporarily restricted. For example, you are cleared for a SID, but given "maintain altitude 4000ft", or "after departure fly runway heading, maintain altitude 3000ft".

Should radio failure occur with a temporary restriction to climb, the procedure to follow is the standard radio failure procedure. Note, however, that the details of the procedure may differ, as mentioned earlier, according to the circumstances, for example, whether under radar vectors, proceeding direct, or on the flight planned route.

Arrival

As mentioned earlier, the procedures for radio failure during initial, intermediate and final approach are usually given on the approach plates for each individual airport and so can be referenced with ease in flight. The procedures for radio failure during descent (i.e. from cruising level to the initial approach fix) are not as easily accessible and may differ due to similar circumstances as given earlier in the list for departure and en-route radio failure.

It is worth highlighting two aspects of the radio failure procedures during arrival as, should radio failure occur, many pilots may be in a certain mindset that is incorrect. These two aspects are as follows:

For the case of radio failure during the cruise, pilots may have the mindset of commencing descent at the normal top of descent point as per any 'normal' arrival (i.e. as given in the FMS or by use of the 'three times height' rule). This mindset can be cemented by the fact that it seems common sense to do so, and similarly pilots would expect ATC to be thinking and expecting the same. However, many radio failure procedures state that such aircraft should proceed to the holding facility for the instrument approach procedure at the filed or current flight planned level and then begin descent in the hold if necessary over such aid. Although this may not seem a very practical level, if it is stated as the procedure then it is what ATC will be expecting. Note that if the filed flight plan is to be used then such details must be reviewed to ensure the correct level is flown - the filed flight plan may be filed with a different level to the current cruising level or with a stepped descent rather than maintaining the cruising level. In contrast, such radio failure procedures for some countries actually state that descent should be commenced from the cruising level to arrive at the holding facility at the specified instrument approach procedure level or MSA if higher.

The second point is that during normal operations (i.e. every time an arrival is flown) pilots will be expecting to, and therefore have the mindset of, flying the appropriate STAR. This mindset can be cemented where the pilot in question has always been cleared for a particular STAR whenever he has visited that particular airport. Note, however, similar to the previous paragraph regarding the appropriate level, in the case of radio failure the radio failure procedure may state to revert to the filed or current flight planned route and proceed to the holding facility for the instrument approach procedure. This may therefore mean that, depending on the airport and procedure in question, the STAR should not be flown even though the pilot may be in the mindset of flying the STAR and think it is what ATC will be expecting. It is often the case that the filed flight planned route is to a beacon/point on the airfield i.e. directly overhead the airfield, rather than to a point at a distance from the airfield where a STAR begins. In such a case, upon reviewing the filed flight plan, the correct course of action is therefore to fly to that beacon (at the airfield) enter the hold as necessary and then commence the instrument approach procedure which, if the associated beacon is at the airfield, is likely to be a teardrop or racetrack procedure. If the radio failure procedure states to follow the current (rather than filed) flight planned route then in most cases the current flight plan will be to route direct to a waypoint, the waypoint also being a waypoint on the filed flight plan. When the waypoint is reached the current flight planned route (i.e. the lateral flight path) therefore becomes the same as the lateral flight path of the filed flight planned route. Note, however, that if the current flight plan is to be followed then the speed and level of the current flight plan must be maintained (unless otherwise specified) although the route (i.e. the lateral flight path) of the current and filed flight plans may become the same as explained.

Note from earlier in this chapter that the radio failure procedure will state when the pilot is to change to or from the current or filed flight planned route i.e. after a certain time period or at a certain waypoint. It may also state, for the case of where a clearance to fly a STAR has been given, whether the STAR should be flown or whether to revert to the current or filed flight planned route or a specified alternative route.

With reference to reviewing the filed flight plan, a copy of the filed flight plan should always be present on the "pilot's log" or "plog" forms that are provided by the dispatcher or the pilot's company operations department. Where pilots file their own flight plans it is therefore necessary to keep a copy of this, as explained, in case of radio failure.

Note that I have purposely used the word 'may' in the previous paragraphs as it is important to reference the exact details for your circumstances in the correct country and for the specific airport should you experience radio failure. This also highlights the need to set transponder code 7600 as soon as possible after radio failure so that the controller can recognise the fact that you may fly a different route and/or level to what would normally be expected or to the clearance issued.

Radio failure whilst receiving radar vectors during either departure or arrival may be considered as one of the more critical occurrences due to the fact that such aircraft are likely to be closer to terrain and in an area of increased traffic density. It is worth noting that radio failure procedures whilst receiving radar vectors may differ depending on whether radio failure occurs on departure or arrival. For the case of departure the procedure is often to maintain the last assigned level and heading for a specified (short) period of time before returning to the flight planned route. For the case of arrival the procedure is often to immediately continue visually or by a suitable navaid. Again these procedures 'may' be in place, so it is important to reference the exact details for your circumstances in the correct country and also to set transponder code 7600 as soon as possible.

Expected approach time

Expected approach times have relevance to radio failure procedures. The subject is discussed in chapter 6.13.

Mobile phones

If it is practical, should you experience radio failure, there is always the option of using your mobile to telephone ATC to establish some form of communication (whilst following the correct radio failure procedure). An appropriate number to store in your mobile is that of an en-route centre (e.g. Swanwick) or a major international airport (e.g. Manchester) as given in the AIP. Such places are ideal as they are large units that can easily get in touch with any other required ATC unit in the country and are also guaranteed to be open 24 hours a day. The en-route centres also have connections to overseas centres, so it would not be unreasonable, should radio failure occur whilst abroad, to telephone the UK centre and ask to pass a message or relay information to the appropriate ATC unit at your location. It may also be an advantage to store the telephone number for ATC at your home base and any airfields that you frequently visit. Again, these numbers are given in the AIP.

Chapter 10.3   Radar failure

The subject of radar failure is encompassed in chapter 6.6.

Chapter 10.4 Emergency descent

This chapter is mainly intended to remove the possibility of a collision during an emergency descent by detailing the subject in a practical manner.

Recommended procedures for use by flight crews in the case of an emergency descent differ between countries and also to that of ICAO. Such differences often mean that the procedures contradict each other, for example, some states recommend changing squawk to 7700 as soon as possible, whereas others recommend keeping the current squawk until otherwise instructed by ATC, and some states recommend a turn away from the assigned track before commencing an emergency descent, whereas others recommend descending on the current track. It is difficult and impractical for pilots to reference and remember each procedure for each country being flown over during a flight. However, if some practicality, common sense and airmanship is used as described in this chapter, then whichever procedure the pilot adopts for an emergency descent the possibility of a collision should be removed.

In the case of an emergency descent due to loss of cabin pressure the mindset, once the oxygen masks have been donned and crew communications established, is often to commence an immediate 'at all costs' descent i.e. the mindset is that 'we must get down immediately'. This will also usually involve the immediate selection of an increased speed and the use of speedbrake giving a very high descent rate. Incidentally, the transponder will still be set to TA/RA (which is discussed later in this chapter).

The reality is that the one and only immediate action required is for the flight crew to don their oxygen masks. Once the flight crew are breathing a suitable oxygen supply then all other actions should be accomplished in a purposeful but calm manner with the appropriate amount of co-ordination and confirmation between the flight crew members. This is similar to the philosophy applied to the case of an engine failure/fire on take-off i.e. no rushed actions, no rushed thinking, diagnose the situation clearly between both flight crew members then action the required items with the agreement of both flight crew members.

Whichever recommended procedure is followed the reality is that on that 'worst day' a collision hazard could still result unless some further airmanship is used. Descending on the current track could produce a head on collision, especially with the navigation equipment in today's aircraft being very accurate and able to follow route centrelines to within a few metres. However, turning off track and descending could equally produce a collision hazard if (either) aircraft have been given direct routeings. Pilots must understand that they are therefore not in a position to assess traffic for possible collision hazards in such situations, the only persons that are, and will have the 'full picture', are ATC. Those that argue that TCAS is a defence mechanism in this situation are incorrect for the following (practical) reasons:

Firstly, current TCAS equipment is only certified for use in the vertical plane. Therefore it cannot and must not be used for guidance in the lateral plane i.e. to avoid potential conflicting traffic. Although pilots generally get into the habit of believing the TCAS laterally, there is no guarantee of any lateral accuracy and there are numerous examples of TCAS displays being very inaccurate laterally and sometimes even displaying aircraft in the opposite polarity i.e. to the left instead of to the right and vice versa. Also, the use of such TCAS derived lateral manoeuvres is of particular nonsense if under radar control – as ATC will have the immediate accurate solution.

Secondly, TCAS equipment fits vary and so pilots must check what height selection the TCAS equipment (buttons or knobs) are set to and know what height band this relates to. Therefore a suitable 'below' setting should be used and the pilot must know the cut-off height that the display will not show any traffic below – is it 2000ft below the aircraft's current level, 6000ft, etc. At high rates of descent any narrow band selections will give pilots a sense of security if no traffic is displayed, but this perception is a false and dangerous one with such a narrow band being 'checked' and a high descent rate. Even the widest height band selections may only give minimal time if a high descent rate is used.

Thirdly, if a TCAS RA is received during an emergency descent what action would pilots take? If the RA was a climb RA would pilots, in the confusion, stop the emergency descent and initiate a climb? If the RA instructed to increase the rate of descent would the aircraft be capable of this? If the aircraft is already near to maximum speed with speedbrake deployed then the answer to this is no. Also, if the emergency traffic is receiving a descent RA then the crew of the conflicting aircraft are receiving a climb RA. In such a case can that aircraft accomplish a suitable climb? At higher levels it may be difficult for a jet aircraft to establish a meaningful and suitable climb rate, especially if the aircraft is close to its maximum weight. At lower levels the conflicting aircraft may be other than a jet aircraft and so is equally close to the edge of its performance at such lower levels. Additionally, for those pilots that set the TCAS to TA during an emergency descent (as is recommended) then this obviously does not remove any potential collision hazards but solely removes the generation of any RA's.

The solution, therefore, is to check with ATC before commencing any emergency descent. This can be accomplished efficiently by adding to the end of the MAYDAY transmission the request for an emergency descent, for example:

"MAYDAY, MAYDAY, MAYDAY, [callsign], cabin decompression, request immediate descent".

The controller will then give an appropriate response with any required instructions in order to avoid any conflicting traffic. If the controller does not specify any manoeuvres or simply replies "Roger" then it is good airmanship to use a suitable clear, slowly spoken phrase before commencing the emergency descent in order to fully confirm that there are no collision hazards, such as:

"Confirm clear of traffic [callsign]", or
"Do we require a heading to avoid traffic [callsign]"

In an extreme case, should the controller give the instruction to maintain the present level due to immediate conflicting traffic then, again, some practicality is required. Although the mindset is for an immediate descent, once the flight crew are breathing a suitable oxygen supply there is no rush to descend and it is much safer to stay level for a short time rather than commence an immediate descent and risk a potential collision. Although staying level in the case of a decompression may seem against all rationale and teachings, an immediate descent and collision is a much greater hazard to flight safety than staying level for a few more seconds whilst checking with ATC to remove any collision hazards.

For those that may argue that taking literally 10 seconds to check with ATC for collision hazards before commencing an emergency descent is inappropriate due to the perception that a descent must be commenced immediately in case there are any 'oxygen problems', then again, some practicality is required. The time of useful consciousness at cruising levels (i.e. above 30,000ft) is in the region of 30 seconds. The time taken to don the oxygen masks, complete the recall/memory checklist items and push, pull and turn the appropriate buttons and knobs to initiate (an autopilot) descent is also in the region of 30 seconds. So if there were any problems with the oxygen flow to the flight crew then it is likely that the crew would be unconscious before descent even if attempting to descend immediately. Also, even if such a high rate of descent as 10,000fpm could be achieved, this would take in the region of 120 seconds to descend below 20,000ft and 180 seconds to 10,000ft from a typical cruising level. Therefore, adding literally the 10 seconds it takes to check with ATC for collision hazards before commencing an emergency descent is an insignificant amount of time to add to such a time scale but provides an invaluable addition to flight safety.

Note that although the phrase "request immediate descent" has been used, it is obvious to the controller that such a request is a necessity. However, this gives the controller the chance to think clearly and reply with any necessary instructions to avoid any potential conflicting traffic. This is a much safer practise for all concerned compared to a pilot stating that he is descending immediately – the controller in this case would face an immediate shock as he may see an immediate collision hazard and has to decide instantly which traffic to manoeuvre first and in which direction. There is also the possibility that the emergency traffic is in conflict with more than one other aircraft. Also the situation may be worsened if the emergency traffic turns as per a recommended procedure, as such procedures often do not specify a direction for the turn, just a 'turn away from the assigned track' or a 'turn left or right by [number] degrees'. As the radar screen takes a few seconds for the returns to portray an aircraft's flight path (as the radar head sweeps round) the controller may be initially unaware that the emergency traffic has turned and may have inadvertently turned other traffic towards it whilst thinking that he was actually turning such aircraft away from the emergency traffic. The controller will be expecting/hoping that such emergency traffic will be following the procedures as recommended by the state of that country being flown over, but again, if practically the pilot is not familiar with that specific procedure or has simply forgotten it or confused it with the procedure to be adopted in another state then any such de-confliction instructions issued by the controller to the non-emergency traffic may be in vain.

When under procedural control it is still good practise to contact ATC before commencing an emergency descent. Although in this case the controller will not have an accurate radar 'picture', he can still provide useful information with regards to traffic in the vicinity that may cause a possible collision hazard, or he may state that there is no traffic to affect. If necessary the controller could, within a few seconds, ask the emergency traffic and other relevant traffic to report the DME distance and radial, or the distance and bearing from a waypoint in order to quickly ascertain the relative position and track of any potential conflicting traffic. Again, although staying level initially may seem irrational, in a non-radar environment pilots do not have any of the instant protections to aid avoiding conflicts that are present with radar i.e. the fact that the controller can instantly see the actual situation (or radar 'picture') or that the radar equipment my even be fitted with a conflict alert system to aid the controller in avoiding collisions. Therefore, such a call to ATC is still in the best interests of all concerned in a procedural environment.

The explanation above has detailed a high rate emergency descent due to loss of cabin pressure. The practicalities discussed are equally applicable in the case of an engine failure or loss of thrust at high altitude/cruising level. In such a case an engine failure or loss of thrust at high altitude may often require a descent to be initiated almost immediately for performance reasons i.e. the loss of thrust at that altitude means that the aircraft is unable to maintain speed at that altitude and the margin to the minimum/stall speed is relatively small, so the aircraft will be in danger of departing controlled flight if a descent (to maintain speed) is not initiated almost immediately. If this is the case then the pilot has no choice but to initiate a descent to prevent a departure from controlled flight, but the practicalities of a collision hazard with other aircraft and checking with ATC as discussed in this chapter are still present. To solve this problem the situation therefore needs to be viewed from a different angle as follows:

It is standard practise for aircraft to cruise at the maximum level for the given weight for reasons of efficiency i.e. fuel and cost. Such levels will be certified as safe by the authorities by having a specified margin from the aircraft's minimum performance boundaries. However, as discussed, such margins may give little time before a descent is necessary in the case of loss of thrust. The solution therefore is not to operate at the very maximum level if such a level provides only a small performance margin. Operating at only 1000ft or 2000ft below the maximum cruising level may give sufficient extra margin (e.g. an extra 10kts to the margin to the minimum speed) which provides sufficient extra time to check with ATC for collision hazards, and this also gives negligible or zero fuel/cost penalty.

It is a fact that in the case of loss of thrust at high altitude, any such descent that is required for performance reasons will be of a relatively low descent rate, especially when compared to an emergency descent for reasons of loss of cabin pressure. However, it is still a fact that the aircraft is leaving its cleared altitude and a collision hazard could exist, so pilots may find it beneficial to give some thought to operating at a level that gives sufficient time to safely react and check with ATC should the case of a loss of thrust occur. To conclude this thinking with regards to the balance of safety and efficiency, on most occasions, the only reason to operate at the maximum level will be for reasons of fuel/cost efficiency.

It should be noted that the details discussed in this chapter are not intended to guide pilots to blatantly disregard any SOP's or recommended procedures. However, the main priority is for pilots to ensure the safety of their aircraft and its occupants. Such practicalities as discussed in this chapter, including that of ATC's perspective, are therefore worthy of consideration by pilots in order to take the appropriate actions in such non-standard situations in the interests of maintaining flight safety.

Bibliography

Manual of Air Traffic Services Part 1   CAP 493

Radiotelephony Manual   CAP 413

UK Flight Information Services   CAP 774

ISBN 142513270-7

Printed in Great Britain
by Amazon.co.uk, Ltd.,
Marston Gate.